"In *Taylor's Gift*, the Storches are an example of an ordinary family that experienced an extraordinary and tragic event. The Storch family transitioned from grieving to becoming a shining example of giving the ultimate gift of life all over the world."

Everson Walls, NFL all-pro, kidney donor

"This is a book about love on so many levels. How grieving parents turned their anguish into joy by seeing their daughter live through others."

Cynthia Izaguirre, WFAA-TV news anchor

"Tara and Todd's courage and strength in the face of tragedy are an inspiration to us all. The entire Storch family's dedication to Taylor's memory and Taylor's gift makes them my heroes."

Ann Lopez, kidney donor

"In *Taylor's Gift*, Todd and Tara Storch take us inside the agony of losing a child. But more than that, they take us inside the unexpected joy that comes in seeing God use the worst thing we can imagine for good, helping us to believe He will do that in our lives too."

Nancy Guthrie, author, *Holding on to Hope* and *Hearing Jesus Speak Into Your Sorrow*

Taylor's Gift

A Courageous Story *of*
Giving Life *and* Renewing Hope

Todd and Tara Storch
with Jennifer Schuchmann

Revell

a division of Baker Publishing Group
Grand Rapids, Michigan

Published by Revell
a division of Baker Publishing Group
P.O. Box 6287, Grand Rapids, MI 49516-6287
www.revellbooks.com

Printed in the United States of America

Library of Congress Cataloging-in-Publication Data is on file at the Library of Congress, Washington, DC.

ISBN 978-0-8007-2188-6 (cloth)
ISBN 978-0-8007-2241-8 (pbk.)

Published in association with Creative Trust, Inc., Literary Division, 5141 Virginia Way, Suite 320, Brentwood TN 37027, www.creativetrust.com

13 14 15 16 17 18   7 6 5 4 3 2 1

We dedicate this book to our children Ryan and Peyton:
This is not just our story; it is your story too.
We love you deeply.

Contents

Contents

Part 3 New Beginnings

Foreword

My initial contact with Todd and Tara Storch came in the form of an email blast. A longtime friend was asking everyone to pray for a player on his volleyball team. She'd suffered a severe injury in a skiing accident. There was concern she might not survive.

And so it was that I became acquainted with the story of Taylor Storch and her family. It is a difficult one. It is a story that causes every parent to grimace, every person to wince.

It is a story that challenges the faith of the most stalwart saint. Why? Why would God give a family a child only to take her? Why so soon? Why her?

These are difficult questions. The Storch family has asked them and a thousand others. They invite you to consider their journey. They don't gloss over their pain. You won't find any pious pretentions or shallow dismissals. Instead, you will find an honest itinerary through the valley of sorrow. Sadness comingled with hope. An alchemy of doubt, determination, regret, and resolve.

Their story makes us think of a well-known Bible verse. "And we know that all things work together for good to those who love God, to those who are the called according to *His* purpose" (Rom. 8:28 NKJV).

Note the phrase "work together." Individually, the challenges of life are daunting and difficult. What good is found in the cemetery or ICU? But mixed together—by God's hands—good will happen.

The story of Taylor Storch is the story of Romans 8:28. On one hand, there is the tragic death of a delightful girl. On the other, there are the needs of ill patients, literally dying for want of a healthy organ. When the loss of Taylor met the needs of these people . . . good happened.

The prayer of this book is this: may good continue to happen. May this story bring hope to anyone who has suffered tragedy. There is life after loss. It comes after a monsoon of tears. But it comes.

May this story alert us to the potential of organ donation. Taylor's gift of life made the difference of a lifetime for the people you are about to meet. In more ways than we can imagine, she lives on.

Thank you, Storch family, for sharing your story. May God continue to bring healing until we are all finally home.

Max Lucado

Part 1

Endings

— 1 —

The Accident

March 14, 2010
Vail, Colorado

The sun wouldn't set for another three hours, but the shadows of the snow-covered pine and spruce trees that bordered the ski run had grown longer with the afternoon. From the top of Beaver Creek Mountain, the view was exquisite. Todd Storch knew he was experiencing the trip of a lifetime, and he wanted to capture every minute of it in pictures and videos.

It was shortly after 4:00 p.m. when the three skiers pushed off from the top of Latigo, an intermediate "blue level" run. Eleven-year-old Ryan took off first. An experienced skier, he'd been on numerous father and son skiing trips with Todd, but this was the first ski trip that also included his mother and sisters. Swelling with pride, Ryan couldn't wait to show them all the things he'd learned and talked about from his past trips.

Thirteen-year-old Taylor was next. She'd graduated from ski school only minutes earlier. The instructors couldn't believe this was her first time skiing. They'd promoted her from her assigned class with her little sister, Peyton, to a much harder class with older teen boys. She handled it just fine. "She's a natural. She's been on blues and greens all day," the ski instructor had said, referring to the color codes that signified the difficulty of each run. "She's good to go."

Seconds later, Todd was the last of the three Storches to push off from the mountaintop. With poles in one hand and his Flip camera in the other, Todd took videos of the kids as he skied behind them. He couldn't have been prouder. Ryan was in the lead, showing off a bit for his older sister. Taylor skied behind her brother, her neon pink and black ski jacket and forest green helmet creating a colorful contrast to the glistening snow. A natural athlete, she looked good on skis. Todd marveled at the sight—his two kids skiing together for the first time. He reminded himself to breathe in the moment.

Back in the alpine village, his wife, Tara, and their nine-year-old daughter, Peyton, ordered hot chocolate and found a seat by the fireplace. Todd told Tara he'd meet them there with Taylor and Ryan by 4:30. The family needed to return their equipment rentals by 5:00.

Earlier in the day, Todd and Ryan had mapped out an easy route to the bottom. They had planned several pit stops along the way, which gave the three skiers a chance to reconnect so they didn't get separated on the mountain. Those stops also gave Todd the opportunity to take pictures with his phone. At the final stop, Todd dropped his backpack onto the snow, took out his good camera, and said, "Okay, guys, we're going to get a bunch of pictures here."

He snapped a few pictures, then posed his children to get the perfect mountain landscape in the background. "C'mon, Dad," Ryan said, "we're supposed to be skiing, not taking pictures."

Taylor was more tolerant of her dad's wishes. She loved having her photo taken; she'd recently opened a Facebook account and wanted to share pictures of her in the snow for all of her friends back in Texas to see.

Todd wrapped up the photo session and gave his kids their final instructions. "This is the last run, so when you finish, wait by the ski lift and then we'll go find Mom together."

Once again, Ryan pushed off first, followed by Taylor. Todd was delayed a few seconds as he put on his backpack, grabbed his poles, and once again held the Flip camera in his hand. Todd had never been so happy. It had been the perfect first day, and they still had four more vacation days to go.

The run got a little busier when their slope combined with another. Ryan, already ahead of his sister, pulled over to wait for Taylor, but when she caught up with him, instead of stopping she seemed to rapidly pick up her pace. Ryan pulled out a few feet after her, while Todd was less than a hundred feet behind them.

As the runs merged, the slopes became steeper. Though the path was extremely wide, trees now flanked both sides of the run, and the number of skiers continued to increase as they neared the bottom. Taylor was now moving too fast for the conditions. At first, she tried to snowplow—a technique used to slow a skier down—but instead, she fell backward into a squatting position, which had the effect of reducing her wind drag, and she began to increase speed at an alarming rate. Ryan and Todd watched, hopelessly unable to help, as Taylor got into trouble.

Witnesses suggested that instead of falling over to stop herself, she tried to stand and put more weight on her right side, which caused her skis to turn. As the slope steepened, she continued to pick up more speed. Like a rocket, Taylor shot toward the woods that bordered the run. Heading into the tree line, she hit a pine tree head-on, but her perilous speed made her bounce off it, and she propelled into a second tree.

Stunned at what he'd witnessed, Ryan snowplowed to a sudden stop on the trail adjacent to where Taylor lay face up, her leg unnaturally bent backward at an angle.

Seconds later, Todd skidded to a stop, overshooting the area by about five feet. He quickly kicked off his skis and ran into the woods toward his daughter. But off the main trail, the snow wasn't packed. With every step he sank into the powder, and he found it impossible to climb up the hill. After backtracking to the trail, he sidestepped up the hill until he was directly next to Taylor, then once again left the trail, tugging his boots through the deep powder until he reached his daughter.

"Is she dead?" Ryan cried out. The sickening alarm in his voice could only be heard by his dad. The other skiers on the hill didn't seem to notice what was being said—or even realize what had happened.

Todd got down on his knees, straddled Taylor, and looked into her eyes. They were dilated and watery. He leaned closer, placing his left ear against her mouth, listening for breath sounds. Then he shouted.

"Listen to me, Ryan. I need you to listen to me. She's breathing! She's just knocked out."

"Okay, okay."

"Do exactly what I tell you. Kick off your skis and put them in the snow so they form an X, and then wave your arms at the skiers as they go by. You can yell, 'Help!'"

"Okay, okay, okay," Ryan said, as he looked at his sister's limp body and the gravity of it all sank in.

"Do it now!" Todd yelled. "We have to get help. Taylor can't ski down."

Ryan immediately went to work and flagged down a skier, who used his cell phone to call the ski patrol. The time was 4:20 p.m. Within minutes, Taylor was taken off the mountain on a sled. Riding in the sled next to her were EMS officials who made sure she didn't code out on her first—and last—run down the mountain.

⚬⟊⚬

At 12:15 p.m. the next day, doctors at Grand Valley Junction hospital pronounced Taylor Storch dead. Her grieving parents wept by her bedside, and the doctor asked a single question that would forever change countless lives.

"Would you be willing to donate Taylor's organs?"

— 2 —

Snapshots of Taylor

Donate Taylor's organs? Her parents had obviously never discussed it. Who thinks about such things? It doesn't even cross parents' minds that their child might die in a skiing accident—let alone whether or not they should donate their child's organs. But now, in Taylor's hospital room, the unwanted question stood at attention before them. Todd and Tara didn't say anything out loud, but they both knew what the other was thinking.

What would Taylor do?

❖

It could have happened anywhere:

In the backseat of a car.
In the lunchroom at school.
In the gymnasium after a volleyball game.
In the bathroom in front of a mirror.
Or even in her bedroom.

All it took was a couple of girls trying to snap a picture of themselves, and Taylor couldn't hold herself back. Just as the girls lined up perfectly in the viewfinder of a camera or cell phone, Taylor would sneak up behind them and position herself in the background of their photo. Sometimes, she stood there looking innocent, like she didn't even know she was in the picture. But more often, her presence was deliberate. She'd pose for the camera with a specific look—an arched eyebrow and pursed lip, a thumbs-up and a big smile, or eyes wistfully looking off into the distance while she made a heart with her thumbs and pointer fingers. No matter the occasion, Taylor had a pose. And she loved sneaking into other people's photos. Her friends thought it was hilarious because no one would know she was there until they looked at the picture.

Taylor was tall—five foot eight—and still growing. She had a lean, athletic build, perfect for a middle hitter on the volleyball team and a forward on the basketball team. She had long, straight brown hair that she wore up, down, in braids, or purposely messed up, depending on her mood and activity. But it was Taylor's eyes that were unforgettable. They were framed by long black lashes, and people compared them to the color made famous by the "little blue box" from the expensive jewelry store. Even strangers commented on the color of Taylor's eyes. Taylor had often heard her mother tell the story about the time she was two years old and an older woman in the grocery store stopped Tara.

"Excuse me, excuse me," she had said in a loud and pushy voice. "Did you put mascara on your baby?"

This was back in the days before toddler pageants made reality TV. Tara was horrified at the thought.

"No! She just has really dark lashes."

The lady turned away, obviously not believing that the little girl's eyes and lashes were natural. Over the years, others also noticed and commented. By the time she was in eighth grade, Taylor had just begun to get a glimpse of what other people saw. "My eyes are my favorite feature," she'd recently told her mother.

But when Taylor snuck into the background (or, occasionally, the foreground) of her friends' pictures, those same stunning eyes were just as often closed, crossed, or rolled upward. She was goofy and not afraid of being the punch line of her own joke—as long as it made other people laugh.

⚬⅀⚬

Tara watched as the students of Coppell Middle School East shuffled into the welcoming gym and found seats in the bleachers. The students were happy to be out of class and were excited for the pep rally. Taylor entered with a large group of friends. The girls were easy to spot in their black and red uniforms with white trim. They found a seat on the floor with the other cheerleaders. Sitting beneath the basketball hoop, with their tricolored pom-poms on the polished wood floor in front of them, the girls laughed and talked. But Tara could see from the look on Taylor's face that she was deep in thought.

Tara knew her daughter was going through a mental checklist. Ever since Taylor had entered middle school two years earlier, she had been a list maker. It was how she kept herself organized. In her notebook she made lists of homework assignments due, and on her nightstand she always had a list of what to bring to school the next day. But Tara's favorite list was the one her daughter made during the school day—a list of things she wanted to tell her mom when she got home from school. One of the items on that list the previous day was Taylor's reluctance to perform at the pep rally. Though she was a great athlete—a starter on the school volleyball and basketball teams—Taylor was not the greatest cheerleader, and she'd confided to Tara that she was worried about the routine. She wasn't sure she could pull it off.

Principal Laura Springer took to the microphone and made some announcements to gain control of the crowd. Before becoming an administrator at East, Principal Springer had been a beloved teacher among students at the local high school. Once she arrived at the middle school, it didn't take long for their little brothers and sisters to take a liking to her as well. They called her "Springer," a name that was fine with her. Laura Springer didn't fit into the traditional models of authority anyway. She preferred jeans and T-shirts to suits and blouses, and she was just as often seen roaming the halls talking to kids as she was seen in her office talking to educators. Tara knew that the kids, Taylor included, loved her.

While Springer spoke, Tara watched Taylor retie her shoes and check to make sure the red ribbon in her hair was securely tied. When the principal stopped talking, she motioned for Taylor to come to the microphone. Taylor bounced up and strode across the floor. Then she stood at the mic to make an announcement about an upcoming event. As she finished and turned to leave, Springer stopped her.

"Taylor, stay here. I have something for you," she said.

At that moment, the volleyball coach appeared and handed Taylor a certificate.

"Congratulations! You're volleyball player of the week!"

Taylor took the certificate with all the poise of a middle schooler, and with a smile spreading across her face, she turned to rejoin her friends on the floor. Halfway there, Taylor abruptly stopped and turned around. Her smile turned to a grin as she passed Springer and the microphone on her way to the chairs where the band sat. She found her seat in the second row next to the other French horn players and checked to make sure her music was there. She was in place and ready to go as soon as the bandleader waved the baton and signaled the first notes of the East Broncos fight song.

Beginning French horn players don't make the sweetest sound by themselves, but when the middle school band played together, they actually sounded good. Taylor had never loved playing the French horn, but Todd and Tara had encouraged her to stick with it and she agreed. As the final notes of the pep song hung in the air, Tara, the other parents, and the students burst into applause. The crowd was there to celebrate all things Bronco, and the fight song was just one more element to cheer about.

As soon as the song finished, Taylor placed the French horn on her chair and scooted out of her row to find her way back to the pom-poms she'd left on the floor. She picked them up and rushed to her spot in the center of the gym to take her place in the cheerleaders' formation. Tara saw the concentration on her face as the music started and Taylor joined the other cheerleaders in a routine she hadn't quite mastered. While the other girls did standing backflips and round-offs, Taylor glanced at her mother in the crowd. "Help me!" she jokingly mouthed to Tara, acknowledging her lack of cheerleading prowess. Tara smiled, encouraging her daughter. Taylor stuck with it and struck a pose, making the best of it until the moment passed and the routine ended.

❖

A few weeks later, in the lunchroom, Springer sat at a table reviewing paperwork and watching the students emerge from the cafeteria line and find seats at the crowded tables. As Taylor walked by she caught the principal's eye. Maybe it was because she didn't take herself seriously, or maybe it was because she was involved in so many activities, but Taylor seemed to get along with everyone. She was outgoing and silly one minute and warm and welcoming the next, traveling easily from group to group and from one social activity to another. Unlike some girls who felt the need to protect their status by remaining exclusive, Taylor was as comfortable hanging out with the loners and the nerds as she was the popular girls in her own crowd.

But Springer also noticed Megan, a girl who wasn't in Taylor's circle of friends; in fact, Megan wasn't in anyone's circle of friends. She was a loner and comfortable with being separated from everyone else. But others weren't as comfortable. Springer had occasionally discussed Megan's aloofness at staff meetings. She worried Megan was spending too much time alone and didn't have any friends. The staff strategized about ways to get her involved, putting her in groups for academic activities, encouraging her to get involved in school clubs and other social activities, but they soon realized that Megan didn't want anything to do with their ideas. Or with her classmates. Megan didn't want to be fixed. She appeared to be as comfortable with who she was as Taylor was. The only difference was that Taylor had tons of friends while Megan had none.

That day, as Megan sat alone at a lunch table reading a book, it was Taylor who couldn't stand it anymore. Springer watched as, without warning, Taylor got up from her table of friends, walked across the sticky cafeteria floor, and plopped her tray down next to Megan. Apparently, Taylor had decided that Megan needed a friend and that she would be that friend.

From where Springer was located she could overhear parts of the conversation.

"I've read that book," Taylor said.

"I'm only halfway through," Megan said.

Springer listened as the girls continued to talk about the book.

"Oh, that part is good. But wait until you get to the next part, it's amazing!" Taylor said.

Megan put down her book and picked up her lunch, and the two girls spent the rest of the lunch period talking about other books they'd read. When the lunch bell rang, Megan picked up her things and said goodbye to Taylor.

"Bye, Megan," Taylor said.

Taylor didn't see Springer until she dropped off her tray.

"Taylor, come here," Springer said. "I want to tell you what it means to me that you did that. For you to take your lunchtime and spend it with Megan instead of your friends tells me a lot about your character. I'm very proud of you."

Without missing a beat, Taylor said, "Springer, I didn't do it to make you proud of me." With a flip of her ponytail, she was off to class.

❧

During Taylor's first year of middle school, Todd and Tara received an unexpected call. When the phone rang, Tara was making dinner, Todd was in his home office working, and Peyton and Ryan were in their rooms. The caller ID said the call was from Coppell Middle School East. Taylor was there, at volleyball practice, so Tara immediately grabbed the phone.

It was Springer.

"I need to talk to you about Taylor," she said. "She did something I think you and Todd should know about."

From the tone of her voice, Tara knew it was something serious, so as she listened, she walked down the hall to Todd's office and motioned for him to listen in. He picked up the other receiver in time to hear Springer say, ". . . the boy had his pants down, and before I knew what was happening, Taylor jumped up and closed the door so no one would see."

"She did what?" Todd asked, unable to comprehend what he'd just heard.

Tara and Springer laughed as they realized what Todd had missed, and Springer began the story again.

"When Taylor and her friends left band a couple of weeks ago, one of the special needs boys was using the bathroom directly across the hall from the band room," Springer began.

Todd looked at Tara, confusion in his eyes, but she just smiled and motioned for him to keep listening as Springer continued.

"He had forgotten to close the door, so when Taylor and her friends left the band room, they could see the boy in the bathroom with his pants down. Some of the kids stood there and laughed at him."

"Oh, that's terrible!" Todd said.

"Well, it was. Except that Taylor sprang into action. Instead of laughing with them, she jumped up and closed the door, so the boy would have his privacy."

Todd exhaled. This was much better than what he'd thought he'd heard.

"I was coming down the hall," Springer said, "and Taylor stopped me and told me what happened. I thanked her and said, 'You were looking out for someone who really needed looking out for. Good job, Taylor.' But that wasn't good enough for her."

Springer described how Taylor peppered her with questions as the conversation continued.

"Why are all these kids down here?" Taylor asked, referring to the isolated hallway far from the rest of the school.

"Well, baby, that's just where the room—" Springer tried to answer, but Taylor interrupted.

"But why are they separated from the rest of us? They should be with us."

Springer attempted to explain. "There are a couple of kids who strip down and run around naked before we can stop them."

"Yeah, but I bet if they're in the middle of the school, they wouldn't do that," Taylor said.

"That got me thinking," Springer said to Todd and Tara, "so I decided to do something about it." Though the incident had happened a few weeks prior, Springer told them where she'd been earlier that day. "I just got back from a campus leadership team meeting where I told them about Taylor's suggestion. I got them to agree. We're moving the special ed kids to the middle of the school, thanks to Taylor."

Twins Allison and Emily Sunshine were two of Taylor's best friends. Matt and Beth Sunshine, the twins' parents, had been good friends with Todd and Tara since before the girls were born. The three girls were only six weeks apart in age, and the families had only grown closer as the girls grew. Though the Sunshine family lived in Plano, about twenty minutes away from the Storch home in Coppell, the families managed to spend almost every weekend and most holidays together. On New Year's Eve they would even have T-shirts made, combining both family names into one—"The Suntorch family."

In the car with both families, on the way home from a very long Fourth of July, Tara suggested a stop at Starbucks.

"Yeah! We're going to Starbucks," Taylor said. "I'm going to get a crap-a-chino!"

"What did you say?" Tara asked. Her friends were puzzled too.

"A crap-a-chino, everybody wants to get crap-a-chinos."

"Do you mean a *Frappuccino*?"

The whole car burst into laughter, and Taylor joined them. "I always thought they were crap-a-chinos." Taylor was never one to let a good joke pass, even if it was on her. She had the self-confidence and poise to laugh at herself often.

When the families got together, Taylor, along with Allison and Emily, would lip-synch to music, write and act out skits, and make movie trailers for their favorite books, recording them on video. They called themselves AET Productions.

But even when her friends were over, Taylor always included Ryan and Peyton in what she was doing. For one video, Taylor cajoled her brother into dressing up in girls' clothes, promising that when she put it on YouTube, "No one would see it."

The video currently has more than two thousand views.

Taylor was always aware that Peyton and Ryan were watching. She took her role as a big sister seriously, and therefore picked her friends carefully. It was as if she were handpicking her girlfriends to be older sisters to her younger siblings. Taylor seemed to have a wisdom and maturity beyond her years.

Other parents noticed.

They would ask Todd and Tara how they had done it. But the Storches never had a good answer. They'd talk about how their parenting was an outpouring of their faith, or how Taylor was putting into practice the things she was learning at church and youth group. They'd tell parents how they always tried to be open with their kids and how there was a lot of laughter in their home.

But how did they tell them that their teenage daughter still wanted to snuggle with her dad while watching TV? That while other girls pulled away from their mothers, Taylor said that Tara was her best friend? Or that while most teens couldn't wait to hang out with their friends, Taylor still wanted to hang out with her brother and sister? The Storches were blessed, and they knew it.

They had a five-piece puzzle and everything fit perfectly.

⁂

The Storches were looking forward to their ski trip. It would be their first family vacation without the Sunshines since anyone in the Suntorch family could remember.

On Thursday night, March 11, 2010, while Todd got the car ready and Tara finished packing, Taylor worked on the "many things" she had due before spring break. One of those things was an autobiographical website. On Monday of that week, Taylor had turned in a poem she wrote as part of that project, and now she was finishing the other pieces. The next afternoon, she turned the rest of the project into Mr. Bush, her language arts teacher, and checked it off her list.

The poem she had turned in on Monday, March 8, read:

I Am
by Taylor

> I am outgoing and friendly.
> I wonder how long is forever.
> I hear support from my family whenever I need it.
> I see myself helping people in every way I can.
> I want to be on the Ellen DeGeneres show.
>
> I am outgoing and friendly.
> I pretend I can do anything I want to.
> I feel touched by the generosity of my sister.
> I touch people's lives.
> I worry about failing.
> I cry at the thought of losing a member of my family.
>
> I am outgoing and friendly.
> I understand how to make people feel happy.
> I say with pride that I am a Christian.

I dream about becoming a teacher.
I try to make every day like my last.
I hope to become successful in life.
I am outgoing and friendly.

Later that Friday, with everything checked off her list, she got in the car with her family and they drove to Vail, Colorado.

They knew it was going to be a trip of a lifetime.

—3—

The Cowboy

JEFF KARTUS
COLORADO

Before he left the house, Jeff and his wife, Vanessa, argued, and she told him not to go. "Your blood sugar is too low; you shouldn't be driving!" she insisted. But when Jeff was in *that* mood, often caused by hypoglycemia (low blood sugar), he wouldn't listen. And that day, the consequences were extreme.

Just blocks from their house, Jeff blacked out behind the wheel of his pickup truck, had a seizure, and lost control of the vehicle. With his foot still on the gas, the truck hit the median and shot into the air. It flipped across oncoming traffic until it rolled headlong into the front yard of a house, where a tree stopped its wild rampage. Broken glass littered the street and the truck was mangled beyond recognition. Witnesses called 911.

At home, Vanessa heard the sirens and cussed. She picked up her cell phone and tried to call Jeff. "Come on, answer the phone!"

But there was no answer.

She grabbed her shoes and car keys, then tried once more.

Still no answer.

She flung open her car door, threw the phone on the front seat, and started the car. Backing out of the driveway, she headed the same direction Jeff had just minutes earlier—the same direction the sirens were coming from. Vanessa had no doubt in her mind that Jeff had been in another car accident. The only question that remained was whether this would be the one that killed him, someone else, or both.

A longtime diabetic, Jeff had a history of blacking out, often at the most inopportune times. He'd blacked out in the bathroom multiple times, resulting in several concussions. He'd blacked out in the field while supervising crews of natural gas construction workers and eventually was put on medical leave. He'd even blacked out at his insurance agent's office. A week later they'd received a letter saying their car insurance had been cancelled.

Over the years, Jeff's diabetes had gotten so bad his kidneys began to fail. His blood sugar level would drop so quickly and so far that he couldn't do anything to prevent the blackouts or the seizures that inevitably followed. Often, he'd just get "stuck" doing the last thing he was doing before his sugar dropped.

One afternoon, after running errands, Jeff backed his pickup into the garage. Unbeknownst to him, his sugar level was already dropping to a dangerously low level. After the bumper hit the rear wall of the garage, Jeff kept applying pressure to the gas pedal. With the truck bed being lighter than the cab, the truck climbed the wall a bit, and the wheels began to spin. By now, Jeff was completely out of it, his hands frozen to the wheel. Unable to comprehend why the truck wasn't working right, he pressed harder on the gas.

The engine revved and the tires began to overheat and then smoke. A neighbor noticed and called the police. Dispatchers put the call out over the emergency radio system, and a friend who worked for the local sheriff's department recognized the address and knew it was Jeff. He also knew Jeff's condition. Immediately, he called his dispatcher and requested an ambulance.

"It's a medical emergency," he told them.

By the time the emergency personnel arrived, thick black smoke was pouring out of the garage and the tires had worn down to shreds. Melted rubber oozed from underneath the truck and spread across the garage, the smell permeating the entire neighborhood. Rescue personnel pulled Jeff out from behind the wheel and dragged him outside to safety before cutting the engine. They confirmed and then treated his low blood sugar. Ambulance drivers tried to coax Jeff to go to the hospital, but he wouldn't listen. Instead, as he often did in these situations, he became combative. Friends in the sheriff's department called Vanessa at her job at the local elementary school. She came home and tried to talk to him. But it didn't matter. He refused to listen. With his lips pursed together, he became unreachable.

Since his diabetes had worsened, everyone tried to tell him what to do and how to take care of it. But Jeff was stubborn. He was a man's man, a modern cowboy who didn't want to be told what to do, even if it was in his own best interest.

Unfortunately, his deteriorating health meant Vanessa had to be with him at all times. She did her best to make him breakfast, or remind him to eat, but even with her there, if he didn't want to eat, he wouldn't. Jeff was the kind of guy who made up his own mind.

It was quickly becoming one of the few things he still had control over.

༚

Jeff liked helping people. It made him feel good. When he was in elementary school, he thought it would be nice to help the elderly, and he started with the lady next door. As he grew, Jeff helped the neighbors by sweeping or shoveling their walks, or doing other chores around the neighborhood. No one told him he had to, and he didn't want money for his work, but he loved it when people noticed and appreciated his efforts. He was a good kid who always respected authority and never got in any trouble.

For as long as he could remember, Jeff had wanted to be a police officer. That kind of position would give him endless opportunities to help others and to gain the respect he hadn't always gotten at home. After graduating from high school, he had called the local police department to inquire about joining the force.

"Have you graduated from high school, son?" the recruiting officer had asked.

"Yes, sir. I just finished."

"Well, then come on in and fill out the paperwork."

"Yes, sir! But I want you to know I am diabetic." Jeff had integrity, and he wanted to make sure they knew about his disease. He'd been diagnosed two years earlier, even though he'd been having problems with his blood sugar for a couple of years prior to that. As soon as he had been diagnosed, they had put him on insulin, and he'd been on it since. He would be for the rest of his life.

"Aw, I'm sorry, son. You can't be a diabetic and be on the police force," the officer had said.

Crushed, Jeff had made more calls. To other police departments, to the state patrol, and to the sheriff's department. The answer was the same—they weren't hiring diabetics.

For a proud cowboy who just wanted to serve, the blow was severe and lasting. Jeff not only felt he wasn't good enough but also now felt different from everyone around him. When his mom told him the diabetes was his fault, that he hadn't gotten it from her, the cut was complete. Made to feel different and unwanted, Jeff felt as though his life was over before it started.

His dad got him a job driving cars for the executives at Excel Energy. Eventually, he moved into oil and gas construction. Because they couldn't move heavy equipment onto a homeowner's lawn, his crew was often required to dig ditches by hand. Early on, Jeff knew when his blood sugar was dropping, and he would take a break to get some food or a drink. But over the years, his blood sugar began to drop uncontrollably and without warning. Numerous times, Jeff blacked out and had seizures in the field, and his co-workers ended up having to call an ambulance. Finally, the company couldn't put up with the potential liability. Though Jeff had done his best for the company, had cracked and dry hands from the manual labor, and had deep tan lines etched in his face from more than thirty years in the sun, he no longer had a job. They placed him on disability.

To Jeff, this was just one more example of how useless and unwanted he was. Though his health was failing, the psychological toll and assault to his identity as a provider for his family were much, much worse.

◦┋◦

In 2008, Jeff's doctor told him he needed dialysis. But once the leathered cowboy heard the news he said, "No way," and turned his boots around and left. As Jeff often said, "I'll be good as long as I stay busy; it's the stopping that kills you." He knew dialysis would take away what little freedom he had left.

At home, before he could even take off his jean jacket, Vanessa announced, "You're getting dialysis."

Jeff tried to argue, but Vanessa insisted. "The doctor just called, and without dialysis, you have less than six months to live."

Reluctantly, Jeff agreed. But it was only a temporary solution. Jeff needed a transplant, and in 2009 he went on the list. Family members were tested to see if they were a match, but they weren't. A new kidney and pancreas would have to come from a stranger.

In the beginning, Jeff called the doctor's office every couple of days until someone finally explained it could take *years* before a match would come up. The waiting list was long, and he was relatively new. But it was his only hope.

◦┋◦

As Vanessa raced to follow the sirens, she prayed.

Jeff's truck had come to a stop in her co-worker's lawn. Vanessa knew it was bad. His truck had left the main street and rolled through a backyard to the front of a house located on another street, where it had hit a tree. Vanessa ran across the street, her heart pumping, to see if Jeff was still alive.

Please be breathing.

A local officer from the sheriff's department recognized her from the many calls he'd made to their house. "It's his wife," he told the officers restraining her, and they let her go. She could see that Jeff was still breathing, but paramedics didn't have much time to talk. She watched as they cautiously braced his neck. It didn't look good.

At the hospital, Jeff was put on a ventilator. He had broken both the C-6 and C-7 vertebrae, and questions arose as to whether he'd ever walk again. But once again, Jeff pulled through. This time his recovery was more difficult. He lay in the hospital for a month, and then they wanted to release him to a rehab center.

Jeff was relieved to hear that Vanessa would have none of that. She took him home and cared for him herself.

During his recovery, doctors had "frozen" his position on the organ donation list. They hadn't removed him, but he couldn't get an organ until he healed from the accident. And recovery wasn't easy. Even after months of rehab, he could barely walk. To get up the stairs, he had to sit down and go up one at a time—backward—while Vanessa helped. But they didn't give up. Together, they got him well enough to walk on his own, to have his trachea tube removed, and to get back on active status.

By now, Jeff had been on dialysis for two years, and he didn't feel well. He'd started swelling and at times he could barely bend his arm to brush his teeth. His Wrangler jeans didn't fit any longer, and the snaps on his cowboy shirts routinely popped open. His blood sugar problems were getting worse. Dialysis wasn't enough. A kidney/pancreas transplant was the only thing that could help him, but he still hadn't gotten a call. No one was sure how much longer he could physically take it.

—4—

The Nurse

PATRICIA WINTERS
ARIZONA

On July 4, 1976, while the rest of America watched fireworks bursting in national pride, six-year-old Patricia watched her father die. Patricia, her brother, and sister had just gotten out of their new pool and were drying off when someone noticed her father's body floating in the water.

"Reno," her mother said, calling him by his nickname, "if you're kidding, I'm going to kill you!" Patricia's mother jumped in—all 120 pounds of her—and dragged him out of the water while Patricia watched. Friends and family tried to resuscitate him, but her father died of a heart attack before the ambulance arrived. All Patricia could think was, *If he's dead, how is she going to kill him?*

Patricia's life quickly changed. After her father's death, her grandmother became her primary caretaker. Her mother became emotionally detached, went back to work, started dating, and got remarried. Within four years of her father's death, Patricia's family moved to Scottsdale, Arizona. It didn't take long for Patricia to become acutely aware that she'd *forgotten* more about her father than she remembered. The memories had faded, and that bothered her.

Now thirty-six, married, and lying on the couch too sick to get up, she watched her own two kids playing. If she died, would they remember her? Sadly, she already knew the answer. Sam was just six—the same age she was when her father died—but Jack was only four. If she died now, Sam's memory would fade over time and Jack might not remember her at all. It was a painful thought, one that devastated her already dysfunctional heart. She was dying and she knew it. Patricia closed her eyes, trying to squeeze back the tears, and offered her kids the only thing she had the strength to give them—a prayer.

Please, God, let them always know how hard I fought to be with them, how much I wanted to raise them, and how dearly I loved them.

Growing up, Patricia thought of herself as healthy. In high school, she was on the track team. She was strong and fast. She had a type A personality and was involved in a variety of activities. Before getting married, she worked full-time as a nurse, started work on her master's degree, ran marathons, and was active in her church. Heart problems weren't supposed to affect people like her. But genetics weren't in her favor. On her father's side, mortality seemed to hit by age forty-two. By that unimaginably young age, everyone had suddenly dropped dead from a heart attack. Her dad was the last to go. Patricia assumed that since she was so active, she was immune. She'd had her heart checked when she was young, she took care of herself, and everything seemed fine. What could go wrong?

During her first pregnancy, Patricia's heart rate occasionally shot into the two hundreds—much higher than it should have been—but it always came back down. As a labor and delivery nurse, she'd seen lots of women overreact to the changes in their bodies, and she didn't want to be one of them. Every pregnant woman had trouble breathing; why should she be any different? But after Sam was born, some of her symptoms persisted. And then new ones emerged.

Patricia began to have episodes where she felt as if she would pass out. Her heart rate would increase and then quickly decrease. She began experiencing tunnel vision. With her history, she knew these new symptoms could be serious. Her family doctor recommended she see a cardiologist.

Her second visit to the cardiologist resulted in a diagnosis of atrial fibrillation, or an irregular heartbeat. The doctor wanted to perform an ablation to fix it and promised she'd feel better once it was done. But Patricia was pregnant again. The procedure would have to wait.

During her second pregnancy, the symptoms worsened. At work, she would be in the delivery room, working alongside a doctor, and she'd break into a sweat. Her heart would start racing, and she'd feel as if she were going to faint. One day, when assisting her OB with a delivery, it happened again.

"Are you okay?" her doctor whispered.

"I'm fine, I just don't feel well," Patricia said.

"Has this ever happened before?"

"A few times," Patricia said. She brushed it off as she focused on the patient.

After the patient had given birth, her doctor pulled her aside and said, "We're putting you on something to keep it from happening again."

Patricia started on a low dose of medication. For a while it lowered her heart rate. She felt great, and was pleased when, in August of 2005, she gave birth to another healthy boy, whom they named Jack.

⸰⸰⸰

On the day before Thanksgiving, almost three months after giving birth to Jack, Patricia entered the hospital for the ablation. Things were going well for the young family. The boys were thriving, and her husband's mortgage business had taken off, allowing them to buy a spacious new home in an upscale neighborhood for their expanding family. Patricia worried more about thawing the turkey than the ablation.

But on Thanksgiving Day, Patricia couldn't breathe. She was constantly short of breath, and it frightened her. She called the cardiologist and he suggested she go back on her medication. She did, but it didn't help. Over the next few days, she felt so bad she couldn't even hold baby Jack.

In the emergency room, the doctors did an echocardiogram and X-rays. These were standard tests for diagnosing heart disorders, but it was the first time they'd been done on Patricia. After looking at the results, the surprised physician asked, "Why didn't you tell us you felt this bad?"

Doctors explained how the ablation had stopped her heart from racing, but the racing had actually been helping her. Now, her heart was unable to keep up with her body's needs.

"We're going to admit you," the doctor said. "You have a 10 percent ejection fraction, and we can't let you go home with that."

"What does that mean?" Joe asked after the doctor left.

"I think it has something to do with the heart pumping," Patricia said. She never liked learning about the heart because it reminded her of her family history. She called a friend, who looked it up.

"It has to do with the volume of blood flowing out of the heart. Normal is 60 percent to 70 percent," her friend said.

"Mine's 10 percent."

"Patricia! It says here that's not compatible with life!"

The cardiologist arrived. "We're sending you up to ICU, and we're starting you on meds, but we're not sure what will happen next. You need to get your things in order—right now," he said.

Patricia had worked in a hospital long enough to know that was code for, "You don't have long to live."

She was eventually diagnosed with peripartum cardiomyopathy, a serious disorder that occurs during pregnancy, which essentially meant her heart muscle wasn't contracting forcefully enough to pump blood to her vital organs. Approximately 50 percent of women with the condition spontaneously recover with medication. Another 45 percent recover, but not fully. The remainder need a pacemaker, possibly even a transplant. Patricia was in the latter category.

In January of 2006, doctors installed an ICD that would zap her heart into rhythm whenever it started to beat erratically. Though it was meant to be used only occasionally, it was soon pacing her 100 percent of the time. Still, doctors were confident that with time her functioning would increase.

⚜

In 2008, doctors at Mayo agreed that Patricia wasn't going to recover as expected. It had been more than three years since the symptoms had started, and even with the pacemaker, her heart was still operating at a mere 10 percent.

"You're going to need a transplant, but not for another five or ten years," her doctor told her.

Patricia wasn't happy with the news. If a transplant was the only thing that would cure her, she didn't want to wait ten years to get one. Constantly short of breath, she prayed, *God, how sick do I have to be before I can get better?*

But things started to deteriorate quickly. By the summer of 2008, her condition had gotten considerably worse. Her cardiologist, Dr. Copeland, decided that Patricia needed to be put on the transplant list as a status two—meaning her name was on the list but at a lower priority. Dr. Copeland expected it would still be a year before she needed a new heart, but now she was on the list in case things got worse.

And they did.

At the beginning of September, Patricia spent most of her days lying in bed or on the couch. The boys were in daycare, and it was all she could do to pick them up from school at 4:30, feed them, and watch them until bedtime at 7:30. At best, she was a mom for three hours a day. There was additional stress too. The economy was taking a toll on Joe's business, and with Patricia no longer working, the new house that had seemed like a reward now became a financial burden.

When she experienced another decrease in functioning, Dr. Copeland changed her status on the list to a B1, which meant she needed a heart sooner rather than later.

In the fall of 2008, Patricia was back in the hospital. Dr. Copeland was on vacation, and a new doctor saw her. "I don't see why you're on this list," he said. "You're on the right medications; you just need to go home and stop being so anxious." Patricia had never felt so dismissed. Not only did the doctor think she was just having anxiety, but he also took away her only hope—he removed her name from the transplant list.

Patricia fell into a dark depression. Was this somehow all in her head? Was she just an emotional woman with anxiety like the doctor said? She knew she'd been under a lot of stress, but her symptoms were very real. With no hope, what was she supposed to do?

For months, she did little more than curl up in a ball, drink, and hope to die. Friends grew worried and sent her medical records to out-of-state doctors, who confirmed her need for a transplant. But the family couldn't afford to move. Joe's business was failing, and with the housing market collapse, they were about to lose their home and their cars. Besides, Patricia was too sick to move.

In January of 2009, Patricia ended up in the hospital yet again, this time with pericarditis—an inflammation of the sac that surrounds the heart. It was more painful than childbirth, and it was the last straw in her ongoing battle to live. Though she would do anything to save her boys from experiencing what she'd experienced—the death of a parent—Patricia was ready to die.

A few days after being released from the hospital, Patricia got a call from Dr. Copeland's office. The transplant coordinator wanted to know what was going on and why she hadn't been in for her regular evaluations—a necessary condition to remain on the list.

Patricia explained how the other doctor had taken her off the list and how she'd given up hope. The coordinator was alarmed and set up an appointment for Patricia to come in immediately.

In the office, Dr. Copeland quickly put her back on the list. Because she was reinstated as a B1, he told her to expect a new heart in about three months. With renewed hope, Patricia did everything she could to fight for life. She wanted to be the best mom she could while waiting for the phone call. Patricia and Joe also promised the boys that as soon as Mommy got her new heart, they'd all go to Disneyland.

❧

The call came at 2:00 a.m. Patricia and Joe woke up the boys and told them to get dressed. "Do you know where we're going?" Patricia asked.

"To get your new heart!" Sam said.

"Yeah, we're going to Disney!" Jack added.

After dropping the boys off at his parents' house, Joe dropped Patricia at the hospital door. But by the time he parked the car and walked up to Patricia's room, she was ready to leave. "The heart was infected. They want to wait for another one."

Sadly, they picked up the boys and went to IHOP for breakfast. Two tired and disappointed boys cried. Patricia wanted to cry too.

Getting a call means that the patient is at the top of the list, so Patricia and Joe weren't surprised when a few days later, at dinnertime, they got another call. But they hadn't even left the driveway when the doctor called them again and said, "This heart wasn't good enough. We need to wait for the perfect heart."

The boys got ice cream instead of Disney. The date was August 4, 2009.

❧

Patricia spent most of Christmas Day 2009 in bed. It was hard to breathe and her energy was spent. She listened to the boys downstairs, playing around the Christmas tree that she'd been too tired to help decorate. It had been *four months* and there hadn't been another call. That's when Patricia decided to give up—in a totally different way.

It had taken time, but Patricia finally realized she wasn't the one in charge, and now she wanted to give control back to the One who was. *It's yours, Lord. I can't control this. It's your timing, not mine.* As she prayed, her body relaxed and she felt a burden lift from her heart.

She had always hoped that the perfect heart was out there. But now, instead of thinking about how she would receive this new heart, she started to think about the person who would be giving it. She began praying for her future donor and her donor's family. In her mind, she saw her donor as a twentysomething young woman. Maybe God needed that perfect heart to spend Christmas with *her* family. Patricia prayed the young woman didn't have children and that she was with her loved ones that Christmas Day.

She finished her prayer for the donor's family by asking for peace for them, regardless of what was happening at the moment or what was going to happen in the future.

She prayed the same prayer for her own family.

—5—

The Bike Rider

JONATHAN FINGER
COLORADO

Alone in his bed, listening to the rhythms of the hospital and the hum of the nurses' conversations outside his door, Jonathan stared death in the face and wondered if he should back down. His doctors were waiting for a decision, but it was his choice to make: dialysis or death. Jonathan had spent the last two years fighting, and he was exhausted. Hopeless, really. At twenty-two, he wondered if a lifetime of fighting was a life worth living. If he decided to forgo the dialysis, it would end. But questions remained. Was refusing dialysis taking the easy way out? Was it a sin to want to stop fighting and just give up on life? Would he be committing suicide?

He thought about the questions a lot. As a believer, he knew there was a great adventure waiting for him on the other side. It was, he believed, a place where he would receive grace, rest, and health. And it wasn't like he *wanted* to kill himself; he just wasn't sure he wanted to prolong the inevitable anymore. Jonathan didn't feel good, and he didn't feel good about himself. His failed kidney transplant, as evidenced by his high creatinine level, was the cause of his physical discomfort. The fact he hadn't taken care of the kidney he'd received less than two years earlier caused the emotional pain.

Jonathan was thoughtful, analytical, and sensitive. He didn't want to make a rash decision one way or the other without considering all the alternatives and consequences of his choice. So despite the fluid buildup in his body and his overall weakened state, he fought through the mental fog and contemplated what he should do.

A knock interrupted his thoughts. He glanced up to see a priest from his parents' church.

"Hello, Jonathan," Father Seraphim said.

Priests from his parents' church often came to visit him when he was in the hospital. They occasionally made Jonathan feel awkward as they prayed over him, read from their service books, or performed other rituals that were unfamiliar to him. Despite his uncertainty about another priest visiting, Jonathan offered him a chair.

Father Seraphim pulled it up next to Jonathan's bed, and Jonathan was quickly relieved to see he was less about the rituals and more about the conversation. The priest asked questions about Jonathan's medical condition and talked about Jonathan's family and his own. As they conversed, Jonathan became more comfortable. So when the father asked if he had any concerns, Jonathan knew it was his opportunity to talk about what was on his mind.

"I'm struggling with whether I should go on dialysis or not, and I only have until tomorrow morning to decide."

"What's the struggle?"

"I don't think I really want to, but I'm not sure it's okay to say that." The priest nodded knowingly, and Jonathan continued. "I feel guilty. I'm not sure, as a Christian, or even as a person, that it's okay for me to throw in the towel and say I'm finished. I'm only twenty-two. Can I really say I've had enough and I don't want to fight anymore? Is this even my decision to make?"

Saying aloud what so far he'd only thought frightened Jonathan, and he searched the priest's bearded face for a reaction. But Father Seraphim's knitted brow revealed only his concern.

"It is your decision to make. And it's not suicide to forsake dialysis," he said. "You're not ending your life; you're just allowing nature to take its course."

Jonathan found his response comforting.

The priest continued, "Of course, if you ask for my personal opinion, I'd hope you'd choose dialysis; you've fought valiantly to get here. But it's okay if you want to go home."

Listening to the priest's words helped Jonathan remove the guilt from his decision. That allowed him to look at both options clearly. The priest was right; Jonathan had fought hard to get to this point. Thinking of himself as a fighter helped give him a new perspective on what he wanted to do next.

◦§◦

Jonathan was in elementary school when a nasty bike wreck tossed him into the air; he hit the pavement with a sickening thud and then skidded across the rough concrete. The results were as expected—scrapes on his arms and legs and a few bruises. Everyone thought he was fine, until some unexpected symptoms emerged— the most concerning was his coffee-colored urine.

His parents took him to the doctor, and tests revealed that the discoloration was caused by blood. "Don't worry," the doctor advised. "He probably just got hit in the kidney when he fell. This happens to boxers and professional fighters all the time." But the doctor also advised Jonathan to come back if his symptoms persisted. It could be a sign of something more serious.

For the next several years, around Christmas, Jonathan seemed to come down with an upper respiratory infection and a fever. Oddly, the coffee-colored urine would also return. But the symptoms always went away. Doctors began to suspect something was wrong, and they performed some additional tests.

"We think you may have IgA nephropathy," the doctor said when the results came in. He explained how the disease impedes the kidneys' ability to filter waste, which is why it appears discolored.

For IgA patients, this frequently happens when they are fighting off an upper respiratory infection. He went on to explain that for 80 percent of patients with the disease, it wouldn't cause severe problems, but the other 20 percent would find themselves with end-stage renal failure. "The only way to know for sure is to do a biopsy."

"But he's only twelve and he feels all right. Does he really need that?" Jonathan's mother asked.

"I don't think it's necessary. His blood work is normal, and he doesn't show any loss of kidney function, so just continue what you've been doing. But you should try to stay on top of it and have his blood checked once a year."

For the first few years, Jonathan had lab work regularly. But the results showed he was fine. Over time, the lab work became less frequent. By the time Jonathan was in his late teens, a few years had gone by since he'd last had it checked.

❦

Jonathan's family owned and operated one of the premier retail piano stores in the United States. After graduating from high school, Jonathan followed in his father's footsteps and became a piano technician. By the time he was twenty, he was ready for the next step—a yearlong apprenticeship at the piano factory in Germany.

Just weeks before he was supposed to leave, someone remembered that Jonathan hadn't had a blood test in a while. To be safe, it was decided he should have a physical and blood work done before he left.

The next day his doctor called. "You need to come in immediately. Your results came back, and you have a 45 percent loss in kidney function."

Jonathan was terrified. He was supposed to leave for Germany in a week; instead, he found himself at Boulder Community Hospital, where further tests showed he had indeed lost functioning. He had the biopsy they'd discussed so many years before, and it confirmed the doctor's original diagnosis—IgA nephropathy.

Why is this happening to me? Why now? he asked himself in a fruitless search for answers. He knew the diagnosis meant he would have to go on kidney replacement therapy of some kind—either dialysis or a transplant. But for now, his doctors felt it was safe for him to go to Germany as long as he saw a doctor there. Despite the whirlwind of medical activity, he left for his year in Germany.

◦◦◦

In Germany, the air had an odd smell to it and things tasted differently than they had back home. His food preferences began to change too. Jonathan had a sweet tooth, and he'd often crave ice cream. But in Germany his sweet tooth disappeared. Now he craved salty foods. He also noticed a taste like metal, or possibly ammonia, in his mouth. His appetite decreased, he tired easily, and he was sleeping more. Jonathan attributed these changes to his new environment.

By the time Jonathan returned from Germany in February of 2000, it was obvious his kidneys had continued to deteriorate. "You don't have another year left," his doctor said. "You're going to need a transplant before the end of the year."

Over the next few weeks, his doctor began the workup required to find a donor and to prepare Jonathan for transplant surgery. Family members were tested, and it was determined his mom was a match. Doctors told him what a privilege it was to bypass the waiting list and just move forward. The surgery was scheduled for November.

◦◦◦

It took almost a year after the transplant before Jonathan was on a manageable dose of steroids, returned to a fit weight, and became more emotionally and physically stable. He moved to his own place and worked as a piano technician. He was also passionate about technology, and on the side, he began building websites. As things stabilized, he went back to school to become an EMT and had future hopes of becoming an RN and a flight nurse. Things were finally starting to look up.

But living alone, with a busy schedule, Jonathan didn't always make the best decisions. There were days he would forget to take his medications. He felt just as good, or possibly even better, on those days, so over time he became even less consistent, then noncompliant. Soon he wondered why he was taking them at all. He stopped taking the medications entirely, and he felt great. The three months that followed were amazing. He felt better than he had since before he went to Germany. His well-being validated his belief that the drugs made him feel lousy. He was right about that—but he was wrong to think he didn't need them.

In the summer of 2002 he got really sick with a fever and other symptoms. He caught what he thought was a nasty flu. As it progressed, Jonathan's mind grew foggy, and he stopped all rational thinking. He lay in bed for weeks, unable to comprehend that he should probably see someone.

One day he woke up smacking his lips, a vague sensation of metal in his mouth. Then he realized it tasted more like ammonia. That was the wake-up call he needed. With an overwhelming sense of dread, he called his nephrologist (kidney doctor) and made an appointment for that afternoon. The tests confirmed what everyone suspected: Jonathan was rejecting his mother's kidney.

He was sent to a hospital in Denver, where they tried drastic drug therapies to stop the kidney from failing, but it was too late.

An angry doctor confronted him. "You've lost the kidney. Do you have any idea how many people are waiting to get one of those? And you just threw it away! In fact," she snapped, "your creatinine level is so high you should be comatose! You took the gift your mother gave you, and you ruined it. Start thinking about dialysis. You'll be lucky if you ever get a kidney again."

He didn't need her admonitions. Though his mind was still foggy, Jonathan understood the gravity of what had happened. But her comments made him wonder: Should he just give up?

He'd already lost hope that he'd ever feel better. Now he was just tired of fighting.

❖

As Father Seraphim got up to leave, Jonathan finally had the clarity he needed to make his decision. Dialysis or death. Jonathan looked them both square in the eye and made his choice.

He chose dialysis.

He believed what the priest had said. He *had* fought valiantly to get here, and he wasn't ready to give up yet. He also knew that going forward, his path wouldn't be easy.

For the next eight years, Jonathan underwent dialysis up to four hours a day, five days a week. He had to give up his job as a piano technician. He started working in Information Technology because he could work from home when he wasn't feeling well. Eventually, Jonathan got trained to give himself dialysis at home. It was more convenient and he felt more in control. But it still wasn't stress-free. He'd scream in pain from the leg cramps. Or a vein would explode, and he'd watch a lump as large as an orange immediately swell up under his skin. If he pulled the needle out and didn't get the gauze over his arm right away, he would spurt blood, sometimes all over the walls. There were simple frustrations too, like wanting to grab a snack, ride his bike, or travel—things he couldn't do while tied to the dialysis machine.

When his name was put back on the transplant list, Jonathan knew odds were against his finding a donor organ his body wouldn't reject. He needed the perfect kidney. Sitting in his chair, his arm hooked up to a machine that cleansed his blood, Jonathan promised himself, and God, that if he was ever given the gift of another kidney, he would treasure it.

— 6 —

The Teenager

ASHLEY ZOLLER
SOUTH DAKOTA

"Ashley, can you help with the dishes?" Dueene asked as her daughter walked from the dining room into the kitchen of JD's Pizza. It wasn't an unusual request; it was a family restaurant and everybody did what he or she could to help.

"No!" Seventeen-year-old Ashley's short, curt reply caught Dueene off guard.

Standing behind the counter, Dueene could see the dinner line was growing longer and the place was starting to fill up. She knew as soon as the pizzas were done some of the kitchen staff would have to leave their posts to make deliveries, and the restaurant would be even more shorthanded. Dueene needed help.

"Please, Ashley," Dueene begged.

A customer drummed his fingers on the countertop.

"What can I get you?" Dueene asked him.

"No!" Ashley said again, and then for emphasis, "And you can't make me!"

Dueene could hear the agitation rising in Ashley's voice, and she knew what was coming next—Ashley was about to flip out.

51

Dueene didn't have time to argue, not with customers waiting. She handed a receipt to the man on the other side of the counter and tucked a strand of blonde hair behind her ear. "Your pizza will be ready in just a minute," she promised.

Dueene was worn out.

She loved her daughter dearly and hated it when Ashley acted this way. It wasn't good for business, and it certainly wasn't good for their relationship. But Dueene also knew that Ashley was right. Though her teenager was quite capable of helping her with the dishes, if she was unwilling Dueene couldn't force her. Dueene knew from past experience that if Ashley wanted to scream and yell, there was nothing she could do to stop her.

"What can I get you?" Dueene asked the next customer.

Ashley was born frail, weighing just three pounds, fifteen ounces. For two weeks, Dueene wasn't allowed to take her beautiful baby home while she was cared for in the Neonatal Intensive Care Unit (NICU) of the Santa Barbara hospital. When she finally got Ashley home, she was so tiny that when Dueene laid a decorative pinecone next to her baby, Ashley was smaller than the pinecone. Dueene tried to coax her fragile baby girl to eat, but Ashley was difficult—she didn't want to eat.

But more was wrong than just Ashley's preemie weight. At two months old, after another stay in the hospital for pneumonia, Ashley started to cry. And she didn't stop crying for *years.*

When Dueene told people that, she knew it sounded like an exaggeration, but it was the truth: all Ashley did was cry. She cried when Dueene held her and when she put her down. She cried when she was hungry and when she was fed. She cried when she was wet and when she was dry. The crying never stopped.

And when Ashley cried, it wasn't sniveling or whimpering; she was full-blown *screaming* at the top of her lungs. She cried every day and every night—Ashley didn't sleep. No one had seen anything like it. The only relief Dueene got from what she affectionately called her "little crying machine" was the twenty-minute bursts of silence while Ashley was in the swing and it was moving. As soon as the swing stopped, the crying started again. The swing was a godsend; it was the only thing that satisfied Ashley. Dueene used it so often the metal actually bent from use.

Dueene knew something was terribly wrong. She took Ashley to the pediatrician, who recommended she see a specialist, who recommended more specialists. "It's like she's screaming bloody murder," Dueene told each of them. The doctors had lots of recommendations: gas drops, stool softeners, different brands of formula, goat's milk, and starting her on rice cereal. But they didn't have a cure for whatever caused Ashley's discomfort.

After eight months of pointless visits with no end in sight, Dueene grew frustrated. The single mom worked full-time and she wasn't getting any help from Ashley's dad. It was too much for one person. Dueene decided to move back to Rapid City, South Dakota, where she had grown up, so she could be closer to family. Ashley cried the entire flight to Rapid City and continued to wail once she was there.

⚹

At age two, Ashley weighed less than twenty-five pounds and had very limited functioning. The doctor visits continued in Rapid City, where one doctor's visit led to a referral for three more. The diagnoses began to accumulate. Doctors' visits were followed by therapy visits. At three, Ashley finally learned to walk, but she didn't stop crying.

Ashley was four when a musculoskeletal specialist thought he heard a heart murmur. A team of specialists flew into Rapid City monthly, and it was recommended that Ashley see the cardiologist to have the murmur checked. Dueene set up yet another doctor's appointment, but she didn't have high expectations. However, this appointment would change their lives.

After taking one look at Ashley—her upturned nose, flattened nasal bridge, small chin, wide mouth with prominent lips, and the starburst pattern on her iris—the cardiologist said the words that unlocked the mystery that was Ashley. "She's got Williams syndrome." Williams syndrome is a genetic mutation of the seventh chromosome that happens in one out of every seventy-five hundred newborns. Approximately twenty-five genes (out of twenty-five thousand) are deleted. Williams syndrome patients all have a consistent set of identifying traits and are vaguely elfin in appearance. The cardiologist called them "pixie people" because of their diminutive size and telltale facial characteristics. Newborns are often colicky, perhaps due to their hyperacusis (sensitive hearing). Feeding problems, low birth weight, and slow weight gain plague them from birth.

As Dueene asked more questions, she began to see how Ashley's medical history lined up with the diagnosis; though it scared her, it also gave her hope. It wasn't all bad news. Williams syndrome kids have special needs, but they also have an intriguing set of personality traits. They are highly social with remarkable verbal abilities and often have an affinity for music.

The doctor spent two hours talking to Dueene. For the first time, Dueene understood her daughter. Armed with a diagnosis, Dueene was able to more knowledgeably navigate the medical system and choose appropriate therapies for Ashley. Within weeks, Ashley stopped crying.

It had only taken four years.

Over the years, Dueene watched her daughter become more independent and discover her own interests. Ashley was crazy about monster trucks and wedding cakes; she often obsessed about them. Dueene couldn't allow Ashley to go to the fairgrounds to watch the monster trucks perform because it irritated her asthma, but she helped her daughter get a ride in one driven by a friend. It was the best day of Ashley's life. After watching shows on TV about decorative wedding cakes, Ashley decided that instead of a bride and groom on the top of her cake, she wanted his-and-her monster trucks. Her eyes lit up, her speech got faster, and she bounced in her seat as she talked about her passions.

Friendly and social, Ashley had so much about her to love, but by her teens a dark side showed up. Every morning started with a mother-daughter struggle. Ashley would get up wanting to fight. Dueene would try to get her to eat breakfast, and Ashley would respond, "I don't want to eat that. I don't like that." Further coaxing only resulted in Ashley screaming, "You can't make me!"

Ashley then refused to take her medications. After much fighting and tears on both sides, Dueene would have to physically make her.

While Ashley was in school, Dueene found a few hours of peace working at the restaurant. Then Dueene would pick her up and the fighting would start all over again. Dueene hated it. It wasn't at all what she wanted, but she also knew that sometimes Ashley couldn't control herself.

The screaming and arguing went on for years. Doctors prescribed mood stabilizers and antidepressants. They didn't seem to help. Dueene knew Ashley was having headaches and those alone made her irritable, but the irritability grew into rage.

As things worsened, Ashley began hitting Dueene, and then Dueene's boyfriend, Jeff, the only male role model in her life. The physical violence got so out of control that there were days Dueene had to physically restrain Ashley. At times, she even thought about calling the police for her own safety.

Though her crying as an infant had been frustrating and exhausting, as a teen Ashley's anger was turning into something more dangerous. Dueene wasn't sure how it would end.

⚘

On a weekday in December, Dueene took eighteen-year-old Ashley to the eye doctor for a routine visit. "Have you been having headaches?" he asked.

Dueene listened as Ashley told him about the intense headaches she was experiencing almost constantly. Dueene was surprised. Though Ashley had mentioned the headaches, she hadn't complained. By this time Dueene was so used to Ashley's medical problems that she no longer got too worked up about anything. There was always something wrong with Ashley; she always had a pain somewhere. But as Dueene heard Ashley describe the severe pain knifing through the back of her eye, she thought to herself, *No wonder she's so mean.*

The eye doctor recommended they see a corneal specialist, who showed Dueene the problem: Ashley's eye was coning, an inherited condition called keratoconus. "This is likely the cause of her headaches and eye pain," he said. The doctor went on to explain that Ashley probably couldn't see well out of that eye.

While several things could be done for Ashley, her vision would continue to deteriorate. Eventually she would need a corneal transplant. "Most of my transplant patients say they wish they hadn't waited so long," the doctor said.

Dueene was shocked that her daughter needed eye surgery, but she was hopeful that the corneal transplant would help Ashley to see and feel better. Since corneas were more readily available than other kinds of donor organs, the doctor decided to go ahead and schedule Ashley for the corneal transplant while they were there.

The date was set for March 22, 2010.

Part 2

Rewriting the Stories

—7—

Waiting Rooms

AROUND MIDNIGHT
MONDAY, MARCH 15, 2010
ST. MARY'S HOSPITAL, GRAND JUNCTION, COLORADO

Tara

"Would you be willing to donate Taylor's organs?" the doctor asked. I looked at Todd and I knew my answer. But I wanted to make sure we agreed. We hadn't spoken to each other about it, but we'd each had conversations with my brother Bill. As I searched Todd's eyes for his answer, the events of the past twelve hours flashed through my mind.

❖

Todd and I had ridden two and a half hours from the hospital in Vail and waited at least an hour in the St. Mary's hospital lobby before the orthopedic surgeon came out to tell us what was going on with Taylor. He was the first medical professional to talk to us since we had arrived at St. Mary's. When he sat down across from us, he introduced himself and his role.

I wanted to scream, "Just tell us how she is!" but I held my tongue.

Finally, he leaned in, rested his elbows on his knees, and told us what we'd been waiting so long to hear: "She has a fractured collarbone, and she's broken a couple of ribs. Her jaw is cracked. She's also lost some teeth, and her left leg shows a compound fracture in several places."

By now it was after midnight, and we were all very tired. I was so cold I was shaking, and I couldn't seem to wrap my mind around his words.

"Both lungs collapsed, so they put chest tubes in before she left Vail," the doctor added.

His list seemed endless. *Had they told us all this at the Vail ER?* I remembered them saying they couldn't operate on her there— that's why she had to be life-flighted to a larger hospital. Denver was out of the question because of the inclement weather, so they had sent us to St. Mary's in Grand Junction. Todd, the kids, and I had taken a hundred-and-fifty-mile shuttle ride on mountain roads while a winter storm raged around us.

"She has a pelvic fracture and she's fractured at least one clavicle," the doctor continued.

My head hurt. I tried to blink back the tears pooling in my eyes.

"We're working on her leg right now. It's pretty bad. I had to set it, and we've attached rods to hold it in place."

The tears started to flow as I thought about Taylor with rods in her legs. Volleyball was Taylor's life. Outside of school, she spent more time on the volleyball court than anywhere else. Her club team had just started playing in out-of-state tournaments. I couldn't imagine anything worse for her than missing a tournament.

"She has a tournament coming up in a few weeks. It's pretty important to her," Todd said. "Will she be able to play?"

"She's not going to make that tournament," the doctor said.

As a consultant, Todd was used to quickly assessing situations, identifying problems, and coming up with plans to fix things. But I could see he was uneasy about this.

"When we see her, I know she's going to want to know, so, how long do you think it will take her to be back on the court?" Todd asked.

"I've already done the surgery on her leg and that should heal fine," the surgeon said. "We can fix the collarbone, broken ribs, and her jaw. Under normal circumstances, if I do everything I can, it would take six months to a year, and with rehab, she would be ready to play in eighteen months, but—"

At the time, the words "normal circumstances" just whizzed right past me. "Eighteen months? That's too long!" I said, looking at Todd. "High school . . ." he said. "She's going to be devastated!"

High school volleyball tryouts were just a few months away, and it was all Taylor and her friends talked about. Making the high school team meant everything to her.

But I couldn't think about it then; the surgeon was still talking.

". . . that's the least of your worries; broken bones aren't life-threatening. Before we can even begin to worry about that, we need to focus on her *head injuries*. Her C7 is fractured, and her brain is swelling. The neurosurgeon and her team are still in surgery trying to relieve the pressure. That's where our attention needs to be focused right now. Until we get the swelling under control, we can't worry about the rest of her injuries."

I felt my heart racing as I tried to comprehend his words. *Fractured C7? Was that the spine? Brain swelling? What did that mean?* The doctor shifted uncomfortably in his seat and then stood to leave. "The neurosurgeon will be out to talk to you as soon as she finishes. Do you have any questions?"

Todd looked at me; his eyes were red-rimmed and watery. After eighteen years of marriage, I knew he had the same question I did. His voice cracked when he asked it. "Are you saying we need to be prepared for a life or death situation?"

The doctor took a deep breath and slowly exhaled before he spoke. "You're going to need to speak to the neurosurgeon, but you need to prepare yourselves for that."

Somewhere deep inside me a scream bubbled up and exploded into the back of my throat in a burst of bile. I jumped up and ran for the restroom.

Peyton and Ryan had gone with a chaplain to get some food, so they weren't present when the doctor gave us the news. But they heard me retching when they returned. When I came out of the bathroom, I saw them searching my tearstained face for an answer, and I knew that they knew something was terribly wrong.

The kids were exhausted. We'd had two days of travel and a big day on the slopes before the accident. After the doctors at Vail had decided to life-flight Taylor, we'd rushed back to the condo and in just minutes thrown everything we'd brought with us back into our suitcases and piled it all into the Beaver Creek shuttle van that had driven us to St. Mary's. After we arrived, we'd taken up residence in the hospital lobby—our weary bodies, our suitcases, and the kind shuttle driver who just wanted to make sure we were doing okay. *How am I going to take care of these kids and be there for Taylor too? I can barely take care of myself*, I thought, looking into my children's tired and sad little faces.

The elevator door opened. The chaplain and a woman wearing black pants and a khaki overcoat walked toward us.

"They're bringing in a counselor!" I whispered to Todd as I started to panic. But the woman held out her arms to me, and I looked at her face. "Kristin!" I said, jumping off the loveseat in the lobby and running to her.

"I'm here," she said.

Kristin Balko was a sorority sister of mine from college. We'd lost touch several years earlier when she and her physician husband, Greg, had moved to Colorado. I hadn't seen her in fifteen years. "What are you doing here?" I asked.

"Greg got a call about the accident. When we heard the name we knew it was you. I figured you didn't have anybody here, so I came to get your kids."

I burst into fresh tears. I didn't know what to say. It was too much for me, watching this angel from God just swoop in and sweep up my kids. I introduced her to Ryan and Peyton, and I was even more stunned that they were willing to go with her. To me it was just proof of how badly they wanted to escape the nightmare playing out at the hospital.

As I walked the three of them to the elevator, I began crying again. The sobs took every breath I had, and suddenly I began to sway, everything went dark, and then my knees buckled and I fell to the floor.

"Oh, honey," Kristin said, rushing toward me. She put her arms around me and tried to console me.

Sobbing, I looked up at her and said what so far I'd only been thinking. "We're gonna lose her."

Todd

After the kids left, Tara and I sat together in a loveseat in the empty lobby and waited for the neurosurgeon to come speak to us. Silently, I prayed for Taylor. *C'mon, God, you've got to heal her*, I begged. Tara was freezing. The staff brought her hot blankets, but even when she was wrapped in their heat, she couldn't stop shaking. We sat there for what seemed like hours, praying and waiting for news. Finally, the surgeon came out and asked us to join her in a small conference room.

"Taylor has a severe brain injury with a lot of swelling," Dr. Pemblee* began. "We operated, trying to do everything we could, but—"

"Oh, God, have we lost our daughter?" Tara said, not wanting her to finish her sentence.

*Some names and identifying features of people mentioned in the book have been changed. In the case of medical professionals, some composite characters were created to simplify the story for the reader. In addition, the time frame of certain events has been adjusted for clarity.

I was on the edge of my seat. My chest burned like an invisible vise was squeezing it, preventing me from breathing.

"In the twenty-two years I've done this surgery, I've never seen anyone survive it," Dr. Pemblee said. "You need to prepare yourselves for that. That's the reality."

There was a long pause as I tried to make sense of her words. Taylor was alive? But, for how long?

Tara grabbed the edge of her seat as if to hold herself back, and then she suddenly started screaming. "Get out! Get out! I need you to leave—right now!"

"Tara, wait!" I said, grabbing her wrist.

"She's not going to die! She's not!" Tara screamed. Dr. Pemblee looked down, busying herself with the notes in her lap.

I wrapped my arms around Tara and pulled her toward me. She buried her face into my chest and sobbed.

"Can we see her?" I asked. I glanced down at Tara, "We *need* to see Taylor."

"Yes, but not yet. She's still in surgery."

Tara continued to sob into my chest. Dr. Pemblee didn't have a great bedside manner, but she was a neurosurgeon giving us neurological facts about our daughter. Facts we didn't want to believe. Tara was angry and she wanted the bearer of this unfathomably bad news gone, but I wanted to learn as much as I could. To Dr. Pemblee's credit, at least she spoke in a way we could understand. I could see compassion in her eyes even if we didn't hear it in her words. I knew that other than God Himself, she was the only one who could save our daughter.

"Once she is out of surgery, they will take her to ICU to get her stabilized. So it will be a while before you can see her. But in the meantime, I want you to be prepared for what you're going to see—"

Tara didn't want to hear any more. She pulled away from my chest and began to rock back and forth, wailing.

"She's going to have a lot of tubes connected to her. She's on a ventilator, so be aware there is a large tube in her mouth and a smaller one in her nose. She has an external fixation device—a rod, basically—on her left leg to hold it in place, and she's hooked up to several IVs. You need to know, she won't look like herself. She's got an incision on her head, and she's pretty bruised up."

It was as if my mind shut down, because I didn't hear a thing she said after that. She finished talking, and I shook her hand. As Dr. Pemblee turned to leave, Tara slipped from my grip and fell on her knees in front of me. From somewhere deep within Tara a primal wail erupted, racking her body with sobs. Once again, I wrapped my arms around her. I pulled her close and buried my face in her hair as I wept too.

"We have to plan a funeral . . . I've never planned a funeral," she said between gasps of air. I tightened my arms around my wife in an effort to comfort her, but it didn't help. She turned her crying for Taylor into crying out to the only One who could save her. "God, please, You have to do something. You have to save her!" Tara begged over and over again.

Soon, her pain turned to anger, and without realizing it she started to pound her fists into my thighs. "This is not happening; we are not losing Taylor. We're not planning a funeral!"

Tara was quickly falling apart. I grabbed her by the shoulders and gently shook her until she looked up at me. Her dark hair was matted to her tearstained face. "We can do this," I said, looking into her red, swollen eyes. "I'm here. I've got it. I'm going to be your rock."

This was the worst thing either of us had been through in our lives, and I was terrified to learn how it would turn out. I already knew I was losing my daughter. Now I feared I was also losing my wife. It broke my heart to see the woman I dearly loved in so much pain. "We're going to get through this," I repeated again and again, with as much resolve as I could. But I knew it wouldn't be okay. There was nothing I could do to fix it. *Please, God, You've got to heal Taylor*, I prayed.

After Tara quieted down, I helped her walk from the conference room back to our spot on the loveseat in the lobby. She was still shaking from the icy cold that only she could feel. After she was settled, I walked across the lobby, but I kept my eye on her while I called Matt Sunshine. Matt and Beth were our best friends. For the past thirteen years, we'd taken almost every vacation together—except this one. The Sunshines were vacationing in England and were scheduled to leave for France in a few hours. With the time difference, I knew I would wake Matt up, but I also knew he would want me to.

"We can leave and come home now," he said, after I'd told him what had happened and we'd cried together over the phone.

"There's no point. Just continue on to Paris like you planned, and when I know more, I'll let you know."

I hung up with Matt and then called Father Fred at our church in Coppell. I told him what had happened. "We've got to get some prayers going for Taylor," I said, and he agreed. We talked a few minutes longer.

I had just hung up when I saw Bill coming around the corner. Bill was Tara's oldest brother. She was the youngest, and they'd always had a special relationship. Bill was also a doctor.

"Bill's here!" I said.

Tara stood up. I grabbed her arm because I knew she was still shaky. Bill met us, and the three of us embraced.

"I'm so sorry," Bill said. "I don't understand how this could happen."

"You've got to tell us what's going on," Tara cried. "I need you to fix it, or we're going to lose her!"

I'd been texting and talking with Bill since we'd arrived at the hospital in Vail. At one point I'd even put him on speakerphone so he could hear what the ER doctors were saying. Bill heard how serious Taylor's injuries were and he wanted to be with us, but he was with his own family in Montana for their spring break. Texting back and forth, he told me there weren't any commercial flights between Montana and Grand Junction. Bill had a private pilot's license and he could fly himself, but he still needed to find a plane.

And then there was the weather. A couple of hours earlier he'd texted me and said he was on his way, but I still had no idea how he'd made it happen—I was just so thankful to see him.

"Let me fill you in," I said as we sat down.

I updated him on what the neurosurgeon had told us, and he told us how he'd gotten to Grand Junction. Through a series of connections he'd finally found a pilot with a plane, but the weather was too bad. But suddenly a two-hour window of good weather between Montana and Grand Junction had opened up. Just enough time for them to make it, if they left immediately. I knew instantly that God had done it. *Thank you.* I marveled at the miracle, but I knew we needed at least one more.

Behind me, I heard doors opening and turned to see who else was coming. A nurse had pushed open the doors that led to the Intensive Care Unit, and she was now walking toward us. "Are you Taylor's parents?" she asked.

I nodded.

"You can see her now."

—8—

Holding On to Taylor

Tara

I jumped up from the loveseat and rushed toward the open ICU doors, *desperate* to see Taylor. The nurse pointed to a room at the end of the short hallway. When I reached the door, I paused before entering. My heart was pumping madly and my stomach churned. *What will I see when I open the door?* Todd caught up with me, with Bill right behind us. I slid open the glass door and Todd entered first. As soon as Todd saw her, he burst into tears.

"Taylor, *no!*" I said as I moved past him to the far side of the bed, away from the tubes and wires that seemed to be attached to every part of her. "Baby, I'm here. Mommy is here!" I said. I climbed into bed next to her. I wanted to be as close as possible to Taylor and to feel her warm body next to mine.

"Taylor, Taylor! The doctors are wrong. Taylor, wake up! Please wake up," I pleaded. In the Vail ER, they'd told us that whenever we spoke to Taylor, her blood pressure would rise and that was a good sign. I wanted the doctors at St. Mary's to see that too, to know she was still responsive. "Taylor, please wake up. Taylor, baby, please! Mommy and Daddy are here. We're here, baby. We're here."

We didn't want much, just a flicker of an eyelid, a twitch of a finger, or even her heart rate or blood pressure to increase slightly. I rubbed her face, her chest, and I kissed her. I saw Todd rubbing her foot and heard him telling her how much we loved her. I tried to think of anything else that would prompt her to respond.

"Show us you're okay, baby, just move something!" Any positive sign would do, just something to show the doctors, and us, that she could respond, that her brain was still functioning. "Please just show the doctors that they're wrong, show them you're still here."

Nothing.

I remained on her right side, trying to avoid the rods that were elevating the sheet on her left leg. I knew I was out of control—the nurses down the hall could probably hear my wailing—but I didn't care. I looked up at my beautiful daughter's face. Even though she had a trach, stitches on her head, and blood in her hair, someone had taken the time to comb her hair and pull it back. I touched her face and saw a slight scrape on her cheek. For all the trauma she'd been through, she looked like herself, like my baby.

With my head resting on her chest, I listened to her heart beating. Bump-*bump*. Bump-*bump*. Bump-*bump*. Taylor's heart had always made a distinctive sound. It had a fast rhythm, and there was a downbeat on the second beat. I remembered how many times we'd lain like this at home, on her bed, with my head resting on her chest as she told me about her day. But, unlike then, when her heart would accelerate as she got excited about something she was telling me, there was no change in the rhythm, no slight increase in her heart rate to signal she even knew we were there.

Everything in the room seemed steady and rhythmic. The whoosh of the ventilator and the slight whirring noises of the other machines were predictable and regular. The only unpredictable sounds were ours—the sobs of a grieving family.

I don't know how long I lay there, but I know why I finally moved; another wave of nausea forced me to run for the toilet.

While I stood over the bowl on the other side of her room, I heard the nurses down the hall sobbing too.

I finished and wiped my mouth on a paper towel from the dispenser. I returned to the same side of Taylor's bed, but this time I sat on the sofa next to her. The world around me seemed to disappear, and time stopped.

I held Taylor's hand and just tried to breathe.

Todd

There is nothing more horrifying than the sound of a mother crying for her dying child—unless that mother is also your wife. It was as if my insides had been shredded and spit out; my guts spilled across the floor. The pain of that single moment in time was unbearable, indescribable. I could feel a burn spreading through my chest and a rage building in my head.

Nurses, lab technicians, and other medical professionals walked in and out of the room for the next several hours. Each time they did, Tara and I asked if they knew anything more. They didn't. Bill would inquire as to what they were doing and why. "Have you checked her oxygen?" or "Has her level gone up or down on that?" he'd want to know. Sometimes he'd suggest a new test or ask about a previous one. The staff seemed to be on top of things medically, and they were always willing to share the results with him. Several times, I heard him have conversations in the hallway, and more than once he was on the phone with the surgeons we'd talked to earlier in the night. At one point, he even went down the hall to view the CT scans with the technicians who had performed them. Each time he learned something new, he'd come back and share it with us in a way we could understand. But he didn't give us false hope.

"The doctors think that Taylor is brain-dead, but they won't know for sure until they run more tests."

Medically, the plan was to watch Taylor through the night. At 7:00 a.m., Taylor was scheduled for another CT scan to look for any signs of brain function. All of our hopes and prayers for the next five or six hours were directed at the outcome of that one test. If it showed brain function, we could continue to hope for Taylor's recovery. If it didn't, it would confirm what doctors already believed—that Taylor was brain-dead.

�֍

Being in the hospital room was like being in a casino in Las Vegas. There were no clocks on the walls, as if to deliberately keep us oblivious as to how much, or how little, time had passed. We must have been there a couple of hours when exhaustion overtook Tara and she passed out on the couch. I was thankful she would have a few minutes of peace. I sat at the end of the bed, rubbing Taylor's foot, trying to keep my anger at bay, trying to prevent the situation from overtaking me. Finally, I couldn't sit still any longer.

"I'm going to get coffee," I said to Bill. "Do you want to come with me?"

"Good idea," Bill said.

I knew we would find coffee near the nurses' station, and as we walked past them I could see their eyes were as red and puffy as ours. It wasn't looking good for Taylor. "Tell me the worst-case scenario," I said to Bill. I wanted to steel myself for whatever was going to happen, and I needed to be strong for my family. "If things don't go well tomorrow, what do I need to know?"

Bill took a deep breath and slowly stirred his coffee before answering. "If she is truly brain-dead, then they're going to ask you about taking her off the ventilator. They'll also ask if you want to donate her organs."

"How does that work?"

"If the CT scan fails to show any signs of brain activity, they will remove her from the ventilator and you can sit with her until she dies. If you choose to donate her organs, they won't remove the ventilator in your presence. Instead, you'll say goodbye, and then they'll take her to an operating room to retrieve her organs.

72

They'll remove her from the ventilator there. The whole process might take a little longer because there are tests they have to do before they can harvest her organs."

"I think that's what we'll do."

"Are you sure?"

"That's what Taylor would want."

"You need to discuss it with Tara," Bill advised.

"Yeah, I'll talk to her."

Back in the room, I could feel the anger building as I became lost in my own thoughts. It didn't look good for Taylor. This was all happening so fast. How would we live without her? In just a few hours, we'd gone from the best vacation ever to saying goodbye to our daughter. It didn't make any sense.

⚬⚬⚬

I don't know how long I had been thinking about Taylor's life coming to an end—maybe an hour or more—but the weight of my thoughts eventually just snapped something inside of me. I felt loaded down with heavy burdens. Trapped. I could do nothing to stop it from happening, and I could find no way to escape. At the same time, I couldn't just sit and let this burden crush me. I had to do something. I needed an escape from the darkness and pain. I needed a way out.

Then it occurred to me: I had one.

I was scheduled to be in San Francisco next week. I started to think about the board meeting and other things that were already planned for the trip. I had a lot of work to do before I left, and more that needed to be done once I got there.

How would I get it done? What does work even look like now?

I glanced at Tara asleep on the couch. *How will I ever be able to leave my family with this going on? Could I even work again?*

My mind started spinning with the possibilities. I was supposed to leave for San Francisco the following Monday and return on Thursday. *I'll just tell Tara I won't be home until Tuesday.* She wouldn't know the difference. *And maybe I won't come back. Maybe I'll just stay on the road.* At any given time, I had about eight major projects going on. *San Francisco, New York, Denver, and then that thing in Hawaii. I could just separate myself from all of this pain.* I shifted in the chair, and for a second, the noise of the squeaky pleather overrode the hospital sounds—the steady beeping of the machines, the hum of the heating system, and the whoosh of the ventilator. Just like the noises from the chair made the hospital sounds disappear, I wanted to do something that would make it *all* go away.

Maybe I could leave this all behind.

I could run.

With my job, I had a great excuse to be on a plane to any major city in America—I had clients in all of them. I could leave early every Sunday and come home late on Friday. Or even Saturday. In fact, I could line up so much travel that I would never have to be home. The thought was tempting.

I could go a step further. I could vanish.

I'd tell Tara and the kids I was going to work. Then I'd take a flight somewhere and disappear off the grid. There was money in the bank. With three or four days of withdrawing the maximum amount, I'd have enough money to make it to an island. I could start over doing something—anything—else. I started to think through the details of how I could make it happen.

⁂

I don't know how long I let the fantasy play out in my mind. Minutes? A half hour? More than an hour? Whatever it was, I indulged it longer than I care to admit. It seemed so attractive. If I left, I'd be free of the pain. Then Bill came in and pulled up a chair next to me, and I looked over at Tara sleeping—and I thought how hurt she would be if she knew what I was thinking.

I can't leave. I'm stuck and there's nothing I can do about it. I looked at her again. *So what? What does it matter? I'll be gone and I won't even know how they're feeling.*

I thought about family members and friends who'd chosen to run when faced with a crisis. In their wake, they'd left hurting spouses, broken kids, and troubled friends. In some cases I was the one who was hurting, broken, and troubled. I knew what that felt like, and I didn't want to do that to those I loved. I thought about Ryan and Peyton. *Right now, they're alone in a hotel room with Kristin, who is practically a stranger to them.* My heart burst for them. No matter how much I wanted to escape, I didn't want to hurt them.

But it wasn't fair. We didn't deserve this.

I didn't deserve this.

Maybe I did.

Lost in my thoughts, I started to ask, *What kind of horrible person would think about leaving their family at a time like this? Who does that?*

I did.

I realized how dark my heart could be. I was capable of further hurting those I loved most when they were already in so much pain. I started to sob at the ugliness that grew inside of me. *How had I come to this?*

I felt a hand on my shoulder and glanced up to see Bill in the chair next to me. His cheeks were tearstained and his eyes were red. I could see the empathy and love in them. *I bet he wasn't thinking about running.* I deeply respected and admired Bill. Not only were Bill and I brothers-in-law, we were also good friends. A few months earlier, we'd attended a Band of Brothers retreat together. We had spent the weekend being vulnerable about our strengths, but mostly about our weaknesses, as husbands and fathers. We'd both grown a lot spiritually that weekend. As a result, I'd learned to trust both Bill and God in new ways.

I wonder if he knows what I am thinking about right now?

Tell him.

It wasn't an audible voice; it was more like a feeling that came from somewhere inside me. Without a doubt, I knew it was the Holy Spirit prompting me to tell Bill what I was thinking. I knew I could trust Bill, but I was ashamed. Just across the room, my wife, his sister, was passed out from exhaustion and grief. My daughter was lying in the hospital bed and she was probably going to die. And I was angry at the world and trying to run away from them both. I cried harder as I realized how lost I was.

"I need your help," I said, choking on my words.

"Anything," Bill said.

"I am going to want to run from this, from my family, from the pain. I need you to help me not do that."

"Okay."

I told Bill how I had been thinking about leaving and the anger building up inside.

"I feel like an atomic bomb, Bill. I'm ready to explode. It's just so powerful. It's this scary, huge thing growing inside me, and I don't know what to do with it. I just feel so much hate and anger. It's like a violent, murderous rage. It's almost warlike. Like something a soldier feels before going into battle. I feel like I want to kill every living thing I can get my hands on."

I buried my head in my hands and sobbed. It was the first time I had really let loose since the accident. Bill put his hand on my back, and I could hear him praying for me.

When I could speak, I continued. "I know what I'm capable of. I'm going to come home from this, and either I'm going to want to save the world or destroy it. I'm not sure which one it's going to be. But I need to stay close to God, and I need your help to do it. I'm scared to death, Bill, and I need you to hold me accountable."

"I'm here for you," he said.

I looked at my hands and fingered my wedding band. "I can't handle this on my own. I can't fix this like I can fix everything else. This is too important, too big, and too horrible for me to face. I need you to hold me accountable to prayer. Help me give this pain to God. I can't do this on my own."

We talked for a while, and then Bill said, "Let's pray." He reached out and took my hand.

As Bill prayed for me, I felt the weight of my shame and guilt lift and my anger subside. I felt as though I had been to confession and now I was being cleansed, forgiven for the dark thoughts I'd been entertaining. By the time he finished praying, I knew what I was supposed to do.

"God wants me to be a husband, and He wants me to be a father. He needs me to be here for my family. I just need you to help me," I said.

"I've got your back. I'm here for you," Bill said.

And I knew he was.

I also knew God was.

The doors of hell had opened, and I had taken a good, long look. Perhaps God wanted me to get a glimpse of the evil I was capable of so I would cling to Him alone. Thankfully, graciously, mercifully, God, through the working of the Holy Spirit, had rescued me from my own thoughts and those doors had closed. I was weary from the battle, but at least my soul was comforted.

I pulled out the footrest on the chair, leaned back, and closed my eyes. My hand was on Taylor's foot, and my hope was in the Lord. I sat back to wait for the scan that would decide our future.

Tara

I opened my eyes, and it took me a minute to remember where I was. Then I saw Taylor lying next to me. Todd was sleeping in a chair, and Bill was awake in the chair next to him. It all came flooding back. I sat up and rubbed my eyes.

"What's going on?" I asked.

"Nothing has changed. We're still waiting for the CT scan at seven o'clock. Todd fell asleep a few minutes ago. You're both exhausted, you should sleep when you can," Bill said.

"I need to know what's going to happen next." The words spilled out quickly because I wasn't sure if I really wanted to know. Bill and I had been close since I was a baby. He knew what I needed to

77

hear and how to tell me. We talked about the scan and how doctors were looking for signs of activity in Taylor's brain.

"Like blood flow?"

"Exactly."

"What happens if they don't see anything?"

"Then they're going to ask you two questions. The first will be about taking her off the ventilator." Bill explained how we could be with her as she died.

"What's the second question?"

"Would you be willing to donate her organs?"

"What would that involve?" I asked.

Bill explained how he and Todd had already had this conversation, and he didn't want to do anything to persuade me one way or the other. "You really need to talk to Todd about that," Bill advised, his voice cracking.

I nodded, and the tears began to flow again. *Bless his heart. Not only is he being a doctor for us, but he's also a brother, a brother-in-law, and a friend. And he's Taylor's uncle!* I knew he was trying to play a lot of roles to support us, but I knew he was also experiencing his own emotion.

Bill wiped his eyes with the back of his hand and then glanced at his watch.

"It's 6:48."

We had twelve minutes before Taylor was scheduled to have the CT scan. "Oh, God, please heal her. Please let there be signs of life," I prayed as I crawled into bed with her again. I slowly stroked her face. "Please, baby, you've got to show the doctors they're wrong."

—9—

Signs of Life

Tara

At 7:00 a.m., the medical technicians arrived to wheel Taylor down for her CT scan. Todd, Bill, and I prayed the entire time she was gone. At 7:30, the technicians wheeled her back in and told us we'd know the results soon.

We thought that meant 8:00.

But 9:00 came and went, and so did 10:00. By 11:00, we still hadn't heard a word. Bill walked back and forth to the nurses' station, checking to see if they'd heard anything from the doctor. Bill had the neurosurgeon's cell phone number, but he didn't want to use it—he knew she'd get back to us when she could. Todd alternated between sitting in the chair, holding Taylor's foot and talking to her, and pacing the room. I stayed as close to her as possible, lying in bed with her or just holding her hand and talking to her. I was still dealing with nausea, but there was nothing left in my stomach to throw up.

By 11:30, none of us could wait any longer. Bill picked up the phone and called Dr. Pemblee. "I hate to bug you," he said, "but the CT scan has been done, and we're all on pins and needles waiting to see what the next step is." Bill listened attentively as she spoke, and then looked at me and raised his eyebrows.

"What did she say?" I asked when he finished the call.

"She's just down the hall. I'm going to meet her so I can look at the scans."

It was such a blessing to have Bill with us. He would think of questions to ask and tests to run that we wouldn't even know about, much less consider. My heart started racing in anticipation of finally getting the news we'd been waiting so long to hear, but my stomach churned at the thought that it could be bad news.

Before he left, Bill paused in the doorway and turned to look first at me and then at Todd. "The two of you should have a conversation about organ donation, just in case."

⚜

Bill and I are extremely close and always have been. In pictures from our youth, Bill was always the one holding me. As soon as he walked back into the room after speaking with Dr. Pemblee, I knew.

"You have to tell me," I said. "You have to!" But he didn't have to. I saw his face, looked deep into his eyes, and I knew. "That's it, isn't it? There's no hope, is there?" I buried my head in my hands and began to weep. Todd was in his chair at the far end of the bed, weeping too.

Dr. Pemblee's cold exterior seemed to have melted a bit as she followed Bill into the room. With red-rimmed eyes, she simply said, "We didn't see anything to indicate brain activity."

"Are you sure? Isn't there anything you can do?" I pleaded.

She shook her head. "I'm so sorry," she said, wiping away a tear. "There's nothing more we can do."

"So, what's next?" Todd asked.

"Well, one small part of her brain looks like it still could have a small blood supply," Dr. Pemblee began. "To officially pronounce her brain-dead, we'll have to repeat the scans until that blood supply dies off."

80

"How many days are we talking about?" Bill asked.

"It could be one or two days, or it could be as much as a week."

"We can't do this," Bill said. "I know there has to be another way."

"Well, there is. We can take her off the ventilator and see if she breathes on her own. We could do a couple of other tests at her bedside to see if she has any involuntary response, which, from the scans, we know she won't. But we can use those tests to rule out any possibility."

"Let's do that. They don't need to sit around here waiting a week for the inevitable," said Bill.

I looked at Bill, standing next to the neurosurgeon, and pleaded with him to do something, anything.

"I'm so sorry," he said.

"There's no hope, Bill? A test? More surgery?"

He shook his head. "I looked at the scans. There's been no change between the scan they did in Vail and the one they did this morning."

Months later, when we could hear it, Bill explained that normal brain anatomy hadn't even been visible in her scans. Taylor's brain had been so badly injured it didn't even resemble a brain.

Todd sat next to me on the small sofa and wrapped his arms around me. I buried my face in his neck, where our tears merged as we wept. When we finally pulled apart, Dr. Pemblee spoke.

"I have one more question," she said. "Would you be willing to donate Taylor's organs?"

I looked at Todd to make sure we were in agreement.

"Absolutely!" he said.

"It's what Taylor would want," I agreed, and then I burst into fresh tears.

Todd

The surgical team asked us to stand outside while they removed the ventilator and performed the bedside tests. They called her death at 12:15 that afternoon, Monday, March 15, but we knew in our hearts she'd left us much earlier.

Doctors told us it would likely be the next morning before they would have everything in place to remove her organs. They said we could stay with her until then. Of course, we both wanted to.

I'd been on and off the phone since we'd left Vail, getting prayer chains started and informing friends and family what had happened. Tara's brothers were on their way to Grand Junction, along with her dad. I'd also talked to Matt Sunshine again, telling him that Taylor had died. When the nurses finished, Bill left to make a phone call. Tara and I were alone in the room with Taylor.

"What are we going to do?" Tara asked. I'd never seen her dark eyes look so sad and lonely. "How do you plan a funeral?"

I didn't have an answer. We sat in uneasy silence, and I could tell she was thinking. Finally, she said, "I'm going to call Mary Marshall." Later, we would look back on that moment and know it had been a divine revelation. Mary became one of the angels who were there for us when we needed them most.

Mary and Tara weren't the kind of friends who got together often or talked on the phone every day, but even when they hadn't seen each other in months, they could still pick up where they'd last left off. Mary had a daughter who was friends with Taylor and a son who was friends with Ryan. Tara had often talked about Mary's exquisite taste and her ability to get things done, and done right. She was the perfect person to help.

I could tell from Tara's side of the conversation that Mary already knew at least part of what was going on. Coppell is a small community. Everyone knows everyone else. As soon as one person found out about Taylor's accident, it wouldn't have taken long for word to spread.

In addition, I was a big social networking guy, both personally and professionally. I'd been tweeting and posting updates to my Facebook page since we'd left Coppell. In fact, right before the accident, I'd tweeted it was a perfect day on the slopes, it was the best family vacation we'd ever had, and that it was the trip of a lifetime.

While we were on the shuttle bus between Vail and Grand Junction, I'd used both Twitter and Facebook to ask people to pray for Taylor. Somewhere, between the mountains and the storm, I'd lost my internet connection, so I wasn't sure how much had actually gone through. But by Monday afternoon, I realized at least some of the prayer requests had. People were responding with notes of encouragement and promises of prayer.

As Tara filled Mary in on the latest details, she'd have to pause as, between sobs, the words just wouldn't come out. I knew Mary was crying with her. At one point, Tara attempted to take a deep breath, and then through her tears, she pleaded, "I just need you to do this for me because I can't."

Immediately, Mary's side of the conversation must have changed. I gathered from the answers Tara was giving that Mary must have gone into "get it done" mode.

"I don't know when her body will be back in Coppell," Tara said. "They think they'll remove her organs in the morning, so it would be sometime the next day, or the day after that at the earliest."

It was heartbreaking to listen to my wife talk about the details of our *daughter's body*. I felt a shiver down my spine. How would I ever get used to talking about her in the past tense?

Over the next hour, I had many similar conversations. While sitting at the end of Taylor's bed, and absentmindedly massaging her foot, I called Father Fred at our church, gave him an update, and let him know Mary would be calling him.

At some point, Tara said, "We should do something. People will want to help in some way; we should do something to honor Taylor's life."

After a brief discussion, we agreed we'd plant a tree at Coppell Middle School East. Taylor loved her school, and this would be a great way to memorialize her. If people wanted, they could contribute to the tree rather than sending flowers.

Tara called Laura Springer, our beloved middle school principal. She finally reached her at one of Taylor's friends' homes. Springer was with a group of middle school students who'd gathered to pray for Taylor. Tara filled her in on what had happened that morning. Together, the women cried over the phone.

"We want a way to honor her life, and we were thinking about planting a tree on the school property," Tara said.

"I'll work it out with the PTO to collect donations, and we'll get something nice," Springer promised.

Tara's brother Kary and his wife, Juli, arrived within the hour. They'd left Texas in the middle of the night and driven sixteen hours. Shortly after that, Tara's brother Chris and her dad, Bernie, made it to the hospital. Bernie had gotten on the first flight out of Abilene and flown to Dallas, where Chris had met him and joined him on the flight to Colorado. We were glad to see all of them, but each time someone new arrived, we had to repeat the whole story all over again. As soon as they hugged us, they rushed to be by Taylor's side. We could see how they loved her and how much they were hurting.

As soon as things settled down and Tara could catch her breath, someone new would show up, or she'd make a phone call, and she'd lose it again. I watched as Tara relived the trauma over and over through each of their reactions. I was worried about her. She hadn't eaten or drank anything in almost forty-eight hours. Through the night, we'd slept only fifteen minutes or so at a time. She had to be as exhausted as I was. I wasn't sure how much more she could take.

Tara

I felt as if I was losing my mind. I was having trouble thinking, and I couldn't recall things that happened only moments before. My brain was like Teflon—nothing stuck. People would ask me questions, and I would look at them blankly, not knowing what to say. Finally, Bill or Todd would answer for me.

It was late in the afternoon when the team came in. They were all wearing green scrubs with a logo stitched on the left side of their shirt, right above their hearts. I tried to read the words, but they didn't make sense. "Transplant" something. While the two men stood near the door, the woman came over to the sofa where I was sitting and knelt down in front of me

"Taylor would make a beautiful candidate for organ donation. You're willing to consider it?" she asked.

I stared at her, unable to comprehend what she was asking.

"Absolutely, absolutely!" Todd said.

When she left, things started to move quickly. Someone mentioned the need to do some tests. A male nurse came in and injected something into Taylor to prepare the organs. A sweet female nurse dressed in cheerful scrubs said, "I know you don't want those stitches showing. How does she wear her hair?"

I looked at her with a mixture of gratefulness and confusion. I wanted to open my mouth, but I couldn't. I didn't even know how to answer her. Fortunately, the nurse just figured something out.

"I think she wears her hair on the side. In a braid," she said, manipulating Taylor's long locks in her hands. While the woman braided Taylor's hair, others cleaned and washed her. I held Taylor's hand, and at one point, I thought it felt a little warm but I dismissed it. When the nurses finished, I climbed into the bed and lay next to her. I could feel Taylor's skin growing hot to the touch. Something was happening with Taylor!

"She's hot! Her body is hot!" I yelled.

A nurse came running.

"What does that mean? Is it a sign?" I asked, desperately wanting to believe they were all wrong.

The nurse tried to calm me down. "It doesn't mean anything; it's just the medications working." It happened several times, and each time the nurses would remind me this was expected and it wasn't a sign of anything.

Todd and I took turns lying with our daughter in the bed. "I'm so proud of you, Tay," he said, using her nickname. "We're both so proud of you. We love you so much. You're Daddy's girl, you know."

We stroked her face and touched her hair. We told her how beautiful she looked. We wanted to soak up every moment we could.

∘⁘∘

It had to be 4:00 or 5:00 p.m. when the medical staff came in and said we needed to leave so they could do some tests on her organs. Kary and Juli were standing outside the door to Taylor's room, talking, and as Todd and I left, they stopped us.

"You guys need to talk to Ryan and Peyton."

"Are they here?" I asked. I knew they'd been to the movies and to a museum, but I'd lost track of where they'd gone next. Ryan and Peyton had been well cared for. After Kristin had picked them up, she'd taken them to a hotel associated with the hospital to sleep. When they woke up, they'd eaten and then gone with Kristin to do fun things. She texted frequently to let me know where they were, but I'd been so caught up in the fast-moving events of the afternoon I hadn't checked my phone.

"They're in the lobby," Juli said. Kristin had brought them back to the hospital, and they'd been waiting in the same lobby we'd waited in the night before. Various family members were taking turns sitting with them but, of course, they wanted to see us.

"You're right," I said. "We need to tell them." I looked at Todd for reassurance.

Todd turned toward Bill. "Where's the right place to have a meeting like this?" he asked. "Our kids are going to remember this for the rest of their lives."

"The chapel would be a good place."

We met the kids in the lobby and hugged them, and then the four of us, trailed by my family, made our way down to the chapel. My family stood outside, guarding the door so no one else would come in.

Inside the chapel, beautiful stained glass windows gave the place a peaceful feeling. Todd and I pulled four padded chairs together in a small circle. I couldn't help thinking, *There should be five of us.*

"We need to tell you something," Todd began. "This is really hard to say, but it's worse than we thought."

"Is she dead?" Ryan asked.

"She is."

"Huh," Peyton said, falling back into her chair as if she'd just lost her breath.

Todd continued, saying how this was God's plan for Taylor, but I wasn't listening anymore. My eyes were fixed on Ryan. When he heard the news, his face contorted for a second as if he couldn't understand how this had happened. Immediately, though, he seemed to refocus and accept the news.

Ryan noticed my look and mistook it for grief. "She's going to be okay. She's happy now, Mom," he said, as if he were the one telling *me* the bad news. "She's in a better place. She's with Sarge."

Sarge was our dog. He'd died five years ago.

Ryan continued to try to convince me. "We're going to be okay. It's good," he said. But in my heart, I knew he was trying to convince himself.

By now, Peyton had moved from stunned to crying. She crawled into my lap and I rocked her.

Todd

I didn't know what else to say as I watched Peyton clinging to her mother and Ryan completely cut off from any feeling of grief. *It's my fault*, I thought. I felt as though I had lied to Ryan. On the mountain while we were waiting for the ski patrol to arrive, he'd said, "She's dead!"

"No, she's not," I'd yelled. "She's breathing. She's alive, and she's going to be okay!" At the time, everything I'd said was true. I felt her pulse, and when the ski patrol arrived and put an oxygen mask on her, it even fogged up. She was breathing. It wasn't until right before they life-flighted her that they had to put her on a ventilator.

Ryan and I had skied down the mountain together. The whole way I'd talked to him. "She's okay, she's going to be fine," I'd said. I had wanted to reassure him he'd done everything right and that she would be okay.

But now she wasn't. And he wasn't either.

Sitting in the hospital chapel, watching him deny his grief, all I could think was, *He shouldn't have lost his big sister. God, he doesn't deserve to grow up this way.*

I reached out to embrace him and Tara, and we did a four-way hug and just clung together as a family. I don't know how long we stayed in the chapel, but I knew it was a long time from the looks of concern on our extended family members' faces as we emerged.

We left the chapel, and Bill offered to take the kids to get something to eat and then take them back to the little hotel for the night. Family members offered to bring food in for us and urged us to come back with them to rest. But we didn't want to. We wanted to be with Taylor.

Back upstairs in her room, I crawled into bed with her, stroked her face and hair, and held her hand. I thought about how many times I'd snuggled with her on the couch or on her bed, our foreheads pressed together as she told me her secrets. "Don't tell Mom," she'd say. "Pinky swear?"

I'd hook my pinky around hers and swear I wouldn't tell. The last time we did that she'd told me about a boy.

"He plays basketball," she'd said.

"Where does he go to church?" I asked. She told me about his church and the activities he was involved in. "What makes him special? Is he funny, or athletic?" When she couldn't stop talking about him, I asked, "Are you guys texting?"

"Well, he texted me, but I'm not sure if I want to text him back."

"Do you really like this guy?"

"He's really cute," she said, with a smile on her face as she avoided my direct question. "But don't say anything to Mom—yet."

Then she made me pinky swear I wouldn't tell anybody.

Lying next to her in her hospital bed, I remembered what it felt like to be lying beside her in her room. I thought about her lime green walls and the posters that hung on them. I remembered the T-shirt she wore and how she'd gotten into bed with those big UGG boots on. She wore those boots with everything—even shorts. It used to drive me nuts.

What I wouldn't give for her to be wearing them now.

— 10 —

Saying Goodbye

Tara

"Has Taylor ever used drugs?"

"No."

"Did she smoke?"

"No."

"How much alcohol did she drink?"

"She's thirteen, she doesn't drink alcohol!"

I knew the woman from Donor Alliance needed to ask these questions, but they were starting to annoy me.

We had just gotten settled back in Taylor's room when the people from Donor Alliance asked if we would mind coming to the conference room to answer a few questions and fill out some paperwork. We didn't want to leave Taylor, but the nurse in the cheerful scrubs said, "Don't worry, I'll take care of her."

The family members who hadn't returned to the hotel wanted to be there to support us. So Todd and I, along with my dad, my brothers, Chris and Kary, and Kary's wife, Juli, all squeezed into the tiny conference room. Todd and I sat in chairs at the table with Myrna, the representative from Donor Alliance, while the others sat in the background or stood along the wall.

At first, the questions were easy.

"Is she on any medication?"

"No."

"Does she have any allergies?"

"No."

"Has she ever been to Europe?"

My patience ran out, and I snapped, "She never had the chance!"

"Okay, it's okay," Myrna said.

I knew she was just doing her job, and she was doing it as compassionately as she could, but each new question was a dagger to my heart, a reminder of what we no longer had. I mourned for all I would miss with her—her first kiss, finding the boy she'd marry, having babies of her own. I folded my arms on top of the table and rested my head on them.

Todd

Something happened to us in the meeting with the Donor Alliance representative. Prior to now, Tara and I had both been moving in the same direction, but during this meeting our grieving paths diverged. Tara took the emotional route and became the center of emotive grief for our family. I took the project manager route and became the point person for all the decisions, the paperwork, and managing the information flow. Tara began to check out while I started to clock in. There was a funeral to plan and decisions to make. It gave me something to *do*.

It gave me some *control*.

"Do you just want to give permission for us to take all her organs, or do you want to choose?" Myrna asked.

"We're choosing," Tara said, her head still buried in her arms on the table.

"Yeah, we want to choose," I added. It wasn't that we wanted her to rattle off the whole list; it's just that we both needed to feel like we had a choice in something.

"Okay. I'll read the list, and then you tell me yes or no. Kidneys?"

"Yes."

"Pancreas?"

"Yes."

"Liver?"

"Yes."

"Eyes?" asked Myrna.

Though she'd been sobbing on and off through most of the interview, Tara lost it at the thought of Taylor's crystal blue eyes being taken. "No, no! Absolutely not!" Tara said, horrified.

"Now, let me explain," Myrna said calmly. "It's not her eyes; we leave her eyes. It's just the cornea. It's the clear layer on the outside. Her eyes will still look the same."

I looked at Tara, and I could see how conflicted she was. We both wanted to help others, but I could understand her reluctance. The thought of them touching Taylor's beautiful eyes was a lot to bear. This one had to be Tara's decision.

There was a pause while everyone in the room waited for her to speak.

"Okay, fine," Tara said. "It's what Taylor would want." She put her head back down in her arms and cried.

Our family was completely supportive. When we said yes, they said, "Good, good." When we said no, they said, "We understand, that's okay." When Tara started shaking because she was cold, someone grabbed a blanket for her, and when I couldn't speak, one of her brothers brought me a glass of water. Their presence made it easier for us to make some difficult decisions.

After a few more questions, Myrna was finished.

"So, what happens next?" I asked.

"I'll give you periodic updates by phone. After the initial organ placement, you'll receive some written communication, and if you want to connect with the organ recipients—"

"We're definitely going to want to connect," I said.

"So you can submit the paperwork, then it will be up to them. Let me just say, not all recipients want to connect. There are procedures that must be followed, and there are some time limits involved—"

"That's fine, but we'll want to connect," Tara said.

"Okay. We'll send you the paperwork, and you can write a letter. Just make sure there isn't a lot of personal contact information in it. All of the communication needs to go through us. And, of course, there is no guarantee that you'll receive a response."

Myrna was doing everything she could to set low expectations. She didn't want us to get our hopes up of meeting the recipients.

But our hopes were already up.

Knowing that Taylor's organs would help other people was the only thing that would allow us to make sense of Taylor's death.

By default, I was the funeral planner. I spent time on the phone with Mary Marshall and Father Fred, organizing funeral plans and making decisions. Bill was back at the hotel working on flight arrangements for the next day. He knew we wanted, *needed*, to be home as soon as this was all finished. I spoke with Matt and Beth in Paris and told them to head back to Dallas; we'd meet them there. No point in them coming to Colorado, as we would be leaving the next day.

Earlier in the day I had tweeted: "Words cannot begin 2 explain our sorrow, sadness & helplessness. God gave us Taylor for < 14 yrs. To know her, or of her, is a blessing."

People were responding to my tweet with comments, questions for more information, and most of all with prayer. Someone started a Facebook page, and by that evening, seven hundred people had joined to pray for Taylor and us. Now that we were back in Taylor's hospital room, I wrote another tweet: "Tara (Taylor's mother) and I are overwhelmed with love from near and far. Thank you."

After our family members visited with Taylor one last time, they left for the hotel. Tara and I planned to stay at the hospital with Taylor. Though we knew she was already gone, we also knew it would be the last few hours we would have with her. Later that night, a priest came in to talk and pray with us. I also spent some time reading my Bible. Romans 8:28 hit me particularly hard: "And we know that in all things God works for the good of those who love him, who have been called according to his purpose." It was fresh hope, and I clung to it with all my faith.

About that time, my client in Vail called. He was the publisher of the local Vail newspaper, and he'd been kind enough to let us stay in his corporate condo while we were on vacation.

"I'm so sorry, Todd. I just heard what happened."

We talked for a few minutes, then his tone changed a bit.

"Hey, listen. There's going to be stuff written about this. It's a huge story here, and the community is going to want to know more about what happened. As the publisher, but more importantly as your friend, I want to make sure we get the details right and we describe Taylor correctly." He paused and then said, "You don't have to tell me anything. And you don't have to give me a quote. But I want you to know there will be things written, and if there is anything you want to tell us, we'll make sure we get it out there, and we get it right."

"Oh, my gosh. I never thought of that," I said. But I should have. All of my clients were in some form of media: radio, television, or newspapers. "Of course, I want to make sure the details are correct."

He started by asking me the correct spelling of all three kids' names. He asked what school Taylor went to, how old she was, and the name of the city where we lived outside of Dallas.

I didn't give him a full-blown interview; it was difficult enough to get through answering his basic questions. The best I could do was fill in some holes, like the fact we were on our spring break vacation.

At the time, I didn't realize how that little trickle of information would turn into a raging flood of media over the next year. At the time, Tara and I didn't know or care. All we cared about was spending our last few precious hours with our daughter.

Tara

All I did was cry. The passage of time simultaneously seemed fast and slow—sometimes it stood still. The only consistent thing through the night of March 15 and into the morning of March 16 was that I never had any idea what time was actually on the clock.

"Please eat," one nurse said, handing me graham crackers and juice. I appreciated her kindness, but I couldn't drink the juice; I was shaking so badly that I nearly poured it on myself.

"Tara, you've got to eat something," Todd said, watching me. "Bill said before he left that you needed to eat." I picked up a cracker and tried to nibble on it. When Todd got busy on the phone, I set it back down.

It was hard to believe that Taylor was already gone and that in a few hours we'd say our final goodbyes and never see her again this side of heaven. *How does that make sense?* I lay still with my head on her chest and listened to her heart beating. I knew it was only pumping because of the machines, but still it was Taylor's heart, and I took consolation in knowing that even after she was gone, it would continue to beat. I thought about the person who would be receiving it and what he or she must be going through. I cried for us, for them, and for the fallen world we lived in that let things like this happen. I also prayed. *God, just help me get through these next few days.*

"I just want to meet the person who gets her heart," I said. "Even if I never get to meet any of the other recipients, I *need* to hear her heartbeat again."

I heard Todd sniffling. Though he was trying to be my rock, I knew he was grieving too.

He wrapped his arms around me. We held each other and wept.

Todd

The next morning, at exactly 6:00, the three people dressed in scrubs returned.

"Is it time?" I asked.

"Whenever you're ready," one of them said. "Whenever you're ready."

I looked at Tara quietly crying while she stroked Taylor's hair and face. *Don't they know we'd never be ready? We're letting our little girl go. How does anyone ever get ready enough to do that?*

Even after they walked out the door, I could sense them standing outside in the hallway, waiting. There was this busyness happening outside the door, and the number of people waiting seemed to continually grow. Everyone was very compassionate, but I could feel their urgency too. The longer we spent in the room, the more the tension outside the room grew.

We were crying, holding Taylor, rubbing her face and hands, kissing her, and telling her how much we loved her. "I need to hear her heart again," Tara said, leaning down to listen one more time to her daughter's heartbeat. We were trying to gather a lifetime of memories in the few minutes it took to say goodbye. I knew we weren't moving as quickly as they needed us to, but how could we?

Someone came in and gently tried to pry us away. "We're ready when you are." More medical personnel had gathered in the hallway. "The surgical team has flown in, and it looks as if she will be helping a lot of people. There's a woman in Arizona waiting for her heart, a two-year-old child will get her liver, another person will get her kidney and pancreas, and someone will get her other kidney. While nothing is confirmed until it actually happens, it looks like Taylor's gifts will help a lot of people."

There was an awkward pause, and then Tara spoke up. "We're holding up the process, aren't we?" Tears were streaming down her face. I knew she didn't want to let go. I also knew the answer to her question. Yes, we were holding them up. But what could they do? They were at our mercy, and as much as we wanted to help others, we had to let go of our daughter to do it.

"Where are you going with her?" I asked.

"We're taking her downstairs to surgery."

"We want to be with her to the very last minute, so can we—"

Before I could finish my question, Tara interrupted with a statement.

"We're going with you."

Tara

We walked alongside the gurney as it moved from her room to the surgical suite, until it stopped. The next doors Taylor would go through were the operating room doors, and we couldn't go in with her. This was the end of the journey for us. Taylor would pass into the next room by herself.

We stood in the cold, sterile hallway and said our final goodbyes. We held her hand and repeatedly told her we loved her. "We're so proud of you, sweet girl. Mommy and Daddy love you so much. Ryan and Peyton love you too. They are going to be okay. We know we'll all see you again soon." It felt like a race to say everything we wanted to say before we had to leave.

Finally, we let go of her hand, kissed her, and stepped backward into the elevator—the aide had held the door open for us. While the elevator doors closed, we watched as they rolled Taylor feet first into the operating room. My last glimpse of her was the back of her braided head.

"Oh, God . . ." I said. I felt like I was going to be sick again.

As we exited the surgical elevators, we heard a commotion moving toward us. It sounded like three or four people running; I could hear the sounds of their shoes squeaking on the floor. Whoever it was, they were in a big hurry. It also sounded like they were pulling something along the tile floor.

We met them at the corner. Four men in white coats were running as fast as they could toward the surgical elevators. Each was holding

Saying Goodbye

a bag or pulling a cooler. Just before the doors started to close, they made it onto the elevator we'd just exited. I made eye contact with the man in the front of the elevator, and there was a sense of recognition. We both looked away before the doors slid shut.

Time had stopped for us, but the clock had just started for these men who were on a lifesaving mission. I looked at the aide who was with us, and I could see the horror on his face. I knew immediately who they were, and it was a sight we were never supposed to see.

The transplant team had come to collect Taylor's organs.

— 11 —

Homecoming

Todd

Before we left Grand Junction, Myrna, the representative from Donor Alliance, called.

We were at the hospital's small hotel, where the kids and Tara's family had spent the night. We were picking up our belongings and getting the kids packed up for a flight that afternoon Bill had arranged. Tara's dad was joining us on the flight home. Her brothers were picking up our car and driving it back to our home in Coppell. They had already left for Vail.

Tara stood in the bathroom washing her face; she still hadn't eaten or drunk anything. I wanted to get some calories in her before we left Colorado, so I'd gone to the lobby to buy her a Coke. My phone rang, and I glanced at the caller ID. When I saw it was Myrna, I sat down. I wasn't sure what to expect.

"I wanted to update you on the latest," she said. "It looks like we're going to put her organs to good use. There's a gentleman here in Colorado who will receive her pancreas and kidney. It is going to be lifesaving for him. A younger gentleman, also in Colorado, will get her other kidney. We think we've placed her heart with a woman in her late thirties in Arizona, and it looks like her liver will save the life of a young child. We also know her corneas are going to be placed, but that's all the information we have on those right now."

"Okay," I said.

I didn't know how to feel, yet somehow that news planted a seed of hope. I was grateful that something good was coming out of all of this. Mostly, I was tired and emotionally exhausted, but I wanted to soak in the information so I could tell Tara once I got back to the room.

"Thank you, Todd. And thank Tara. You have no idea what this means to the people who are receiving Taylor's organs. Thank you so very much."

∘⁑∘

We didn't talk much on the flight home. What was there to say?

My sister-in-law Wendy, Chris's wife, picked us up at the airport in Dallas. I helped Tara into the car before loading the luggage in the back, and we took off for home. We live less than five miles from the airport. It typically was about a ten-minute drive. But Wendy was driving extraordinarily slowly. It had been at least twenty minutes, and we hadn't arrived yet.

Wendy turned right onto Bethel School Road, and I could hear her on the phone, telling someone we were almost there. Just then, a small pickup truck pulled out of the parking lot in front of us. I stared in disbelief as the driver put on his flashers, driving even slower than Wendy. Unbelievably, he made a left onto the same street we were turning onto. Still on her phone, Wendy said, "We're turning onto Heartz Street now," and that's when I remembered.

Earlier that morning, I had read on a Facebook page something about picking up balloons at Tom Thumb or Kroger and meeting at a church. There was a note that alerted people we'd be home around 4:00 p.m. At the time, I wondered what they were planning and whether or not it would be appropriate. Now, it made sense. There were probably people holding balloons in our front yard.

I leaned over and whispered to Tara. "Just want to give you a heads-up. A lot of people want to welcome us home. There may be some people at the house with balloons or something, so don't be surprised when you see them."

We made the left turn onto Heartz, and as far as we could see, people were holding blue and purple balloons—Taylor's favorite colors. We were at least a half mile from our home, and people stood lined up on both sides of the street.

"Oh, wow!" Peyton said. "Look at that!"

Wide-eyed, Tara, the kids, and I stared at the crowd in disbelief as we drove down the street. Coppell is a small town, a bedroom community in the northwest corner of the Dallas/Fort Worth Metroplex. There are fewer than forty thousand residents, but it feels smaller—everyone seems to know everyone else.

When we looked at the people lining the streets, we saw friends, kids from the local elementary and junior high schools, and neighbors standing two or three people deep along the route to our house. As we crawled by in Wendy's SUV, each of them slowly released their balloon and let it float away.

Soon the Coppell sky was filled with blue and purple balloon-tears rising to heaven.

Our car was filled with tears too. Tara was bawling and calling out names of friends as soon as she made eye contact. I saw people from church, from local businesses, and kids and parents from teams I had previously coached.

The closer we got to our house, the larger the crowd grew. By the time we turned onto the street in front of our subdivision, people were standing twenty deep. News trucks lined the street, some with satellite dishes lifted into the air. Reporters with microphones roamed through the crowd, while cameramen focused their lenses toward the heavens as a thousand balloons filled the sky. Later, I learned that the mayor of Coppell had called DFW International Airport. The city is on a flight pattern, and she was worried that the balloon release would become a safety hazard for planes during takeoffs and landings.

As the pickup truck with flashing lights alerted them of our arrival, reporters and cameramen started to run toward our car, filming as they jogged through the street. The CBS, FOX, and NBC affiliates were there. I either knew people, or knew of the people, who worked at these stations. They were friends and former co-workers of mine, but I never expected them to be at my house. I never thought *we'd* be the story.

From the car window, I made eye contact with Laura Springer, standing next to a couple of Taylor's friends from middle school. Laura let go of her blue balloon the moment we passed, and I let loose the tears I'd been trying to hold back. It seemed as if the whole city had shut down and lined the streets for our sad welcome home. Family, friends, and caring people from the community—everyone we knew was there.

We turned into the driveway, and I saw our mailbox. I began to cry harder. It reminded me of a game I used to play with Taylor. When we were in the car we acted goofy, being silly and cracking each other up. One day, we came up with a game. We called it the Game of Random. I would say something like, "Adjective, adjective, noun. Noun has to be an animal."

Then she'd respond, "Okay, the *silly, magnetic hippopotamus*." She'd laugh and then say, "Your turn!" Then I would have to come up with one.

One day, my response was "Red-painted flying monkey horse!" For months afterward, she remembered that answer, and every time she thought of the visual of a "red-painted flying monkey horse," she would burst out laughing.

Over time, the game evolved. I began giving her just one word, and she would have to make up a whole commercial about it. Last time we played, I'd said, "Mailbox."

Immediately, she'd responded with, "Is your mailbox driving you crazy? Well, don't let that happen anymore. You can have the mailbox of your dreams . . ."

At the time, the game seemed so silly.

Now it seemed like the most important thing in the world.

Tara

I had been crying off and on the whole way home, but once we turned onto Heartz Street, I lost control and just bawled the last half mile to our house. I was totally overwhelmed by the number of people who had turned out to welcome us. I knew I would never forget the pain on their faces, the love in their eyes, or the sight of nearly a thousand balloons filling the sky.

Wendy had planned ahead, and we drove straight into our garage, closed the door behind us, and left the public outside. But even the inside of our garage was packed with people. Our closest friends and relatives were waiting for us, and more poured out of the house once Wendy parked the car. When I looked up, I saw my best friend, Beth Sunshine, running toward me. Oh, how I'd missed her.

"Beth!" I sobbed, as I stepped out of the car and immediately fell into her arms.

"Matt!" She yelled for her husband's help when she couldn't support me. He came running, and the two of them carried me into the house and sat me on our family room sofa.

The house was bursting with people and activity. Someone had brought in our bags, and my friends were busy unpacking them. Others were in the kitchen organizing trays of food. Todd stood crying and confused. His dad hugged him from behind, and he bawled.

I had no idea where the kids were. I assumed friends or family were helping them get settled. I didn't have the energy to investigate.

The whole scene seemed like a montage from a movie. I heard snatches of conversations, or I'd look up and see only one person in a room of twenty people. The bits and glimpses I caught didn't add up, and nothing seemed to make sense to me. I was physically spent. I hadn't eaten in three and a half days. I'd even thrown up the graham crackers I'd nibbled on in the hospital. Todd's brother, Terry, kept offering me orange juice, but I had the shakes so badly I couldn't hold anything in my hands. "No, thanks," I said repeatedly.

Someone brought me a blanket.

I overheard someone else say, "She has to eat. She's not eating or drinking anything." I didn't realize they were talking about me until someone tried to put a Coke in my hands. I refused it.

People were coming and going. The doorbell would ring, and someone would answer it. A new person would come in to give us their condolences, drop off a casserole, or leave flowers. Todd came and sat near me. We were home, but we didn't have a plan or a purpose. We didn't know what we were supposed to do next.

My brothers Chris and Bill arrived later that evening, along with Kary and his wife, Juli. The four of them had driven our car back from Colorado.

People kept bringing me orange juice and encouraging me to take a sip. It was really starting to tick me off.

I overheard Matt saying something to Todd.

"I've tried. I can't get her to drink anything," Todd replied. This time, I knew they were talking about me.

Somehow, I found myself sitting at the table in our dining room. Bill sat across from me, and he said, "Tara, if you don't drink something right now, I am admitting you into the hospital. You can either eat or drink, or we can go to the hospital. If we go to the hospital they will give you IVs and put a feeding tube down your nose. That's the last thing your kids need to see right now."

I drank the orange juice.

❖

After my brothers got back to our house, Chris didn't stay long. Chris and Wendy had planned to go to Austin for spring break but had cancelled when he'd left for Colorado. Now that everyone was home, and we couldn't have a funeral for a few more days, their trip was back on. They planned to take their three boys to the hill country near Austin and go ziplining. "We'd really like to take Ryan with us, if that's okay," Chris asked. "I think it would be good for him to be away from all of this for a few days."

Chris had mentioned something about this while we were in Grand Junction, but that seemed like days ago. "What day is it?" I asked.

"Today's Tuesday, March 16."

"When will you have him back?"

"We'll have him back tomorrow, if you want him tomorrow. You let us know, and we'll bring him back," Chris said. "I just think Ryan needs to get away."

"Okay, but he'll need a bag," I said.

Allison, one of Beth's twins, spoke up. "I'll get it," she said. So she and Ryan packed a bag, and a few minutes later, he was gone.

Peyton had been distracted most of the evening with relatives who were loving her and keeping her busy. It was obvious that Todd and I were in no shape to parent.

"We'll take her home with us," Todd's dad and stepmother offered. As Peyton kissed me goodbye, she seemed relieved to go. On one hand, I hated for them to leave, but on the other, I knew it was the best thing. Neither Todd nor I could offer them the comfort they were each looking for, and they needed a way to escape the craziness.

⚬⚬⚬

As evening turned to night, fewer people remained in the house, and all I could think about was getting clean. I hadn't showered since Saturday night. I felt disgusting, and I wanted to wash off three days of hospital odors.

"I want to take a bath," I told Beth, sniffling. Someone filled the tub and called me when it was ready. Beth helped me up from the sofa and a few women, family and friends, followed as I shuffled into my bedroom, then the bathroom.

Bathing had always been an escape for me. For a few minutes, I could soak and relax without worrying about anyone or anything. That's all I wanted—a few moments of peace. Somehow, the thought of that simple pleasure set me off again. As soon I got into the bathroom, I fell onto the floor. I heard someone screaming Taylor's name over and over again. I didn't recognize the voice. I curled into a ball and tried to make myself as small as possible. When I buried my face in the bath mat the screams became muffled. *Am I the one screaming?*

It was like an out-of-body experience. On one hand, I could hear the most blood-chilling screams, "Tay-lorrr, Taaay-lor," coming from somewhere outside of myself. I became the observer of this woman and her pain. I'd never heard anything like it before or since.

Yet, at the same time, I was also the woman curled into a fetal position with her face buried in the bath mat, pounding her fists on the bathroom floor. I couldn't stop the screaming, and I couldn't stop hearing the screamer.

The women in the bathroom surrounded me on the floor as they tried to console me.

I have no recollection of what happened next, or of how I got undressed. The next thing I remember I was in the tub, my mom was in the bathroom with me, and Beth was leaning over the tub, shaving my legs. I was too helpless to do it myself. I was still sobbing and crying out for my daughter, but the screaming had stopped. They tried to talk to me, and it made me feel better that they tried, but I couldn't stop crying.

Someone laid out pajamas for me and pulled the covers back on the bed. When I climbed in, other women climbed in with me. Beth was on one side of me, and my friend Kathy was on the other, stroking my face. When I shivered, they got under the covers to hold me and keep me warm. Three more women sat with my mom at the end of the bed.

One was rubbing my leg, and my thoughts alternated between *stop* and *keep going*. It was frustrating and comforting at the same time. I wanted everybody to leave me alone, but I needed everybody there.

Someone had called my doctor and gotten a prescription for Xanax to help with the anxiety and Ambien to help me sleep. I finally drifted off, surrounded by these women who loved me.

I woke up five days later.

— 12 —

Honoring Taylor

Todd

When each of our three kids was born we experienced this beautiful, intimate moment where no one else seemed to exist besides Tara, our new baby, and me. But the moment was always quickly stolen when a doctor or nurse took the baby away from us for an examination. Each time someone left with our precious new baby, it bothered me. Emotionally, it made me feel helpless and insecure, as if there were things that doctor or nurse could do for our child that I couldn't. Intellectually, though, I knew it was exactly what had to happen.

Listening to Tara screaming our daughter's name from the bathroom, I felt the same way. Helpless. As if I wasn't enough. I couldn't give Tara what she needed. In that moment, as Tara's screams penetrated the walls of our house and our hearts, I could only stand by while the women in our lives tried to console her. I felt as if I'd lost her, as if she had been ripped from my arms and taken away.

It was also exactly what needed to happen. As Tara was surrounded by her sisters-in-law, her mom, and her best friends, these women were the doctors and nurses who cared for her in ways that I couldn't.

❧

We weren't expecting the local attention our story had generated. My stepbrother had to chase a cameraman from a local affiliate out of our yard after he tried to film through the windows. But apparently, it was also *regional* news. When Tara's brothers arrived that night, they showed me newspapers from Colorado, New Mexico, and Texas they'd collected on the way home; each had stories about Taylor, the accident, and, most importantly, the gift of life she'd given others through organ donation. All this attention seemed a little crazy.

A lot of people tried to reach out to us. People were calling on our cell phones and our home line. We were doing the best we could. I didn't answer my cell if I didn't recognize the number, and I asked my brother, Terry, to take care of answering the home phone. At one point, he came to me.

"We need to talk," he said. "There are a lot of people calling, and they all want the same information. We need to figure out a way to handle all of this. What if I set up a 'Remember Taylor' Facebook page?" Terry asked. My brother was a pastor for a local church and was responsible for all of their digital media, so he knew an online presence could help with some of the communications issues.

"That would be great," I said. I also asked him to contact people we wanted involved in the funeral.

I was so thankful to have someone as capable as Terry to handle things for me. By the next day, he had set up a Facebook page and uploaded pictures and videos of Taylor. For those who knew her, it became a central spot for them to share their memories. For those who didn't, it became a place they could learn more about her. The page went on to receive more than three thousand "likes."

I parked myself in the dining room, away from all the noise and chaos in the kitchen and living room. As friends and family asked questions, they came to me wanting to know everything from, "Where does Tara keep her medicine?" to "Who do you want to write the obituary?" I answered their questions, signed papers, and delegated tasks I couldn't do myself. Everybody wanted something, and sometimes they had to wait in line to get it. I was busier than my busiest day at work, except I wasn't consulting with clients; I was planning my daughter's funeral.

In the moment, I thought I was just doing what needed to be done. But occasionally, I would step back and realize that God had given me the gift of busyness. Planning the funeral and helping coordinate the household gave me purpose. As long as I was being asked to make a decision, give an opinion, or suggest a next step, I didn't have to think.

Looking back, I am so thankful to God for each one of those seemingly small tasks. They gave me something to focus on. Each one made me feel useful and needed.

Early the next morning, I woke up to the sound of Tara's screams. She'd slept fitfully through the night, and then once the sun rose, she suddenly bolted upright and started screaming. Her panicked eyes were open wide and a look of alarm filled her face. I tried to comfort her, but she was unresponsive. When she finally looked at me, it was as if she didn't recognize me. My heart began pumping wildly. While she continued her bloodcurdling screams, I jumped up, got dressed, and then raced up the stairs to wake Beth. I needed help.

Matt and Beth Sunshine had basically moved in. They came straight to our house after arriving home from Paris and would spend almost two weeks living with us.

I pounded on the guest bedroom door. "Tara's screaming and I can't get her to stop! I've tried everything! I don't think she even knows I'm here," I said, crying.

Matt and Beth both jumped up. Beth ran down the stairs and I followed her, but I just couldn't go back into the bedroom. From where I stood in the hallway, Tara sounded like she was hyperventilating.

"Tara, I'm here," Beth said, holding her close. "You're gonna be all right."

Matt turned toward me. "Are you okay?"

I shook my head. I was *not* okay.

I walked into the living room, sat on the sofa, and put my face in my hands. Matt made coffee for both of us. We sat together listening to Tara dry-heaving in the bathroom, while Beth did what she could to help.

I was so grateful for Matt and Beth, but I also worried about what would happen after they left us and the kids came home. I had to get back to my job too, but how would that work out? Tara and I didn't have a plan for this new season we found ourselves in. There were no role models. And the sand was shifting under our feet.

⸎

That day, I needed to work on funeral arrangements. Mary Marshall, who so far had been handling all of the details, joined Matt and me at the funeral home to pick out a casket. I had wanted Tara to come, but she was still in bed. She was so out of it that there was no way she would be capable of making any decisions. So, once we had one picked out, I waited until Beth gave her approval before finalizing it. Over the next few days, Beth became Tara's surrogate when I needed a female opinion.

While finishing up the paperwork at the funeral home, the director asked a simple question: "Where would you like her buried?"

It hadn't occurred to me that in addition to planning Taylor's funeral, I also had to pick out a place to bury her. I knew I couldn't do it on my own, so I asked Matt to drive me.

We drove out to Restland Cemetery and spoke with a representative.

"Is there anything special you're looking for?" he asked.

I remembered something that Tara had mentioned when we were in the hospital. "Texas summers are so stinkin' hot, we'll need someplace with a tree nearby because my wife will want some shade," I told the man.

We found one spot that was perfect. There was a shady tree nearby. Matt and I both agreed it was the best spot.

"If Taylor is going to be buried here, what about you and Tara?" Matt asked. "And Ryan and Peyton?"

I kicked the dirt. "Seriously?" I said, looking at Matt. "First, I've got to pay for this and now you're telling me I have to plan my whole family's burial?" I was ticked! Not at Matt, but at the situation. I knew he was right. If I didn't buy them now, someone else would. *Oh, dear Lord, when will this end?*

I bought five plots that day.

⚛

I spent most of the day working on funeral plans. Tara spent most of the day in bed crying. Beth and the other women who surrounded her started to keep a log of everything she ate and drank. They'd update Bill or me as they saw progress.

"I got Tara to drink half a cup of orange juice."

"She just took her pill; she'll probably sleep for three hours now."

"Two bites of scrambled eggs and four sips of juice."

Her doctors prescribed anxiety medication and she was supposed to take it on a regular schedule, but she began to rebel against Beth whenever she tried to give it to her. So when someone new wanted to go in and visit Tara, Beth handed them the pill and a cup with a line on it.

"You can't come out until she's taken the pill and drank at least this much juice," Beth would tell them, pointing to the line. The medication would then knock Tara out for a few hours. She'd sleep until she woke up screaming, and then the process would start all over again.

There was always someone in bed with Tara, holding her. Whenever I went into our bedroom to check on her, the group of women tending to her would scatter like pigeons to let me through. When I left, they flocked back.

❦

At some point during the day, I got a call from Cynthia Izaguirre. Cynthia and Tara were friends, and Cynthia was also an anchor of WFAA Channel 8 News—the local ABC affiliate in Dallas. Not coincidentally, they were the only local affiliate who hadn't been in our yard when we'd arrived home.

"I know you're getting a lot of pressure from media to tell your story," Cynthia said. "But I want to do it myself. I've been friends with Tara, I know your family, and I want to make sure the story is handled right from the get-go."

"What are you planning?" I asked.

"I just want you and Tara to tell the viewers what happened, why you decided to donate Taylor's organs, and how you're doing now," Cynthia said.

As an anchor for one of the largest ABC affiliates in the country, Cynthia didn't do much reporting herself. So when she told me that *she* wanted to be the one to do the interview, I knew there would never be a better opportunity. Tara would feel safe talking to her, Cynthia would protect our family, and our story would be a way for us to honor Taylor.

Cynthia was our friend. We loved her, and I trusted her to tell the story. We agreed she could come to the house with a crew later that afternoon.

"I promise to give this story the grace it deserves," she said.

❦

When Cynthia and her crew arrived, Tara was still in bed. We went in together to get her.

"Remember that interview we talked about? The WFAA crew is here with Cynthia," I said. Tara stared at me blankly as if she had no recollection of our conversation. Her eyes were red and her face looked gaunt.

Cynthia stepped past me and gave Tara a hug.

"I look terrible," Tara said, tears lining her face.

"You just stay there. I'll take care of your hair and makeup," Cynthia said.

Beth and the other women helped Cynthia as she combed Tara's hair and powdered her face. When they finished, Tara took one look in the mirror and said, "This isn't how I look!" She grabbed a hat and put it on to hide her hair.

We sat in the dining room and told our story. I was concerned that Tara would be out of it, but shortly before we went on camera she said, "We need to do this to honor Taylor." She took one deep breath and focused every ounce of energy she had on the conversation. Cynthia was easy to talk to, and I was proud of how well Tara did. Of course, all three of us became emotional during the interview.

After we finished, Tara went back to bed. A few hours later, she'd forgotten she'd even done the interview. Nonetheless, Cynthia managed to create a beautiful story out of it. Her piece led the ten o'clock news that night.

Between the interview and the new Facebook page, we hoped all the questions and concerns people had would be answered. Most of all, we hoped they would honor Taylor.

ago

The five days after we got home seemed to follow a similar pattern. Tara would wake up screaming hysterically. Shrieks of pure terror would echo through the bedroom walls. The sounds would wake up Beth, and she'd come running. "Do you need me to help? Is there anything I can do? I can go away if you want me to." But I always wanted Beth there. She and the other women who came would take over for me. "You guys give it a try," I'd say, feeling helpless.

Eventually, Tara would calm down. Then she'd mostly be a zombie, going through the motions of living, but without any real emotion. That's when people would try to coax her to eat or drink, and she'd mostly refuse.

I'd go in to check on her and just love on her. If she was able to listen and take in information, I'd tell her the latest. "We picked out a casket." Or, "We found a plot by a tree." Often, it was just simple things. "A friend from church stopped by."

Sometimes she'd talk and tell me things that Beth or the other women had told her. Invariably, she couldn't remember half the details, so it was like playing connect the dots. She'd have a few of the details but not enough to make sense of the whole picture. Sometimes she would remember what we talked about, but most of the time she didn't. I wasn't sure if it was the medication, the lack of sustenance, or the grief.

Throughout the house, the organized chaos continued. Pockets of people mingled in the kitchen, on the back porch, in the bedroom, and in the dining room, which had now become the central planning and meeting area. Dozens of people scurried in and out of the house every day. Food and flowers filled the countertops

Beth organized the women who were all busy cleaning, packing, unpacking, and moving things. To this day, I have no idea what all they were doing. Matt and Terry were my point people and helped me do what needed to be done, especially as far as planning the funeral went. I sat at the head of mission control of funeral central, issuing orders and making decisions—thankful for something to do that made a difference.

I couldn't comfort Tara, I couldn't take care of the kids, and I couldn't make anyone's pain go away, including mine. But I *could* plan a funeral that Tara would be proud of and that would honor Taylor.

I poured everything I had into that.

— 13 —

A Wake

Tara

Juli, my brother Kary's wife, walked in and sat down next to me on the bed. "Tara," she said, "it's been five days. Don't you think Ryan and Peyton need to come home?"

"Five days?" I looked at her, puzzled. "How could it be five days?" It didn't seem as if they had been gone that long. "What day is it?" I asked.

"It's Sunday, March 21," Juli said.

"Sunday?" The last memory I had was of Tuesday night. *How had so much time elapsed?* "Yes, of course, they need to come home," I said.

Beth was standing near my bed, and I searched her face for answers. "Have I been that out of it?"

She nodded. "You were completely shut down. You were like a zombie. We were all here, but it's like you didn't even see us."

I considered the past few days, trying to remember. They were a blur of faces, of people trying to get me to drink or eat. But I couldn't remember any details; it was like a Sunday afternoon when you intend to sleep for just a few minutes and wake to find you've been sleeping for hours. Only in my case it was *days*, and I hadn't been sleeping. It frightened me. *Have I even talked to Peyton and Ryan in five days? Surely, I have. I've got to get a grip. I can't let this happen again.*

I had disappeared into the grief, and Juli's question about the kids helped me fight my way out of the fog. Though the pain of living in the present was intolerable, I vowed to do my best to fight through it. It was the least I could do for Ryan and Peyton.

∱

Later that night, Todd asked me to join him, Matt, Beth, and some of the others to go through details for the next few days. Todd had arranged a funeral mass on Tuesday, March 23, at our church, St. Ann's. There would be a visitation the night before at the funeral home. "When Monsignor Duesman and Father Fred came over—"

"Wait, Monsignor Duesman and Father Fred were *here?*" I asked.

"Yes, they were here yesterday," Todd said. He looked concerned. "Don't you remember?"

I shook my head. I remembered we had spoken about including my brothers Bill and Kary, his brother, Terry, the Sunshine family, Laura Springer, and Taylor's friend Kate Dicken in the funeral mass. But I didn't realize he'd picked out the pallbearers or created a first draft of the funeral program until I saw it.

"I just want you to approve everything before I confirm it," he said, putting the document in front of me.

I was amazed at my husband. How could he manage all of this, while I still couldn't even keep food down? When I needed a shoulder to cry on, he was gentle and tender with me, but as I looked around the table, I could only marvel at his strengths—a rough draft of Taylor's obituary, photos for a slide show, and a funeral program with red ink encircling the typos. *Surely, God is protecting him*, I thought.

"What do you think of this?" he asked, sliding a piece of paper in front of me.

"It's fine," I said, barely glancing at it.

"Here are the Scriptures I picked out. Are these okay with you?" He slipped another piece of paper in front of me, and I read the first verse: "Jesus replied, 'What is impossible with men is possible with God,' Luke 18:27."

"It was on Taylor's Facebook page," he said, pointing at the verse.

Below that one was another, 2 Peter 1:17. I recognized the verse from the paraphrase that Todd said to the kids many nights when he tucked them into bed. "You're my son/daughter with whom I am well pleased. You are my delight." I started to well up, thinking how he'd never again say that to Taylor.

"You're going to be really pleased with the casket Todd picked out," Beth said, trying to change the conversation. As she and Todd went on to describe it in painstaking detail, all I could think was *I'm never going to be happy with that*. But I was thankful that someone else had taken care of it for me.

"I know you haven't had a lot of input on this," Todd said, once again referring to the funeral plans. "Is there anything you want?"

"I think someone should sing 'Finally Home,'" I said.

I remembered Taylor sitting at the bar in our kitchen, her feet swinging, as she listened to the Mercy Me song that spoke of what we'd say to God when we finally made it home.

Taylor was now home. *What was she saying to God?* I wondered.

Beth interrupted my thoughts with a question. "Do you have something you want her to wear?"

I hadn't even thought about it.

"Umm, her jeans. And her UGG boots," I said. "But I don't know what else." The tears flowed freely now, and I tried to think. I knew there were other things. *A ring she always wore, a special bracelet, and a necklace Todd's mom had given her.* But I couldn't put it all together in my mind; it was just too much. "Could the girls go shopping and maybe pick out something for her?" I asked.

"We'll take care of it," Beth said.

Emily and Allison were glad to help. Not only did Beth take them shopping for Taylor but she took care of dressing all of us.

⚘

We arrived at the funeral home for the visitation about an hour and a half before it officially began. The funeral director greeted us at the door and asked if we had any requests. "Can we turn these monitors on?" Todd said, pointing to TVs mounted in the corners of the room. "We'd like to have the slide show playing when people come in. And can you unlock the door to that room, so if we need to get away for a few minutes, we can go in?"

It was obvious Todd had been here before. His ability not only to think through the details but to think *at all* overwhelmed me. I had no idea how he did it. His strength was incredible, and as we walked toward the room where the visitation would be held, I clung to him physically and emotionally.

I could barely stand. Though nausea had made a permanent home in my stomach and I had gotten used to the feeling, my stomach now began to toss and turn violently. Peyton hung by my side, and Ryan just followed without saying a word.

As soon as we walked into the visitation area I could see Taylor's casket, and my eyes were immediately drawn to it. My heart started pounding. It became difficult to breathe. The closer I got to the coffin, the more my body shook. When I finally got a good look, I burst into tears and had to fight the urge to throw up. I stared at the young woman in the coffin with copper-colored lipstick and dark rouged cheeks, and I lost it.

"It's not her! It's not her!" I yelled. "She doesn't look like Taylor!"

Ryan and Peyton had been standing next to me, but when I started panicking, they immediately stepped back. Todd wrapped his arms around me and tried to console me. "Tara, it's her. It's Taylor," he said, holding me tight.

By now, several funeral home employees were starting to gather near us.

122

"It's not her! She doesn't wear lipstick. Her hair would never look that way; it doesn't look anything like her," I said, pounding my fists into Todd's chest. It didn't look like Taylor. I had a vision of what she would look like, and in my vision, I pictured Taylor looking like she was asleep. But the girl in the coffin looked like she was *dead*, and I couldn't bear that.

I turned and ran out of the visitation room, busting through the crowd of family members and intimate friends who had come to support us. Once I got to the hallway, I leaned against the wall and cried.

The makeup artist arrived with her kit. "Tell me what to change, and I'll change it," she said.

"That lipstick!" I shrieked. "She would never wear that color!"

"What color would she wear?" she asked.

I wanted to scream, "She was thirteen! She didn't even wear lipstick!" But I didn't have to answer her. Suddenly, every woman there pulled out her own tube. I looked up to see my mom, my sisters-in-law, and Beth each holding out their personal colors.

"Come with me," the makeup artist said, gently tugging my elbow.

I had a choice. I could stay in the hallway and cry about how unfair the whole situation was, or I could go with her. No matter how much I wished differently, I knew there was nothing I could do to bring Taylor back, and the visitation was going to happen with or without me. I took a deep breath and balled my hands into fists as I tried to pull myself together. *You can do this,* I told myself, digging my nails into my palms.

"Come with me," the woman said again. "We'll fix it, I promise."

I took another deep breath and forced myself back into the room. I walked toward the casket, alongside the woman holding her kit. I took another look at Taylor and fished in my purse for a Kleenex. Then I scrubbed the copper color off of Taylor's lips and applied the lipstick that Beth had given me.

"What else can I do?" the woman asked.

"Change that," I said, pointing at her heavily made-up cheeks. "She would never wear that much makeup." The makeup artist took some of it off, rubbed some of it in, and then asked for my approval. "How's that?"

"That's better. But see if you can fix her hair," I said, pointing to a lump. I knew I was being unpleasant, but I wanted it to look like Taylor. The woman did as I directed and turned to me once more for approval.

"Thank you," I said. "That's better."

Ryan and Peyton had remained in the room with Todd after I ran out, and they stayed away when I first returned. But slowly, they felt more comfortable, and soon Peyton was back at my side.

"Is everything okay now?" Todd asked, after I finally calmed down.

I nodded. But it felt as if I would never really be *okay* again.

Todd stood next to me, and I suddenly felt *his* body shaking. I looked over, and he was wracked with sobs. He had waited for me to be okay before he allowed himself to break down.

◦⟡◦

We were almost two hours through the visitation when Matt came up and whispered to us, "We've got to find a way to speed this up. People are standing in a line outside that wraps all the way around the building."

I knew there was a line to see us; I could see that from where we stood, but I had no idea until later that people had waited up to two and a half hours to talk to us. All I could do was concentrate on talking to the person in front of me and sucking on peppermints so I didn't lose my stomach.

Todd wanted to talk to every single person. When a flood of teenagers came in, it was as if Todd became more engaged, and his face lit up. I just wanted to retreat.

"I am so glad you came," he said, looking a young boy in the eyes and shaking his hand.

"I want you to know you are loved," he said, hugging each of Taylor's close friends.

"Thank God, you're here and that you're okay," he said to those who had traveled a distance to be with us. It was like he wanted everyone to know they were important and loved. He was energized by taking care of them. I was exhausted.

A bunch of girls from Taylor's summer camp came. They stood in a corner wailing, as their mothers tried to comfort them. *They're in shock*, I thought.

So am I.

The line continued to snake past me. Matt and others did their best to keep it moving, so we didn't talk to anyone for too long. But there were people we hadn't seen in years. One moment, I felt like I was going to fall apart, and then the next, I would see someone I hadn't seen in a long time. Their presence made me feel so loved and protected that it helped me make it through the next few minutes.

I kept my eye on Peyton and Ryan. Fortunately, some of their friends came, and they were able to escape for a few minutes to talk and play with their pals. At one point, I saw Peyton sitting alone in a chair by the casket, but before I could get to her, someone was there kneeling down talking to her and hugging her. And when that person left, there was another, and then another.

At one point, I looked to the right of me where Todd had been, and he was gone. I tried to continue talking to the person in front of me, but I could feel panic rising in my chest. I noticed Matt was nearby talking with someone else. I called his name until I got his attention and then asked, "Where's Todd?"

He could see I needed him, so he started looking for Todd. But so many people were milling about that he couldn't move and he had to strain to see the entire room. He couldn't find him either. Finally, Matt grabbed Charlie Hellmuth, a friend of ours who stands six foot three, big, and bald. Charlie looked around the room. When he located Todd, Charlie interrupted the people talking with him. "Excuse me, Todd. Tara needs you." Nobody was going to argue with Charlie. Or with a grieving wife. They let Todd go, and he rushed back to my side. I was comforted by his presence. I needed to lean into his strength.

After almost five hours, things finally wound down. By the end of the night, I was spent. But I'd done what I needed to do. I'd held myself together for Ryan and Peyton.

Lying in bed that night, waiting for sleep to kick in, I thought about Matt crying when he saw Taylor in the casket. We'd been friends for a long time; I'd never seen Matt cry before, and it touched me. Then I worried about the kids seeing her in the casket.

When we walked out of the visitation room, I'd stopped for one last look of Taylor in the casket. The kids had too. That would be their final memory of her. Todd and I had debated letting them see her in Grand Junction, but we were afraid it would be their last image of her—bloody, bruised, and hooked up to machines. Now, I realized their last image was of their sister in a casket.

Had we done the right thing?

✤

We arrived early the next day at St. Ann's, and a church staffer shuffled us off to a holding room. Family members came in to give us a quick hug, and somebody who dropped by left a fuzzy blue elephant for Peyton, which she clung to the rest of the day.

The church was massive, with soaring ceilings, and we'd walked down that aisle countless times—practically every Sunday since we'd joined the church. But that day the aisle seemed different. Endless. The church was packed—I would later learn that more than eighteen hundred people had attended—and I felt each of their eyes on me as I followed my daughter's casket down the aisle. *Why are they staring?* The whole thing was surreal, like an out-of-body experience. It felt as if I were watching someone else in a movie. I just wanted to disappear.

Father Fred was the perfect priest to conduct Taylor's funeral. He was loved by the adults but even more by the kids, because he was appropriately light and funny when the moment called for it—like wearing tennis shoes under his sacred robes at the funeral. As the service continued, his ability to connect with humor and compassion was much appreciated.

All of our kids had been coming to church with us since they were babies, but during the funeral Ryan acted like this was the first time he'd ever been. "Why is he doing that?" Ryan asked early in the service. "What are they doing now?" he asked a few minutes later when someone got up to read Scripture. "Who is that?" he asked when someone else got up to speak. Throughout the whole service, he couldn't sit still and he couldn't stop asking questions. It was as if he had regressed from a mature twelve-year-old to an antsy six-year-old who couldn't sit still.

I tried to be patient. Sitting there with him, I realized this was the longest time the four of us had been together in one space since the accident. Maybe he was just trying to engage me in the only way he knew. Or maybe he was trying to distance himself from soaking in the emotion of the moment by asking questions rather than feeling it.

Peyton was doing something similar, in her own way. She sat quietly staring off in the distance, holding the stuffed elephant under her chin.

I understood their need to be removed from the situation. Though I was there physically, at times I felt as if I checked out emotionally, as if my body had gone into a protection mode by separating me from what was happening. Instead of being fully present, I was catching only snatches and glimpses of the funeral and then processing them in small bites. Even when Todd got up to speak, I don't remember hearing what he said.

But one moment during the funeral stood out.

On Sundays, when we recite the Lord's Prayer, the parishioners typically hold hands with the people standing next to them. So when it came to that particular moment in the funeral, I reached out to take Ryan's and Peyton's hands. Todd joined us by putting his left hand on top of ours. Since no one was sitting to his right, he had a free hand. As the prayer began and people bowed their heads and closed their eyes, I watched as Todd stretched out his arm and laid his right hand on the casket.

It was our final prayer as a family, with Taylor.

— 14 —

Finding Purpose

Todd

At almost 10:00 p.m., I thought I heard a knock on the front door. Though the house had been overflowing with people for hours after the funeral and burial at the cemetery, by now everyone except our parents and Tara's aunt had gone home. The kids were upstairs getting ready for bed. Matt and Beth, thinking things would be calm for a few hours, took the opportunity to run to their house in Plano to pick up a few things they and their girls would need for the upcoming week. When I heard a second knock, I got up, walked to the front door, and glanced out the window.

"Hey, Father Alfonse!" I said, quickly opening the door. "C'mon in!"

Like Father Fred, Father Alfonse was popular with the kids. His primary job was at the local Catholic school, but he occasionally did youth masses at St. Ann's and spoke at youth retreats. He'd been at the burial hours earlier, and we'd spoken briefly. At the time, I'd thanked him for coming and told him how much Taylor had loved his masses. "I have to leave now, but may I come by later?" he'd asked. I told him he was welcome anytime.

I showed him to the kitchen and introduced him to everyone around the table.

"Can I get you something to eat, Father?" Tara's mom said, jumping up from the table. One way Tara's mom showed her love was through serving others, especially food. She believed that when there were guests in the house you needed to feed them.

Father Alfonse took the pie she offered, sat down at the table, and asked how everyone was doing. The conversation turned to the funeral, and Father Alfonse expressed his sympathies. At some point the ski accident was brought up, and he said, "It was all part of God's plan."

Most people just nodded or sat silently contemplating his words, but Tara's dad, Bernie, couldn't let the statement go unchallenged. "Are you *kidding* me? It was an accident," Bernie said. "God didn't *plan* this."

The two men got into quite a discussion with their differing views on how a merciful God could allow pain and suffering. The sticking point seemed to be whether or not God was active and involved in every part of our lives. Tara and I stayed out of it. It didn't matter to us; whatever their conclusion was didn't change the outcome for us. Plus, we had no energy left to argue.

"I don't know how else to explain it," Father Alfonse said at last, "than to say God had a purpose in all of this and this was Taylor's purpose."

About this time, Peyton walked up to the table. She was carrying the journal someone had given her to record her thoughts and feelings about the loss of her sister. "Peyton, show Father Alfonse your journal," Tara said, to change the subject.

"You have a journal? Can I see it?" the priest asked, and then in mock seriousness he added, "Unless you wrote about your boyfriend, and you don't want me to read it."

Peyton giggled and handed it to him. "I haven't written in it yet. And I'm too young to have a boyfriend!"

Father Alfonse flipped through the blank pages. "Look at that, there's a Scripture at the bottom of every page."

"Yep," Peyton said proudly.

"Let me pick one and read it," Father Alfonse said. He randomly flipped to a page and read, "And we know that in all things God works for the good of those who love him, who have been called according to his purpose. Romans 8:28." He finished reading and then slowly looked up, glancing first at Bernie, then Tara, and then me.

As the words he read sank in, it was as if they struck a match. The Scripture was illuminating the darkness inside of me, and I wasn't sure what to do with it. I looked at Tara. From the expression on her face, I could see she felt the same way. It could have been a mere coincidence that out of all the pages in the journal, he opened to this one, but we didn't believe in coincidences. It was clear to us that God was trying to tell us something. *Could there be a purpose in this? Could Taylor's death be used for good in some way?*

Peyton interrupted my thoughts with a question for Father Alfonse, and the conversation changed direction. It grew late and Father Alfonse got up to leave. Clearly, he'd been affected by the timing of the verse he'd read too. "Can we talk another time? I'd like to check back with you and talk more about all of this," he said, as I walked him to the door.

That night, for the first time in over a week, Tara and I went to bed together at the same time. As we lay in bed, facing each other, our arms and legs intertwined, we discussed what had just happened. "Do you really think God could have a purpose for Taylor's death?" Tara asked.

"I don't know," I said. It was an honest answer. I didn't know. It was hard to understand how something so painful could ever be good, but I also knew God was God, and my ways were not His ways. I pulled Tara close and said, "If there is a purpose, or even the possibility of one, then I think it's important we try to figure out what it is."

She snuggled deep into my arms and said, "Mm-hmm," and immediately fell asleep.

❖

I woke up the next morning and stared at the ceiling. The funeral that had kept me busy for the past few days was over and our child was buried. *What am I supposed to do now?*

The calendar said I should be in New York. But how was I supposed to work? I needed to be home for my wife and kids. John and Jim, the company executives, had told me to take as much time off as I needed, but sooner or later that would end. The thought of getting on a plane and leaving my family alone without me was—well, unthinkable. They couldn't function without my help; let's face it, I could barely function myself. How was I supposed to help my clients when I couldn't help myself?

The first thing I had to do was for myself.

I had to learn to live without my daughter.

I heard Tara moan and knew screams would soon follow, but to my surprise, they didn't. Tara woke up, and for the first time since we'd been home, she didn't start screaming. Instead, she rolled out of bed and ran for the bathroom—the screams had gone, but the nausea hadn't.

"Are you okay?" I asked when she returned.

"There is a heaviness in my chest," she said, crying, "and it's making it hard to breathe."

I knew what she was feeling; I felt it too. It was like the lead bib they make you wear at the dentist's office while having an X-ray. A heavy weight wrapped around my shoulders and across my chest. It engulfed me. When I tried to breathe, the weight pressed down harder on my chest. The previous night's conversation played through my mind and I remembered something Charlie Hellmuth had told me at the visitation.

"I have never seen such an outpouring like this for a family before," he had said. "You're going to have to realize that people will want to give, but you're not going to want to receive."

What Charlie said was true. I'd much rather help someone else than have them help me.

"I know you well enough to know you're going to want to do it all yourself. And you're going to tell people 'we're fine' and 'we don't need anything,' but if you deny people the opportunity to help, you're taking away their blessing. You're taking away a gift they want to give you. So, you're going to have to figure out how to let other people help you," he said.

At the time, I hadn't been able to fully reflect on what he meant, but I was starting to get a better understanding. This wasn't going away, and there wasn't some future marker where everything would be okay. This would take time, and as much as I hated the thought of asking others for help, I would have to learn how to do just that.

Charlie went on to remind me that though I might feel abandoned, my faith would be the strength that would help me survive. "Be open to hearing, seeing, and feeling God through all of this," he said. "It's not about you, but it's about a much, much bigger picture, and there is a reason behind this that will help carry you through."

Was Charlie talking about the same thing as Father Alfonse? Could there be a purpose to Taylor's death? Could God be working even through this?

I thought about the call from Myrna I'd received back at the hotel in Grand Junction, when I'd learned that Taylor's final gift was helping so many people. In the midst of our tragic loss, knowing her organs had saved other people's lives was our only glimmer of hope.

చ్చ

The kids went back to school that day. Ryan was appropriately upset but did his best to make it through. Peyton was numb but she craved the distraction of normalcy that school offered. At home, the day passed with the usual visitors coming and going. Everyone except Tara had at least a few bites of the abundant food that continued to arrive in Tupperware and aluminum tins. The hours passed quickly, and soon it was night again. Everyone else was in bed but I was still restless. I sat in my office, composing an email. When I finished, I opened a browser window and googled "organ donation."

Maybe I was looking for purpose and meaning, or maybe I just wanted to know more. Regardless, I was reading everything I could find. The first link led to an article, which led to a blog, which led to an organization, and they all led to more links. It didn't take long to realize how many people were desperately waiting for organs and how few organ donors were readily available. The articles showed how hard it was to get people to register for organ donation. And without registered donors, there would always be a lack of organs for those who needed them. My inner consultant came alive, and I started asking questions. "Why is it so hard to get people to register?"

To answer that question, I did more research and quickly saw the problem seemed to stem from a lack of education. People believed the myths and didn't know the truth. They never discussed it or tried to consult anyone who had real answers. Even for those who thought it was a good idea, a conversation was never broached around the dinner table. Without good information and a clear directive from a loved one, when someone died people didn't know what to do. When they didn't know what to do, they failed to donate organs. It got me thinking. *What could I do to help educate people and lead them into conversations about organ donation?*

❧

The next day Laura Springer, the principal from Taylor's school, called to check up on us. After we returned from Grand Junction, she was one of the people who regularly called or stopped by. We'd sit out on the back porch and have a Dr Pepper, and she'd tell Tara and me stories about Taylor at school. We loved spending time with her because we treasured hearing stories about our daughter. We chatted for a few minutes, and then I asked, "How are the kids doing up there?"

"The kids aren't doing well; they're hurting. Taylor was an important part of this school. We've had counselors in, and I've asked some of the local churches to provide youth ministers to come up and hang out during lunch, in case the kids want someone to talk to."

"What can I do?"

"Would you be able to talk to them? Not only are they missing Taylor, but they're also worried about you, Tara, Ryan, and Peyton. You're all part of this community."

I didn't even have to think about it. "I'll be there tomorrow."

I had always liked Taylor's friends, but after talking with them at the visitation, I had a renewed sense of connection with them. I wanted to take care of them and let them know it was going to be okay. I wanted to be their friend and hear how they were doing.

Tara was sitting out on the back patio. When I found her, I told her about the conversation I'd had with Laura and how we'd been invited to come up to the school for lunch.

"I can't, Todd. I can't," Tara said. "You go."

I understood. It had been hard for her to see some of Taylor's closest friends at the visitation and funeral. Tara didn't receive the same kind of strength from them that I did. Though she hadn't woken up screaming for a few days, she still cried and had that same vacant look in her eyes. The nausea prevented her from eating, and now chest pains were making it hard for her to breathe. She was in no shape to leave the house.

The next day, I met Laura in the cafeteria. After all the kids got their food and sat down, she stood on the stage and said, "We've had a tough time here the past few days. We're all missing Taylor. That's why I've asked Mr. Storch to talk to you." Then she turned it over to me. I looked out across the cafeteria at the round wooden tables and watched some of Taylor's closest friends tearing up. Their heartfelt emotion touched me.

"First, I just want you to know we're surviving as a family and it's because of the love you've shown us. We're so thankful for those of you who have prayed, stopped by, sent cards, or written notes for us. Thank you for loving us."

I could hear some sniffling in the crowd. I turned in that direction and said, "It's okay to cry. We're going through all of those crazy emotions at our house too. I know this is just as tough for you as it is for the adults. But our family is going to be okay, and though it will be hard, you will be too."

Trying to lighten the mood, I talked about Taylor's sense of humor and some of the funny things she did. I told them things they might not have known about her and things they could relate to. I reminded them of how she would sneak into their photos without their knowledge. I mentioned organ donation and how it had given us great hope because even though she was not with us any longer, she was still here in some small way, by making life better for others through her gifts.

The somber mood seemed to have turned as the kids responded to the stories I told. The lunch period was almost over, so I concluded by saying, "If you see me in the grocery store, and you want to give me a hug, you can. Or if you want to come by our house, come by. We don't always know how to respond, so it's okay if you don't always know what to say. I just want you to know we're here for you if you need us."

A girl in gym shorts and a T-shirt asked, "Can I come by your house today?"

Another girl with short blonde hair asked, "I have a note I wrote to Taylor. Is there somewhere I can leave it?"

"Of course, all of you can come by anytime. You can leave the note in her bedroom, if you'd like." As I said it, I immediately realized what was happening. The kids didn't have a place to mourn or pour out their grief. They needed a place. They were too young to drive, and even if they could, they wouldn't visit the cemetery or hang out in a big church all alone. They needed somewhere to gather individually, and in small groups, to remember their friend.

Taylor's room was the place they needed.

"Pull out your cell phones," I said, "and I'll give you my number. That way you can call or text me, or you can just show up at the house. You can go upstairs to her room and just hang out for a while. Or you can write a note and leave it there, if you want. Whatever you want to do, know we love you, and we're all going to get through this together."

Afterward, I followed Laura back to her office. On the way, we talked about how the kids seemed lost. They really didn't have a place to go and needed their own space.

I sat down in her office, and I mentioned the tree account. "I know people have been making donations to the PTO account to buy a tree in honor of Taylor. Maybe we could somehow make that a spot for the kids."

"Todd, you realize that account has more than thirty thousand dollars in it, right?"

I was speechless. "Thirty thousand dollars?" It took a moment for the number to sink in, and when it did, I said, "We're not buying a thirty-thousand-dollar tree!"

Laura laughed.

"Look," I said, "I don't know how any of this stuff works, but if we've got all this money, let's use it to do something great."

She thought for a moment and then said, "The seventh grade class has the responsibility of a garden, but it has a lot of meaning to Taylor's class because they were the first ones to start it."

"Great. We'll use some of this money to spruce it up. What do you need?"

"Oh my, we need everything! It's nothing but some sad little plants, a couple of weathered picnic tables, some old bricks, and a lot of kids trying to do good work."

"Perfect. If we fix it up, maybe plant a tree or two and do a little landscaping, not only will it become a way to honor Taylor but it will also become a place for the kids to talk and grieve."

We agreed on a budget for the garden and decided the rest would be used for scholarships. Jay Praytor, who owned a local landscaping company, was also a former student of Laura's from her high school teaching days. I offered to call him and see what he could do for the budgeted amount. Laura thanked me for coming, and I thanked her for the opportunity to talk to the kids.

But I should have thanked her for giving me a purpose.

— 15 —

Opening Doors

Tara

My brother Bill knew what he was doing even if I didn't catch on right away. Somehow, he convinced me to go for a ride by telling me I needed to get out of the house. He was right. I did. So many people and so much chaos filled the house during the days immediately following the funeral that I spent most of my time either secluded in the bedroom or out on the back porch.

We'd been driving around for about ten minutes when he decided he was hungry and needed to eat. *Why didn't he just eat at the house? There is so much food available, and he could have eaten anything.* I had been trying to eat, but I just couldn't keep anything down. Bill had prescribed Phenergan Gel for my wrists. It was supposed to stop the nausea, but all it did was make me sleepy.

"Anything sound good to you?" he asked.

I shook my head.

He made a left and then a quick right onto the main road. Up ahead, I saw a Taco Bueno, and I immediately knew that's where he was headed. Bill and I were both crazy about Taco Bueno. I loved everything on their menu. If I ever had to choose a death row meal, it would be Taco Bueno.

Before he placed his order, he asked again, "Are you sure you don't want anything?"

"I'm sure."

"I'll have four bean burritos, three beef tacos, and four tostadas. And extra salsa, please."

As the cashier repeated the large order back to him, I realized he had purposely ordered all of our favorites. After paying at the window, he handed the sacks to me. "Can you hold these, please?"

Driving back to the house, I could feel the heat from the food warming my thighs through my pajamas, and it felt good. I was always cold. The aroma of the spicy food began to fill the car. Surprisingly, it didn't make me feel queasy; it made me feel hungry.

We got back to the house, and Bill asked me to join him in the kitchen while he ate. I sat down as he plated some food and purposely left it sitting in the middle of the table. It didn't take long for me to have a bite.

For days, I had only sipped protein-packed smoothies and nibbled at crackers. Finally, Bill got his way. I ate. My first real meal after Taylor's accident was a tostada from Taco Bueno.

ॐ

For the next eight weeks, I was never left alone. Just when things seemed to settle down, someone else would show up—friends dropping off cards, delivery services with flowers, or people bringing trays of food. Finally, someone got smart and attached a basket to the door with a note that said, "Please leave the family a note if you come by. Please don't knock at this time." That helped to calm things down a bit. Each time someone new came, they wanted to hear details about what had happened from Todd or me. They had questions, or they wanted to see how we were doing. In those rare times when I *did* want to talk, I didn't want to talk about any of *that*.

When friends came over all dressed up, wearing jewelry and makeup, it would anger me. It would tick me off that they were going on with their lives, spending time shopping and looking cute, while I was struggling just to breathe. Even smelling their perfume after they left made me mad.

But I knew the issue was me, not them. They were simply doing what they knew to do, just like all the friends who showed up to take care of us. While I didn't have the mental or emotional capacity to thank them, I couldn't have done it without them. These faithful women would come over and do laundry, make dinner, empty out cabinets, and organize the pantry. They'd make the kids' lunches, help them with their homework, and give them rides to practice or school activities, if they needed it. They cleaned, dusted, and vacuumed.

One friend even organized a meal calendar, so when anyone wanted to bring a meal, they would just call her. One day, she said to me, "I got a call from someone at your church who wanted to bring a meal to you tomorrow night, and I told them we already had it covered. They asked if there was a day next week when they could bring one, and I said we had that covered too. Then they wanted to know when the next available day was, and I laughed and told them—July 19."

It was still March.

The generosity of this community of women was surprising, and at times overwhelming, but I couldn't have made it without their help. There was a gaping hole in our lives without Taylor, but these women made sure nothing else fell through the cracks. Their presence allowed me to fully grieve.

⁂

The same afternoon that Todd visited with the kids at Coppell Middle School East, he started getting text requests to come to the house.

"Hey, Mr. Storch. It's Jordan. Is it okay if three friends and I come by at 4:15 today?"

I was in our bedroom when Todd told me he'd offered to let the kids visit Taylor's room, and now they wanted to come.

"Do you care?" he asked.

"No, I'm staying in here," I said.

But it wasn't just that day. It was *every day*. Sometimes they would text or call Todd. Sometimes they'd just show up. The doorbell would ring, and when Todd opened the door, three or four girls would be standing on the front porch. "We want to write a note to Taylor. Can we go to her room?" they'd ask.

They almost always came in groups, with the mom who drove escorting them to the door.

"Sure," Todd would say. "You know where it is; go on up."

The mom who drove would stand at the door, awkwardly trying to express her sympathies. Todd would engage her in conversation and make her feel welcome. She'd say something like, "Should I wait or come back later?"

"You can go, if you want. I'm sure they'll text you when they're done," he'd say.

Todd was a kid magnet, and he never wanted them to feel awkward. He stayed away while they were in Taylor's room and tried to make them feel comfortable when they weren't, or while they waited for their moms to pick them up. When they left, they'd hug him, and if I was there, they'd hug me too. He loved it. To me, it was just more beep, beep, beeping at the door and chaos in the house. Their cute little UGG boots, Nike shorts, and talk of volleyball tournaments were more painful reminders of what I'd lost.

⸎

A few days later, Kim Dicken came to visit me. Her daughter, Kate, had been best friends with Taylor. Like she had with Emily and Allison Sunshine, Taylor had made a lot of videos with Kate and uploaded them to YouTube. They would lip-synch to their favorite songs, and when people commented about what gifted singers they were, Taylor and Kate would laugh—the truth was they couldn't sing at all.

Like so many of my other good friends, Kim had been helping out. On this particular day, only she and I were in the house. Early in the afternoon, I got up from the bedroom and walked to the kitchen to get some water. About the same time, Kim was walking down the stairs with a basket of dirty laundry. Though I hadn't been in Taylor's room since the accident, I immediately recognized the little basket she kept in her closet.

Kim had gathered up Taylor's dirty laundry—pajamas, Nike shorts, a couple of T-shirts, and volleyball socks. When I saw her come down the stairs with that basket, and I realized what was in it, I was like a two-year-old who didn't have the words to express her anger. I instinctively did the first thing that came to mind, and I slapped the basket out of her hands, knocking the laundry all over the floor. I reached down and picked up Taylor's clothes and started to bawl, and then I threw them down again.

Stunned, Kim hesitated for a second and then reached out and hugged me. She held me while I sat on the floor and cried. I was surprised at how childish I acted. I knew it was stupid, but at the time, it was just one more connection with Taylor I felt was being scrubbed away. When I finished crying and got up, Kim picked up the clothes, put them back in the basket, and went to do the laundry.

❧

My neighbor Trista was our "Grief Fairy." She had a way of sneaking into the house to do what needed to be done, then leaving again without anyone knowing she had been there. One minute I would look up and she was doing my dishes, and then I'd look again and she'd be gone. I would walk through a room, and the next time I was there things had been organized or rearranged. I'd go outside with dirty dishes standing in my sink, and when I came back in they'd be gone. Those were sure signs the Grief Fairy had been there.

One day, while Trista was sitting with me on the back porch, people kept entering and leaving the house. Each time someone went in or out, the alarm would make its annoying beeping sound.

"We've got to do something about that blasted alarm!" Todd said, as annoyed as I was.

Trista jumped up. "Where's your alarm pad?"

Todd showed her, and thirty seconds later she was back. "I fixed it so it won't beep every time you go in and out of the door," she said.

"Are you kidding me?" Todd looked at her incredulously. "Someone should have done that ten years ago!"

That was just like Trista, always there with the right thing at the right moment.

◦⦿◦

My days were still filled with bouts of uncontrollable sobbing, nausea medication, and long periods of darkness when I disappeared into my thoughts. Days would pass and I barely realized it.

Every morning I woke up lying on my side, and the first breath I took was a good one—free, easy, and peaceful. Then, with a start, I would think, *Taylor isn't here anymore!* I'd try to remember if it was a dream or if it had really happened, and then, quickly, I'd figure it out. *Yes, this happened. Oh, God, help me! This really happened.* That's when I would awaken to the nightmare. In that horrible moment I wanted to die, but I never did. I wanted to swear, and sometimes did. I wanted to scream, and though I don't remember it, they told me I did. Though the uncontrollable screaming had stopped by now, the uncontrollable crying had not. Some days I cried until I nearly hyperventilated. Even on the days that didn't start out that bad, I dreaded everything that was yet to come.

One more day to get through.

I would roll onto my back and place my palms on my forehead. Then grief, wearing work boots, would step up onto my chest. I would be overcome by a crushing feeling. It weighed heavily on my shoulders and chest, and I could feel the weight of it spreading to my arms, legs, feet, and toes. The crushing feeling was a physical sensation I wore every moment I was awake. The weight was so heavy that I began to slouch, my chin dropping toward my chest because I could no longer hold it up. My back ached because of the hours I sat slumped over, huddled in a blanket.

The only thing that relieved the pain—both physical and emotional—was sleep. It was the only time I didn't hurt. From the time I woke up in the morning and took that second breath, I couldn't wait until it was time to take an Ambien and go back to sleep.

I missed Taylor like crazy. She had been taken from me so suddenly that I just wanted to be with her one last time. I wanted to see her, touch her, smell her, and hear her. I wanted my little girl, and I wasn't sure I wanted to live without her.

Every day I woke up, I felt disappointed she was gone and I was still here.

One afternoon, I was having a really bad day and I missed Taylor so much. In addition to the crushing weight on my chest, I felt like my heart had been shredded. The pain was so real and so unbearable that I just couldn't take it a minute longer.

"I have got to find the person who has her heart," I said to Trista, my Grief Fairy.

"Are you serious?" she asked.

"Yes. I just think it would make me feel so much better to hear her heartbeat again."

"Do you know anything about the recipient?"

"All we know is that she is a nurse from Arizona."

I told Trista about the conversation with Donor Alliance back at the hospital in Grand Junction, and how Myrna said we could write letters to the recipients but we had to wait at least six months, and then there was no guarantee they would respond.

"I have to hear her heart again, I just have to," I said. Maybe hearing *her* heart would help to heal *mine*.

— 16 —

Opposing Grief

Todd

I loved having Taylor's friends over to our house. But I also knew their presence pained Tara in ways I couldn't feel or understand. Our mourning paths had first diverged in that meeting with the Donor Alliance representatives in Grand Junction, and they'd only grown wider since.

I was looking for meaning and purpose from Taylor's death, and when I couldn't see it, I wanted to create it. But Tara's grief was unfocused, unpredictable, and uncontrollable—even to her.

Before we married, Tara and I were best friends. Afterward, we became partners in everything. Now it seemed as if I had lost my best friend and my partner. Most days, her grief confined her to the house and often to her bed. She couldn't remember simple things like what day it was or conversations we'd had only hours earlier. Her emotions ranged from anger to profound sadness. She cried uncontrollably and without provocation. People had to remind her to eat, drink, and bathe.

I began to think of her as disabled.

⸎

Laura Springer and I met with Jay Praytor, and together the three of us walked the school property where the current garden sat unattended. We decided that somewhere between five and eight thousand dollars was the right amount to spend on the project.

"What can we get for that?" I asked. I hoped maybe some nice beds that would be easy for the kids to maintain, and maybe a long hose from the water source, which was located in the back of the school. That way, they wouldn't have to water the garden by carrying buckets back and forth.

"Let me see what I can work out," Jay said, promising to get back to us with a quote.

A few days later, he was back with elaborate drawings that included stonework, lighting, sidewalks, and underground sprinklers. As he talked Laura and me through the architectural designs created by a professional architect, I could see his enthusiasm building. But I cringed, knowing we didn't have the budget for all the extravagant things he wanted to do. Finally, I couldn't take it any longer.

"Jay, the budget is seven thousand dollars—eight max. We can't do all of this."

With a sparkle in his eye, Jay looked at us and said, "Every single landscaper and company I've talked to wanted to donate something. This is an eighty-thousand-dollar project, and it's basically costing us nothing!"

I was stunned.

"So, when do we get started?" Jay asked, a smile growing on his face.

We decided it would be really nice to dedicate the garden on April 19—Taylor's birthday—but that was less than a month away. "That's a pretty ambitious goal," Jay said. "If we're going to get it done in time, we need to get started immediately." He turned to Laura. "How long will it take to get permission to build and dig on city property?"

"Just get started," Laura said. "I'll ask for forgiveness later."

After that incredible meeting, anytime I drove by the school I would see backhoes chomping the dirt, stonemasons laboring, and landscaping crews sodding, planting, and trimming. They even brought in work lights, and the progress continued well into the night.

༄

A little more than a week after I spoke to the kids at Coppell Middle School East, a dad of one of Taylor's classmates sent me a beautiful email. In his email, he told me how his daughter had been so touched by the things I'd said that day that she wanted to do something to help.

He was a big supporter of organ donation, and we immediately hit it off. I invited him over to the house, where I learned he was also a website developer. During one of our conversations, I told him how I wanted to direct people to one place on the web where they could learn more about Taylor, be educated about organ donation, and sign up to be an organ donor.

"Would you be willing to help me build a website that did all that?" I asked. He agreed. Soon I had assembled a team of people to create a new online portal. Each night, after Tara and the kids went to bed, one or more team members joined me at the kitchen table or out on the back porch. I'd tell stories about Taylor and together we would work on the design and function of the new website.

"I just want to make something good out of something so bad," I told the team. "Maybe it is just a gift we can leave, maybe it's Taylor's gift," I said, thinking out loud.

"What are we going to call this?" someone asked.

I thought for a moment and said, "What about Taylor's Gift?"

Soon, we were all referring to this thing we were building as "Taylor's Gift Foundation."

Within a few days of the funeral, I was spending hours every day working on something that had the potential to change and save lives. I would stay up until three in the morning talking with friends who agreed to partner with me. And, just like they had the school garden, the community of Coppell embraced the idea. A law firm offered to help us file the necessary paperwork to become a 501(c)3 tax-exempt organization, so we could receive donations. Friends volunteered their time and expertise. I assembled a team of advisers. Each of these advisers introduced me to new people who wanted to help, and soon I had volunteers with marketing, publicity, legal, social media, and film backgrounds offering to help create not only a foundation and a website but also a documentary that would encourage people to donate their organs.

Taylor's Gift Foundation was a positive thing into which I could channel my energy. It gave me purpose.

◦§◦

In the past, when one of the kids celebrated a birthday, Tara would wake up early and decorate the kitchen. She'd arrange signs that said "Happy Birthday" and hang crepe paper streamers, banners, and balloons. She wanted to make the day extra special for the birthday boy or girl. She even did it on *my* birthday. It was an expected tradition in our family. But this year when I woke up on March 28, I knew there wouldn't be signs and streamers. No banners or balloons. I didn't want or need any of that, and Tara didn't need any pressure on her to do that sort of thing. Without traditions to navigate my choices, I spent the early morning hours thinking, *It's my birthday, what do I want?* Then the answer came. *I want to be with people.*

I called a friend who lived across the street and asked him if he would bring his fire pit into the cul-de-sac later that evening. "I want to get some people together tonight," I said.

It was a chilly day, and a bunch of friends hanging out together around a fire pit seemed like the perfect way to spend the evening. I composed a text that said, "Come to the cul-de-sac. It's my birthday," and then sent it to some of my closest friends. Immediately, people started texting back, saying they would come. The day was shaping up to be a good one.

I got busy working on things for the foundation and for the memorial garden, and the hours quickly passed. When Tara woke up, I went in and sat on the bed, and explained my plan.

"So, a few hours ago, I invited friends to come over and hang out in the cul-de-sac for my birthday. We'll have a fire pit, and we'll smoke a few cigars . . ."

A shadow crossed Tara's face as I talked.

"About forty guys have already said that they're coming," I said excitedly. "I guess the word got out."

"I cannot believe you're doing this," Tara said through clenched teeth.

"What? Inviting some guys over for my birthday?"

"It's like you think nothing's happened. And now you're throwing a party?" she said, raising her voice. I could tell she was mad.

I got up from the bed, walked to the door, and closed it. I didn't want the kids to hear us fighting. I turned back, looked her in the eyes, and said, "How *dare* you think I'm acting normal! How *dare* you think I'm not suffering! I'm trying so hard just to get through the day!" I could feel the blood pulsing in my head, and I knew my face was red with anger.

What was she thinking?

"If it hadn't been for me, the visitation, the funeral, the funeral plot, none of it would have been done! I'm the one spending hours a day trying to create a memorial garden for Taylor while you're sleeping. I'm working day and night on a website so more lives will be saved through Taylor's story. I'm the one trying to make something good come out of the pain! And yet, you have the audacity to say I'm acting like *nothing happened*?"

It wasn't like I was having a huge party with cake and balloons. It was barely a celebration. I just wanted to hang out with a few friends on my birthday. Why shouldn't I? Tara was the one lying in bed crippled by grief; should I be crippled too? *I deserved this.*

"Just let me have it; it's what I need," I added, and quickly left the bedroom before I could say something I'd later regret.

⁂

A chill filled the night air. We all wore jackets and tried to stand as close to the fire pit as possible. All my buddies came. My dad was there, along with Tara's dad, Bernie, some of my brothers-in-law, and a number of my neighbors. When we were all assembled, I looked to my friend John Lookabaugh and said, "Would you say a prayer to bless this evening and get it started?" John and I have been friends for a long time. Not only do we share a faith in God, but we also share the same sense of humor. He prayed a beautiful prayer, and I was thankful he was there. After he finished praying, he offhandedly made a remark. I don't recall what it was, but for some reason, I found it hysterical. I doubled over in laughter.

It was the first laugh of the night, but it was also my first laugh since Taylor's accident. I wasn't sure how I felt about that. Things still weren't right between Tara and me. I tried to put it out of my mind. I just wanted to be present for the guys, but it was hard.

About midway through the evening, Ryan came running out.

"Dad, Dad!" he said, trying to get my attention. I turned to look at him. "You have to come; we've got to show you something."

I excused myself from the guys and followed Ryan into the house. Tara and Peyton were sitting on the couch in the family room and looking out the back window. The backyard looked dark. Other than the full moon, I couldn't make out much else. "Look!" Ryan said excitedly, pointing out the window. "Isn't it cool?"

"What are you looking at?"

"There's a cross around the moon!"

I looked harder and there it was—a full moon with a radiating light coming from behind it. The brilliant beams of light formed the shape of a glowing *cross*.

"Ah," I said.

"Grab a camera," Tara said.

152

The kids were excited, Tara was excited, and I was too. The cross felt like a sign. I missed my daughter, I'd fought with my wife, and it hadn't been much of a birthday. Yet, God wanted to remind me of His love for me—for all of us—and He had decorated the moon to do it.

After we took pictures, I kissed Tara and told her I was going back outside. "I hope that's okay with you," I said.

"Go," she said. I knew it wasn't what she wanted, but she was willing to let me go. Besides, neither one of us had the energy required to be upset with the other. I went back to the fire pit, and with the moon watching over all of us, I felt free to enjoy myself. I did my best to lose myself in the moment. I talked, told stories, and laughed at other people's stories. Everyone had a great time, and it was nearly 2:00 a.m. before they all went home.

I helped the neighbor pull his fire pit around back before returning home. Tara and the kids had been sleeping for hours. I climbed in bed and wrapped my arms around my sleeping wife, and fell asleep remembering how good it had felt to have fun.

❧

Soon after my birthday, someone introduced us to Randy and Pam Cope. They'd lost their son, Jantsen, to an undiagnosed heart condition when he was fifteen. They were the first people we knew who had also lost a child. They invited us to their home, and they quickly became friends, confidantes, and a source of inspiration to us.

At that first meeting, we were sitting on their couch when Pam said, "You were handpicked—chosen—for this burden."

I could immediately see Tara didn't like that thought, but it aligned with my thinking. *Was there a purpose in Taylor's death? In our grief? Was this all, in some way, a part of God's plan?*

A few visits later, Randy and I went outside for a walk to give the women some privacy. I told him how difficult it was to watch Tara crying all the time, unable to get out of bed.

"It's okay that you don't want to see her sadness," Randy said. "And it's okay when she's sad and you're not. It's even fine to be mad at her because she's sad; just don't act on it. Don't do anything that would drive a wedge into your relationship."

Pam and Randy gave us permission to grieve separately and differently. Randy taught me how to accept Tara's sadness and her need to sleep away the days. Pam told Tara it was okay if I wanted to laugh, get lost in my work, or go outside and hang out with friends. We each needed what we needed. We didn't have to like it, but we had to respect it.

Finally, someone had given us a plan for our grief—something we could follow. It was the best advice we'd ever been given.

It saved our marriage.

— 17 —

Purpose in the Pain

Tara

I hated waking up.

It was a few weeks after Taylor's funeral, but each time I woke up, it started all over again. Every day, I relived the horror that Taylor was gone.

As soon as the kids got off to school, I'd take an antianxiety pill, and it would knock me out for four hours. If I went back to bed by eight, I wouldn't wake up until noon. Someone would force me to eat lunch, and afterward I'd go back to bed. When the kids were home from school, I'd fight through the fog and exhaustion to do my best as a parent. But it was obvious to everyone—everyone but me—I wasn't doing it well.

One day, Beth Sunshine planned to stop by for a visit. Since she lived in Plano, a thirty-minute drive from us, it was a special treat. I hadn't seen her in a while, and I was looking forward to talking with her. Beth knew me better than probably anyone except Todd, and I wanted to share a few things and get her feedback.

As soon as she walked in the door, I hugged her. "I've got so much I need to talk about."

Peyton was sitting in a chair coloring. When I led Beth past the family room, Peyton spoke up. "Mommy, come watch me color."

"Baby, I'm going to talk to Aunt Beth right now," I said.

"Please come see me color," she protested. Her coloring book was spread open on her lap and crayons littered both arms of the chair.

"Sweetie, I'm going to talk to Aunt Beth. It's been a while since I've seen her." I was already tearing up. I'd waited all day for Beth to get there, and I desperately needed her to listen while I unloaded.

I opened the back door to the patio, and Peyton said, "Mommy, you don't even see me." She didn't look up or wait for my reaction. She just kept coloring.

I took a deep breath. Peyton was right; I hadn't been there for her.

I knew the dynamics in the house had shifted. Peyton and Ryan used to get along, but I'd come to realize it was because Taylor helped keep the peace. Without Taylor to stop the bickering, their squabbles rose to new levels—both kids had been sniping at each other and picking fights. They didn't have to tell me it was because they were afraid of losing another sibling; I understood. The spats were a way to protect themselves from another potential loss.

Other changes occurred too. The first few days they were home, they slept on the floor in our room. They were now afraid to sleep upstairs in their own bedrooms. When it became obvious they weren't going to leave, someone loaned us an air mattress. Now, our bedroom had become theirs. At night, they wouldn't even go to bed unless I went with them, which meant I had to go to bed around eight o'clock. While they would quickly fall asleep, I couldn't. If I attempted to leave, they would hear me and get upset. They wanted me there beside them. So I lay on the bed, with them next to me on the floor, and prayed. Then I would text on my phone as I counted down the minutes until I could take my Ambien.

Standing behind her chair, I watched as Peyton put down one crayon and chose another. During the day, everyone who came to the house wanted a piece of me and a piece of Todd. Ryan and Peyton got pushed to the side. *I've got to be present for her*, I thought. *She's fearful of losing me too.* I glanced at Beth, and she motioned for me to go talk to Peyton. I knelt down in front of my daughter's chair, so I could look her square in the eye and really see her. "What do you want me to do, Peyton?"

"I want you to watch me color," she said. Then she quickly changed her mind. "Will you take me to the park?"

The park? I didn't feel like going to the park. The short walk would require more energy than I was capable of, but what choice did I have?

"I'll wait here," Beth said.

I grabbed a hat and Peyton's hand, and we walked to the park. It was the longest walk of my life.

She talked the entire way. I didn't say two words. She was ebullient, skipping and tugging on my arm, trying to get me to bounce along with her. All I could manage was to shuffle alongside her. I had concrete blocks for feet and a cement cape wrapped around my shoulders. Each step was slow and painful.

When we neared the park and I caught a glimpse of the distant duck pond, I knew I'd blown it. "I didn't bring any bread," I said. "I'm sorry, I forgot."

"Oh, Mommy!" Peyton said. "That's the reason we came!"

Every time we went to the park, we went to feed the ducks and we always took bread. "I'm so sorry, baby. As soon as we get there, I'll just call home and have someone bring it." I knew I couldn't make it home and back to the park again in the same day, let alone the same hour. Someone would have to help me out.

I mentally kicked myself for being so stupid. Nothing seemed right in my life. My memory was screwed up and my concept of time was completely missing. Even the simplest habits in my life—like bringing bread to the park—were messed up.

We walked up the path to the pond, and Peyton let go of my hand and skipped on ahead. I suddenly stopped short. Peyton chatted away about nothing, until she noticed that I'd stopped. She turned back to see why I'd stopped.

"What?" she asked when she saw my face.

"Look!" I said, pointing to an area just off the sidewalk.

There in the grass, someone had mowed a perfect cross, and the cross was littered with bread crumbs. They weren't mowed in and they weren't dirty; to my amazement, they had been freshly sprinkled over the grass cross. To me, it was duck manna from heaven. Tears welled in my eyes as Peyton and I picked up handfuls of the fresh crumbs. *Someone had brought bread crumbs.* That someone had left a trail of bread crumbs to the cross. It was a reminder for me that, in the midst of my mess and my pain, *Someone* saw me and loved me.

❧

My brother Bill's wife, Sandi, was at the house one day helping me sort through a pile of cards we'd received. We were busy opening hundreds of envelopes and sorting them into piles when Sandi stopped and said, "Is this a joke?"

"What are you talking about?"

She handed me a card that didn't look anything like the muted pastel cards with flowers and flowing Scriptures that we'd been opening for the past twenty minutes. This one was square shaped and bright yellow. Dancing girls were lined up on the front. I opened the card and read, "Have you planted your tomato plant? Waiting for your call, so you can get your ten points."

I looked at Sandi. "I have no idea what this is. Who is it from? I don't get it." The envelopes had already been separated from the cards, and there was no way to match it. The next day Sandi came back and we started again. As we neared the bottom of the pile, I opened a card from Angie. It wasn't a sympathy card. It was the kind of card you send a good friend when you share an inside joke about something stupid. But Angie and I weren't that close. Her daughter had played volleyball with Taylor, so we saw each other a lot. We were friendly, but we weren't good friends.

I looked at the card in my hand. Under the preprinted message, she'd included a handwritten note: "Plant a tomato plant, call me, and you'll get ten points."

"I know who sent that card you found yesterday," I said to Sandi. "Apparently, it was the second one. Here's the first," I said, handing it to her.

Sandi looked baffled. "I still don't get it," she said after reading it.

"I think she's trying to get me to do stuff, to get over my sadness," I said. "And it kind of ticks me off. Who does she think she is?"

❦

Randy and Pam Cope were becoming good friends. They had given us lots of solid advice, and I had great respect for Pam. Though I didn't like her saying we'd been "handpicked" for this, I liked *her*. She was the only person I knew who'd experienced what I was going through.

Pam started coming by the house, and if she thought I needed to talk, she'd ask me to take a car ride with her. Sometimes, we'd go to the park and she'd pull into a parking space. She'd turn off the car, look directly at me, and say, "Okay, talk to me." I appreciated our time together because I knew she would understand things no one else did. The next time we were alone in her car, I told her about the cards I'd gotten from Angie.

"I got another one yesterday," I said, fuming. "It said, 'Have you planted your tomato plant yet? Waiting for ten points. Your next challenge is to get a pedicure. If you do that, you'll get twenty points.'" I pounded my fists onto my pajama-clad thighs and said, "Who does she think she is? How dare she challenge me!"

Pam listened with a smirk on her face and then tried to stifle a giggle. When I exploded, she couldn't hold it back any longer, and she roared with laughter. When she got hold of herself, she simply said, "What do you know? That's really creative!"

I was dumbfounded by her response. She was supposed to know better than anyone why that was so thoughtless. "I am not planting any stupid tomatoes, Pam! I'm not. I'm constantly in my pajamas. I'm barely out of bed. I'm not doing that."

A few days later, I was sitting on the back porch when Pam walked out with a large green pot. Inside was a bag of soil, a watering can, fertilizer, and a hand tool. "C'mon," she said, handing me the trowel, "we're planting this darn tomato plant."

Later, I texted Angie and said, "Got ten points."

And that was the beginning. Over the next few months, lots of cards followed—at least one a week. Angie encouraged me to earn points for taking showers and getting a pedicure, and she even gave me a book on sex and romance, with the opportunity to earn bonus points.

Some of her challenges were easy, while others were hard and I'd have to work up to them. Her challenge for the first week of May was to go to a museum. I still wasn't showering, and I couldn't control my sobbing. How was I supposed to go to a museum? Before I could figure it out, another card arrived with a new challenge to go downtown, take a ride on the trolley, and stop at Sprinkles Cupcakes. The thought was entirely overwhelming. But it coincided with another overwhelming day.

I handed the card to Todd and said, "Here's what I want to do for Mother's Day." I knew the day would be hard, and I knew I needed to spend it with Ryan and Peyton doing something that wouldn't flood me with memories of past Mother's Days. So that's what I did on my first Mother's Day without Taylor. I visited a museum with my family, we rode a trolley, we ate Sprinkles Cupcakes, and I earned thirty more points.

I never knew what the points were for; it could have been an ice cream cone for all I knew. But the challenges got me moving again and they helped me find my smile.

◦❖◦

I was sitting in my usual spot in my chair in the backyard, a blanket wrapped around my shoulders, staring off vacantly into the

Our five-piece puzzle of a family fit together perfectly as these pictures from Florida show.

We loved hanging out together . . .
and when we were all together we could be really silly!

The Sunshines are like our extended family, and New Year's together as the "Suntorch" family is a tradition.

Taylor always included Peyton in her life, on big occasions and small ones.

Taylor cherished her relationship with Ryan and Peyton.

Sometimes it is the ordinary moments like this one of Taylor and Ryan that we miss the most.

Taylor challenged herself to try new things—like cheerleading—even when she felt awkward. She knew that smiling and laughing at herself always made it better!

Volleyball was a big part of Taylor's life—and became a big part of ours.

Laura Springer, Taylor's principal, with Taylor in 2009. Springer continues to look out for Ryan and Peyton.

Taylor never lost the opportunity to be a ham and make the most of a camera.

Taken on the slopes on the first day of our vacation, this photo became one of the hardest to look at in the months to come.

Bill is so important to us, and his presence in the days after the accident was a gift.

We looked out at a sea of blue, one of Taylor's favorite colors, when the memorial garden was dedicated on Taylor's fourteenth birthday. Now it serves as a beautiful gathering place for students.

It seemed whenever we didn't think we could make it one more moment, God would send an image to remind us He had not forgotten us. This image was not possible under normal circumstances at that time of day.

When we forgot bread crumbs on a walk to the park after Taylor died, God did not—even placing them within the sign of a cross.

We were nervous to meet our first recipient of Taylor's gifts, Jeff Kartus, who received Taylor's kidney and pancreas. Yet a day with Jeff, his wife Vanessa, and daughter Brooke made us realize—it was our privilege to make a decision that gave life.

Ana Lucia Cottone is a gift to us; her loving yet outspoken approach helped our family regain its footing.

A search for the perfect dress for a foundation event became one more place God confirmed His presence in our lives. This label was an answer to Tara's quick prayer.

Before receiving Taylor's kidney, Jonathan spent four hours a day on dialysis; now he lives a physically active life and has become a vital volunteer for the foundation.

When Ashley received Taylor's cornea, it not only improved her vision but also finally relieved years of intense daily pain.

Photo Credit: Michael Rozman/Warner Bros.

One year earlier, Taylor wrote in her "I Am" poem, "*I want to be on the Ellen DeGeneres Show.*" Now she was.

Patricia watched Peyton's face as she lifted the stethoscope up to her chest. As soon as Peyton heard Taylor's heartbeat, she looked up at Patricia. I was so thankful to capture the moment of their connection on my camera.

Meeting Patricia Winters—and hearing Taylor's heart—became the most significant step forward in our healing, and in our motivation to share Taylor's story.

Photo Credit: J. Ann Photography

Photo Credit: Denise Stivers

We're so proud of Ryan and Peyton, who are now both in middle school. They were our inspiration to keep going during our darkest days. (For more photos, visit TaylorsGift.org.)

distance, when my friend Gayle walked out of the house. She handed me a box. I opened the gift, expecting it to be a blanket or maybe a book. I'd gotten a lot of those recently. But instead, there was a plate inside. On the plate was hand-painted Taylor's "I Am" poem.

I remembered Taylor writing the poem. It was due the Monday before we left on spring break. At the time, it was just another piece of homework. The assignment was to create an autobiographical website, and the poem was just one element among many. We first saw the poem shortly before the funeral, when her language arts teacher emailed us the password to Taylor's website so we could decide what to do with it.

Since then, Todd had read it at the funeral and to the kids at school during lunch. It had taken on a life of its own, spawning "I Am Taylor" videos of her friends reading it on YouTube. With tears in my eyes, I thanked Gayle for her thoughtful gift. Later, I found a special spot to display the plate in our kitchen.

༄

"Tara, listen to this," Todd said one day. He'd been holed up in his office, and I knew he was working on something related to the website or the foundation. "I was doing some research on organ donation, and I just downloaded the annual report from Donate Life, and it says that only 37 percent of Americans are registered donors."

"That's not very high," I said.

"But listen to this: Texas is the second lowest state, with only 2 percent registered! That isn't right! We can do something about that."

"How?"

"I don't know, but I'm going to figure it out," Todd said. Though it was a huge issue, I knew Todd well enough to know that if he got his mind around it, he'd figure out a way.

A few days later, Todd came to me with a request. "Look, I know you don't like doing interviews, but WFAA has been wanting to do a follow-up piece to see how we're doing, and I've been holding them off," Todd said. "But in light of the low number of organ donors registered in Texas, I think telling our story could help more people register."

Though it had been weeks since the funeral, and the foundation was only getting started, there still seemed to be a lot of interest in Taylor's story and our desire to promote organ donation. The media continued to call, and it wasn't unusual for Todd to do a radio, newspaper, or occasional TV interview. Though he wanted me to be a part of them, I mostly stayed away. However, in light of the statistics he'd recently shown me, I now felt differently.

"I think we should do it," I agreed.

Cynthia personally picked the reporter who would interview us. His name was Gary Reaves, and we immediately liked him. We were seated in the dining room when Gary noticed the plate Gayle had made. He asked about it, and we told him the story behind the poem.

"Can you read it out loud?" he asked.

I picked up the plate without thinking and began to read it. Certain lines jumped out at me, like I was hearing them for the first time: "I wonder how long forever is . . . I want to touch people's lives. . . ." *If she only knew how many lives she's touched and is continuing to touch*, I thought. "I cry at the thought of losing a member of my family." *I wonder if she knows how many tears we've shed for her.* By the time I finished, I was crying. The only good thing to come out of Taylor's death was the lives she touched—some through inspiration, but five through direct organ donation. Though I didn't like it, I was starting to see a purpose in our pain, and it was a purpose she'd written about in her poem.

During the interview I said to Gary, "I can't wait until I can hug the person who has her heart." It was the one hope I'd clung to—the hope that I would one day hear her heartbeat again this side of heaven.

The interview ended, and as we said goodbye to Gary and the crew, I realized that if we really wanted to promote organ donation, there would be more interviews in the future just like this one.

Oh, God, if this is what You want for us, if there is some purpose in Taylor's death for us, I need a sign. And I need You; I can't do this on my own.

—18—

Looking for Confirmation

Todd

I'm a light switch guy. I'm either on, or I'm off. When I read about the low number of registered organ donors in Texas, something in me clicked on. It infuriated me and made me resolve to work harder to get Taylor's story out there. The foundation was the mechanism to make that happen, and I truly believed we could get the needle to move higher than 2 percent.

Things were already happening. The website was up and volunteers were working in several areas. A documentary producer and crew were in place, and they were beginning their initial interviews of people who would tell Taylor's story.

Not only were my days filled with the details of the upcoming garden dedication but I was also having numerous conversations regarding the foundation's evolving mission and vision, associated website photos and graphics, and the educational strategy for organ donation. While I tried to include Tara in these conversations, she couldn't participate in long drawn-out discussions; she didn't have the focus. But she helped to make simple choices, like deciding between two fonts for the website. I wanted to include her but not overwhelm her.

⚛

On April 19, a month and four days after we lost Taylor, we celebrated her birthday by dedicating the newly completed garden at her school. It was unbelievable how much work Jay, his team of professionals, and the community volunteers had gotten done so quickly.

Hundreds of people turned out. It reminded me of the visitation, except this time everyone was wearing Tiffany blue (the color of Taylor's eyes) T-shirts. Taylor's friends had designed them, and everyone who came wore them—students, teachers, neighbors, volunteers, and the community at large. The crowd looked like a sea of blue, with swelling waves of purple balloons. The guests sat on the freshly mowed grass. Several people spoke, including two of Taylor's friends, Father Alfonse, and Principal Laura Springer.

I planned to speak and I looked forward to it. When I spoke in front of the kids, it energized me and fed my soul. I had no expectation that Tara or the kids would get up too; I was just pleased that Tara had come. But when I stood up, Tara, Ryan, and Peyton all stood too. They wanted to stand alongside me. As I spoke, I thanked those who had made it happen and encouraged the kids to make this garden their own. In many ways, they already had—students had painted the stones lining the garden with their original artwork. Though the space started out as a way to honor Taylor, it had truly become a community park.

The ceremony ended with tearful voices singing "Happy Birthday" to Taylor.

After the ceremony, I spoke to some parents. Out of the corner of my eye, I could see a girl waiting to talk to me. I didn't remember meeting her before, but I could tell something was troubling her; tears were streaming down her cheeks.

"Hi, I'm Mr. Storch," I said.

166

She started to talk, then sob. I could barely make out what she said.

"When my mom died, Taylor was the only friend who ever asked how I was."

"Oh, sweetie," I said, hugging her. I calmed her down, and she told me the whole story. Her mother had been in a car accident. People asked about the accident, and they asked about her mom, but Taylor had asked about *her*. She told me how Taylor made a point to stop every day and ask how she was. Taylor texted and sent her notes.

Through her tears, she said, "You have no idea how much that meant to me."

That young lady had no idea what her story meant to *me*. It was one of the first times since Taylor's death that I'd heard a story about my daughter that I didn't already know. Learning about this beautiful thing my child had done was amazing. If the garden never served another purpose, to me it was worth creating just to hear that one story.

⁂

It had been more than a month since Taylor's death—and since I had last been to work. I had an amazing job at the Center for Sales Strategy helping media companies develop their digital initiatives. Until we lost Taylor, I'd loved my work. But going back would be hard. If I was having a bad day, I didn't have the kind of job where I could hide in a cubicle pretending to answer email while crying inside. In my job, I had to fully engage one on one with clients, give presentations for as many as sixty people at a time, and lead team meetings. I didn't work out of an office; I worked at my clients' offices. There was no place to hide and no way to fake my emotional state.

Jim Hopes was the chief executive officer, but I reported to John Henley, the chief operating officer. Both were really great guys to work for. Though John was technically my boss, a better description would be to call him a dear friend or a brother in Christ. When we were in Grand Junction, John was one of the first people I called. We had several deep conversations as I told him what was happening with Taylor, and many times he prayed with me over the phone.

John and I hadn't yet talked about my starting back up, but I knew it probably would be soon. I wasn't sure how, or even if, I could return to work. I certainly couldn't travel. Tara was still deeply grieving. In my absence, she couldn't take care of herself, let alone the kids.

With my mind preoccupied with thoughts of the future, I needed to keep my hands busy. Tara had planted some tomato plants, and I started fertilizing them. Then I bought more dirt and planted rosemary and mint. I found some larger pots and carefully replanted the tender tomato shoots. Each day, I'd water them and check for new growth. My time with the plants became a kind of therapy. While I was outside tending to them, I would think and pray. Sometimes I cried, and often I cried out to God.

What is it that You want me to do? What is Your plan for my life? How am I supposed to serve You in the midst of all this?

When Tara was awake, she spent a lot of time outdoors, and she would watch me work in the yard. One day, I sat down next to her and said, "I feel as if there is something more for me. I feel like I need to quit my job and be the executive director of the foundation."

Tara and I weren't talking much at this time, which, in hindsight, was a good thing. Instead of asking for her advice, I had been seeking God and praying harder than ever. While I knew my words came as a surprise, she listened as I explained my thoughts and prayers. More than anything I wanted to follow God's will. "So, I am waiting. I'm waiting to see what God is doing," I said.

⁓

Grieving people are hard to be around. Grief can get ugly. It's messy. Some people don't want any part of it. Others choose to get involved. They enter your story without concern as to the sacrifices they'll have to make to love you. Father Alfonse was one of those people. He left our house late the night of the funeral, but he came back. And he came back often.

Father Alfonse was only a couple of years older than Tara and me, but he was experienced in life's mountains and valleys. He understood faith issues, not only from his priestly duties but also from walking with families through God's Word as it met up with the messiness of their lives. I didn't know why he took Tara and me on, but we were glad he did.

Since the funeral, we'd see him at least once a week, sometimes more. He'd come over to visit and hang out with Tara and me at night. Sometimes we'd call and see if he wanted to have dinner with us; other times I'd meet him for coffee. He and I would spend hours discussing suffering and grief. Occasionally, Tara would text him questions about God or just let him know how we were. He became a sounding board as we tried to figure out God's plan for our lives.

Father Alfonse encouraged me to read about Christ's suffering on the cross so I could understand my own pain. That led me to read about other people who had suffered. I began to pray and read my Bible more, something I had never done regularly. I felt the need to get up early in the morning and spend time reading and praying before I officially started my day. Often, I returned to the Scriptures late at night as I searched for purpose in my own life. Father Alfonse encouraged me, answered my questions, and comforted me as I tried to find meaning in my suffering.

I wanted to make something good come from Taylor's death. As a consultant, I often came up with solutions for my clients. That was my first instinct—to *do*. To create. To write a report. To research it to death. To fix it. But instead, a very different feeling now washed over me—God was doing something. I needed to wait on Him to see what it was.

Part of me wanted to go to work to escape my life at home. But I was also scared. I knew the statistics of how many couples got divorced after they lost a child. I'd stood by helplessly as my own parents divorced, so that also fueled my thoughts. I wanted the best for my kids, and that meant being home with them.

Then there was the foundation. We were getting ready to file paperwork for a business license and our tax-exempt status. It was time to decide whether I was all in or not. It wasn't an intellectual decision; it was a spiritual one. In the past, I wouldn't have waited for God; I would only have waited for Him to catch up with me. This time, I didn't want to get in the way of what *He* was doing. So I waited on Him.

⚘

Each day, I heard new stories of how our work was affecting people. Instead of stagnating, things seemed to be growing. Nearly every day, God brought a new volunteer to join me in our work. These weren't just idle people looking for something to do. These were gifted professionals with busy careers. If I had an unlimited budget, these were the people I would have gone out and hired. Instead, I randomly met them at a Starbucks, was introduced to them by a mutual friend, or they contacted me after hearing our story. Each one was a gift from God and filled a much-needed spot on my advisory team.

At times, I'd be so busy working with or talking to my advisers that I'd go a few days without talking to friends or neighbors. Inevitably, one of them would say something like, "Tell me what's happening with the foundation," or, "Catch me up since the last time we talked."

I'd honestly have to say, "I can't. I literally can't. Dude, you miss a day, you miss a year. Things are happening that fast."

I was working closely with a few key people who had volunteered their time and talents to work alongside me at a dizzying pace. Even they felt it. Pauline, one of my advisers in my innermost circle, would call in the morning and then again late in the afternoon.

"It's been six hours since we last talked. Catch me up," she'd say.

She knew from experience that even in that short time span things were popping. And some of those things were likely to be big—interview requests, offers of introductions to experts who could help, or opportunities for new fund-raisers. Each day, amazing new opportunities presented themselves. The documentary crew was working hard and connections were opening up. The website was receiving hits from around the world.

One afternoon, I picked up the phone. It was a representative from Donate Life who'd heard about our work. "We'd love it if you would come to our banquet in June. We'd like you to present an award to the producers of *Grey's Anatomy* for a show they did about organ donation."

"I'd love to!" I said. "But I need to ask my wife."

I wasn't sure how Tara would feel about traveling. It would mean flying to California and leaving the kids at home. Taking Tara on a trip to Hollywood was unimaginable when a trip to the living room was still a big deal for her.

I waited for the right moment to talk to her. I anticipated her reply, knowing it was a lot to ask. "It's okay if you want to say no. I understand," I said. But to my surprise, she agreed.

"It would be good for the foundation and another way to honor Taylor," she said.

This was a defining moment for her, and one that only God could have orchestrated. *Thank you!* I prayed, both for the opportunity and for Tara agreeing to go.

⁕

Too many things were happening for me to ignore God's direction. Everything seemed to be pointing toward my leaving my job and working for the foundation. At the same time, I realized how dumb it sounded to give up my job. I worried that Tara would think it was a stupid idea when I told her. But I had to. I couldn't shake the feeling that this is what God wanted.

A few nights later, my opportunity arose. We were out on the back porch, sitting side by side and staring at the stars. I told her about the incredible things occurring with the foundation. In passing, I mentioned that John Henley, my friend and boss, would be in town the next week and that we needed to talk.

"I feel there is a higher purpose for me than my job. I can't imagine going back to my company and leaving y'all," I said, trying to hold back tears.

"So, what do you want to do?"

"It's been wearing on me, but I think I want to quit my job. I could work at the foundation full-time. I don't know if it is stupid or not, but I feel my attention needs to be on it and our family."

I knew this was hard for her to hear. For one thing, I couldn't answer any of her questions—like how we'd survive financially. I wiped my eyes with the back of my hands, but the tears were flowing too fast.

"I *need* to make a difference. When I see Taylor again, I want her to say, 'Good job, Daddy! You did it!'"

This was the first time I'd been so vulnerable with Tara, and I was nervous. I wasn't sure if she would cry, scream, yell, or just stare at me. But she did none of those things.

"If this is what you need to do, I'll absolutely support you," she said.

She told me she could see how much this decision had been weighing on me, and gave me a long hug.

"You've changed," she said, her warm cheek pressed against mine. "In the past, you would have made a decision and followed up on it, but now it's as if you're waiting for something," she said.

That night, we discussed all the what-ifs. I didn't have many answers except to say I was trusting God to do it. If He called me, He would equip me.

"I agree. He will take care of us," Tara said. "And you've always taken care of us. Honestly, though, it scares me a little bit."

I didn't say anything out loud, but I thought, *It scares me too.*

ojo

I sought my closest friends' and foundation advisers' counsel at a breakfast meeting soon after I talked with Tara. I told them what I'd been thinking and praying about. "I give you full authority to tell me I am just a grief-stricken dad or I'm going to bankrupt my family. Tell me it's a dumb idea. Whatever you need to say, please say it."

I wanted them to talk me out of it.

In the end, nearly everyone I sought advice from thought this was something I needed to do. That God was calling me to do it. They cautioned me, they gave me advice, but they didn't say, "I don't think you should do this."

With the leading of God, the approval of my wife, and the encouragement of friends, the old Todd would have put together a financial strategy and plan for how I could quit my job and work full-time for the foundation. Numerous opportunities had presented themselves. All I needed was a strategic plan to know which ones to go after first, and then I would be off and running.

But *I* wasn't doing this. God was. So I did something completely out of character: I waited on God for a confirmation that this was what He wanted. If this was to be, I needed Him to confirm it.

— 19 —

Showers of Emotion

Tara

Before we lost Taylor, taking a bath or hot shower was my favorite way to relax and get away from it all. But while I was mourning, the shower wasn't a place to relax; it was a place to escape the world and to cry.

One night, after the kids had fallen asleep on the air mattress in my room, I couldn't stay in bed any longer. Sorrow overwhelmed me, and I deeply missed Taylor. I went in and turned on the shower so the water could wash away my tears and drown out the sounds of my sobs. Under the hottest water I could tolerate, I just stood and bawled. My nose was running, my head ached, and it was difficult to breathe. I couldn't breathe deeply, so I breathed faster, which caused my chest to constrict and resulted in a stabbing feeling every time I inhaled. I tried to get a grip, but sobs wracked my body. I was too overcome by grief to even wash my hair.

I can't recall ever feeling so alone.

So very alone.

It was close to bedtime, and that meant sleep. I welcomed sleep, but I couldn't stand the thought of waking up the next morning and reliving the pain all over again. I stood in the shower and silently begged, *Oh, God, please take this pain away. It feels like it will never stop. I miss Taylor so much, and I can't stand the hurt anymore. I would rather be there with You and her than down here, living with all of this pain.*

A fleeting thought raced through my mind. *What if I didn't have to wake up in the morning? I have a bottle of Ambien on the nightstand. How easy would that be? One swallow and the pain disappears.*

I suddenly understood why people chose that option. *It makes complete sense. This could be over. The pain would be completely gone, and I wouldn't have to deal with this anymore.* Instantly, I felt released from the pain. I felt happy and empowered. Just thinking about it energized me. I quickly got out of the shower, and as I dried off, I thought, *This is how it can all be over!* The weight on my chest lifted, and I felt lighter than I had since the hospital. I couldn't wait.

As I walked to my dresser and pulled out a clean pair of pajamas, my brother Bill came to mind. I remembered him sitting me down and saying, "If you ever feel like you want to take your life, and you think you might act on it, you'd better call me."

I put on my pajamas and snuggled into bed. The kids were asleep, and Todd was in his office reading or working. I picked up the Ambien bottle and looked at it, thinking. My phone was also on the nightstand, so I kept my promise and I texted Bill, "Are you there?"

I fingered the bottle while I waited for Bill to respond. But time went by and I didn't hear from him. I didn't care; I felt good knowing the pain would soon end. While I continued to wait for Bill, I texted Father Alfonse. "Are you awake?"

"Yes, what's up?"

"I need to talk to you about something, but this is between you and me."

"Of course."

I took a deep breath and then decided to go for it. "I've got a plan," I texted. "The pain is too much, and I can't do this anymore."

"Are you saying what I think you're saying?"

"I would much rather be with her than be here." While I waited for his response, I set the phone down and took the lid off the bottle so I could count the pills. His text arrived before I could finish the count.

"What makes you think if you did that, you would see her?"

I hadn't thought about that. I'd never thought about something like that before, because I'd never, ever gone down that path. *How does God feel about that? Would He turn me away?*

Before I could respond, more texts came in from him. "What makes you think that if you did it, God would welcome you with open arms?" Then, "How selfish of you to leave Ryan and Peyton like this!"

Suddenly, the idea was more complicated than it had seemed a few minutes earlier. I thought about my response and was just getting ready to text him back when he sent me a real zinger. "Do you really think Taylor would be proud of you?"

His words took my breath away. I knew for a fact she wouldn't be happy with me. *She would never be proud of me if I did that.*

It was my lowest moment ever. But through his texts, Father Alfonse helped me realize it was because I was focusing on myself—on my own pain. I'd never looked at it from Taylor's perspective. I hadn't considered her reaction at all. Neither had I thought about what it would do to Peyton and Ryan.

I certainly hadn't thought about what God would think.

I put the cap back on the bottle and set in on the nightstand. I knew then I could never do it. Ever. Father Alfonse was right. I *was* being selfish. We texted back and forth a few more times. He made me promise I wouldn't do anything.

"I promise I won't," I texted back. I meant it.

◦⟡◦

My brother Kary was at the house one day, and he asked if Todd and I were seeing a counselor. We weren't. Todd had seen one a few years earlier to deal with his parents' divorce and some depression he had in the past, but I didn't believe in counseling. Counselors were for weak people with problems. That wasn't me. I was just sad, and I had every reason to feel sad.

"You might want to give this woman a try," Kary said. "Her name is Judy, and she lost her son four years ago."

I didn't want to go. I'd already lost too much control in my life. The last thing I wanted was someone else telling me what to do, how to act, and what to feel. But after much urging from friends and family, and cajoling from Todd, I finally agreed.

Our first two appointments were rough. We were supposed to go back again for a third appointment, but we couldn't find a date and time that worked for both of us to go together. Out of necessity, we went separately. And we both kept going separately. It was one of the best decisions we ever made for our marriage. Judy helped us individually understand our grief—why I wanted to sleep, and why Todd wanted to work—and how those choices played out in the context of our marriage. Like Pam and Randy Cope, she told us it was okay if our grief wasn't the same, but she also taught us how to deal with our feelings about our spouse's grief.

Counseling was hard work, but it was also very helpful. Some days I would just roll out of bed, take the kids to school, and then drive to Dallas in my pajamas for my 10:30 a.m. appointment. I would sit on her couch with my wild, uncombed hair, crying while we talked. She became a lifeline for me. Because she saw Todd and me individually, she knew what was going on with the other person and could use that knowledge effectively to help each of us. As our relationship grew, I realized that counseling wasn't for weak people—it was for strong people who wanted to get stronger. I looked forward to our visits each week. Judy and I were a lot alike, with the same sense of humor. If we had met before all of this happened, I think we would have been good friends.

c๕ว

My new life looked drastically different from my old life. Before we lost Taylor, I was the center of the hive and life was always buzzing around me. If the kids needed rides, I picked them up or took them, or at least told Todd what time and where to go. If the kids wanted a friend over after school, they asked me. I knew what homework they had and when it was due. I was central to everything that happened in our house; the calendar of activity spun around me.

The nausea had stopped, I was sleeping less, and I was up more. But now I had zero purpose. I went from full days to having nothing on the calendar but grief. On one hand, it was good not to worry about all of those things, but it was also damaging because it left a lot of room for me to think negative thoughts. Other people had taken over my parenting duties. They were the ones picking Peyton up from school and taking Ryan to basketball. They filled the mom role because most days I couldn't physically or emotionally do it. In some ways, I felt like my only purpose was to grieve, so that's what I did all day, every day.

I didn't want something to keep my hands busy or to occupy my time; I wanted something to occupy my mind. Something like Todd had. His grief seemed to be channeled into doing something *good*. The activities of the foundation occupied his thoughts, and he had things to do all day. I wanted that too.

A few days later, Todd walked in and sat down beside me on the bed. "Why, Todd? Why us?" I asked. I struggled with that question often. It was probably a question I'd asked him before, but that day his answer was different.

"It's not even a question of why," he said. "Why not? Why not us? I can handle it." He went on to talk about how he'd seen purpose and meaning in Taylor's death.

"Great, so maybe you've found a purpose. But what about me? I used to be a mom of three; what am I now? I'm not even that. I wake up every day with this crushing feeling in my chest, wishing the morning had never come."

"I don't, Tara. I don't wake up that way at all. I wake up feeling like I can't wait for the day to get started. I hope what I said didn't hurt you. It's just the truth."

But his comments angered me. Why was God allowing him to be so strong when I felt so weak? "We are so opposite right now," I said. "How can you wake up with joy?"

"I don't know, but I do."

I wasn't angry at Todd. I was angry at God. I put my hands on my hips like a petulant two-year-old and said to God, *I'm not talking to You. You are not important to me anymore. You had control over this, and You could have made this turn out differently. I prayed and asked You to change this, and You didn't, so we're no longer talking.*

As if I needed any more proof that God and I weren't friends, I checked my Facebook later that night and saw a friend of mine, whose son had been very ill for quite some time, had posted a new status update: "Thank God! My son almost died, but God answered our prayers and healed him, and now he is completely better."

Before I could stop myself, I wrote a comment. "How lucky you are that God decided to save your child." Then I posted it and went to bed.

Lying in bed, I knew I shouldn't have written that, but it was just further proof that God answered other people's prayers but He didn't answer mine. He saved other people's sons but He didn't save my daughter. I was angry.

By the next morning my anger had faded, and I got up and deleted the comment because I regretted writing it. Unfortunately, all of our mutual friends had already seen it.

After that, it seemed like everyone's desire to fix me only increased. "Why don't you just make her get up?" they'd ask Todd.

People had expectations of grief. If I was good one day, they expected me to be better the next day. If there were faith practices that worked for them in their normal, happy lives, they thought those same faith practices would help make me normal and happy too. Pray more. Fast. Go to church. Read your Bible. Memorize Scripture. The people who made these suggestions meant well. What they didn't know was I had already tried those things and they hadn't achieved what I really wanted—my daughter back.

⁂

One morning when I woke up, I had the usual question of why. *Why* swirls and never stops at an answer. Just like the mornings before it, on this day I moved past the why only to land in more dark thoughts. The cycle was starting again.

I looked above our bedroom door. We'd hung a crucifix on the wall when we moved in years earlier. Though God and I still weren't talking, I focused on the cross and tried to concentrate on my thoughts to get out of the darkness swirling around me, but my mind remained confused. I picked up a book near my bed and opened it—a devotional. I looked at the page, but the words just swam and ran together. I closed the book and looked back at the cross.

I felt so abandoned by God. I was lost and alone, and not even the God of the universe cared.

Somehow, one clear thought made its way out of my fog. *This is all for Your glory.* It was so distinct from everything else swirling in my mind that I said it out loud. "This is all for Your glory." For someone who wasn't talking to God, it was at once jarring and peaceful at the same time.

Then I said it again. "This is all for Your glory."

And again. "This is all for Your glory."

Soon, I was repeating it over and over. Even as I said it out loud I thought, *How can this ever be for Your glory?* But somewhere in the saying of it I believed it, and I started to cry. I didn't have any answers, but for some reason, I had a tiny bit of faith.

"This is all for Your glory!"

The more I opened up to the idea, the more I cried. Soon I was bawling. My faith had been—and still was—shaken, but it wasn't broken.

God and I were talking once again.

❧

Before Taylor died, everything in our house ran by the clock. It had to. Three busy kids, a husband who traveled, and my volunteer work all meant that things had to happen on time and on schedule. Now, I never looked at a clock. I had no concept of time. There were days I felt too weak to shower, or even to simply stand under the hot water, and sometimes those days flowed into each other without my realizing it.

One day, Sandi came to me and said, "Tara, you have got to shower. It's been five days. People are coming over to see you, and you stink."

I had already lost fifteen pounds and I continued to lose more. I was weak and tired. Tears rolled down my cheeks because she was probably right, and I didn't have the strength to argue—but neither did I have the strength to shower.

She helped me up, and I leaned on her as we walked into the bathroom. She stripped my clothes off me, turned on the shower, and held the door while I stepped in. Once I was under the water, I didn't even have the strength to lift my hands to wash my hair. Even the water was painful as it hit my head and back. Through my tears, I could see Sandi standing on the other side of the door, watching me.

"Oh, honey," she said. I saw her take a deep breath and blow it out. "Okay, I know this is weird, but I'm doing it." Then she got in the shower with me and shut the door. "I'm going to wash you and wash your hair," she said. "I'm going to wash everything but your who-ha." She grabbed the washcloth and soap, and she kept talking as she washed my arms and legs. "Girl, I'll do everything for you, but I'm not touching that."

I couldn't take it anymore. I didn't mean to, and I certainly didn't plan to, but I smiled.

And then I chuckled, just a little.

Then I let out a big laugh.

It was my first laugh since Taylor's accident, and it had snuck up on me when I least expected it—in the shower. That moment was important. It helped me to see that there would be smiles and laughter in my future, even if I couldn't see them coming.

—20—

The Cowboy's Daughter
Connects on Facebook

JEFF KARTUS
COLORADO

Nothing was ever easy for Jeff.

After two years, the cowboy finally got the kidney and pancreas he'd been waiting for. During the surgery, the doctors thought they had done a successful transplant, but somewhere a blood vessel started to leak. Because he was on blood thinners, Jeff bled out.

He actually died on the operating table.

Fortunately, doctors were able to give him a transfusion—ten pints of blood—that revived him. Because of complications, Jeff was in the hospital for nearly a month—his wife, Vanessa, and his daughter, Brooke, by his side. When he was finally released and able to go home, it was as if he had amnesia; he remembered very little about the two years he'd spent on dialysis.

But other changes were easy to see. The new pancreas cured his diabetes. No longer did he have to eat at certain times, prick his finger to test his blood sugar levels, or take insulin. The results were dramatic.

Living in Colorado, Vanessa and Brooke had seen the news reports on the local television stations about the girl who died while skiing. And while Jeff was in the hospital, one of the medical staff mentioned his donor was a young girl. Jeff had to have received her kidney and pancreas—the timing was too coincidental.

Brooke did a little bit of online detective work and came up with an email address. With Jeff and Vanessa's permission, she carefully crafted a letter telling them how much her dad's life had changed and that while they would love to make contact, she understood if it was too difficult for the family. Then she hit send.

A couple of weeks went by and she hadn't heard anything back. She wondered if she ever would.

— 21 —

Confirmation

Todd

I picked up my phone and scrolled through my list of favorites until I found John Henley, my good friend and boss at CSS. I paused for a moment, then tapped his number. It was one thing to talk to Tara and my friends about quitting my job, but quite another to tell the guy responsible for my paycheck. If he cut me off after this call, I had no backup plan. We had some money in the bank, but we weren't wealthy. It certainly wasn't enough to hold us for long.

John answered, and we made small talk. He asked how Tara and I were. I asked about business and about his wife, Cricket. I knew he could tell I was nervous, so I got right to the point.

"John, there's something I need to tell you," I started. I took a deep breath and dove in. I thanked him for being a good friend and told him how much I appreciated him as a leader. "I hope we'll still be friends, but I can no longer work for the company." I explained how Tara still wasn't well. "I can't travel like I used to, or do the job that's required, with all that's going on in my personal life."

I brought him up to speed about the foundation and all the amazing things that were happening. "John, I am so sorry, but

I need to quit so I can work full-time with the foundation. I've prayed about it, prayed with Tara about it, sought counsel from friends, and everything just seems to be leading me to this decision. I simply feel as if I'd be disobeying God if I didn't do it," I said. Then I paused to give him a chance to react.

He didn't hesitate. "I knew it before you did."

Of all the reactions I'd thought he might have, this wasn't one I'd considered.

"Not long after we heard about Taylor, Cricket said to me, 'You know, Todd's not coming back. You know there is something he has to do.' I agreed, Todd, because I knew it too. I knew."

Chills ran up my arms as he continued, "I just want you to know we're here, and we're going to support you. We'll be the first company to support your foundation. I don't know what that looks like yet, but we'll talk more next week."

John had a layover in Dallas the following week. We'd have six hours to sit down and talk face-to-face. I hung up the phone, grateful and excited. I still didn't know how it would all work out, but this was the sign from God I'd been waiting for. It was official: I would work for the foundation full-time.

⊱⊰

A week later, John and I met in a Dallas restaurant. "What are your plans?" he asked. John knew me well enough to know how I operated.

"I haven't worked it all out yet," I said honestly. I didn't divulge that I was trying *not* to plan. I didn't want to get ahead of God.

"Well, Jim and I want to contribute five thousand dollars of start-up money for Taylor's Gift on behalf of CSS. If you need more, let us know. If you don't need it all, then just keep the balance as a donation."

I couldn't believe it. We'd just filed the paperwork the last few days of April. Now it was early May, and we'd already received our first major donation! It was an unexpected and generous gift. But

John wasn't done. "We'll pay you a full salary through August," he continued, "and we'll keep you on the company insurance for a year."

I'm sure my mouth was hanging open. It was beyond anything I could have hoped for or imagined. In addition to giving the first and biggest donation to Taylor's Gift, John had removed my financial worries for the next ninety days. And he'd provided insurance for my family for the next year.

"And, Todd, here's the deal: if in thirty or sixty days you think this was the stupidest decision you've ever made, you'll have a place to work. I'm not sure what your job will be, but we'll figure it out."

I couldn't wait to tell Tara. I'd asked for one more sign, and God exploded blessings like fireworks on the Fourth of July. I began to see how much better His way was than mine. If I had put together spreadsheets and business plans to make this happen, I probably would have talked myself out of leaving, because, financially, it didn't make sense. But God's math was different from mine. God had helped me stay open to what He was doing—no matter how ridiculous it sounded—and then He revealed himself to me in ways I couldn't have imagined.

I was no longer concerned about failing. With God on my side, how could I?

⁂

Now that I was actively seeking God's plan in my life, I saw Him every day. Things other businesses worked *years* to achieve, or other nonprofits one day *hoped* to have, were being handed to us. Various groups began to organize fund-raisers for us. Bracelets, hats, and T-shirts with foundation logos were being printed and sold. The media stories led to more media stories. Friends in the volleyball community offered to host a tournament with proceeds going to the foundation. The first annual 4T (Taylor's volleyball number was 4) tournament was held less than two months after Taylor's death.

The documentary on organ donation went from being a good idea one day to a fully staffed crew the next. While several documentaries had been done from the perspective of the recipients, we weren't aware of any that had been done from the perspective of the donors. By telling our story, we could encourage others to become organ donors while also honoring Taylor. It was exciting to think about the impact we could have.

Our first fund-raising dinner and kickoff event was being held in June, a week after we got back from our presentation at the Donate Life Film Festival in Hollywood.

We hoped to roll out a new version of our website, one that encompassed everything we'd become since the first website was put out. New opportunities to tell our story and encourage organ donation happened every day, and the number and quality of volunteers continued to climb.

As cofounder of the foundation, Tara needed to be brought up to speed. As my wife, her involvement and approval were important to me. But Tara wasn't ready, and even if she was, she still couldn't handle the pace. "You've got to give me only little pieces of information. I can't handle more than that right now," she said one day.

I knew she felt as if I were the strong one, but there were times I also felt weak. I missed my wife and my best friend, and I wanted her by my side while these amazing things were occurring. So, we compromised. Once a week we would sit down and I'd update her on the major highlights. It wasn't perfect, but it was the best we could do under the circumstances.

We didn't have much of a relationship at the time. She was at the lowest spot in her life, and I felt like her caretaker. She needed to grieve in her own way, so I didn't want to push her to be a mom or a wife before she was ready. And despite my outward productivity, I was still grieving too. I felt broken. And alone.

Occasionally, I still had fantasies of running away like the one I had in the hospital. *If I took money out of the bank, paid cash for an airline ticket, and flew somewhere, I could disappear off the grid for at least a month before anyone found me.* Then I'd remind myself of all of the reasons I didn't want to run.

Other days I was mad at Tara. I resented that she got taken care of, while I did all the caretaking. At times I couldn't take one more minute of hearing her cry. I would call a friend to come stay with her, and I'd leave the house.

Grief counseling with Judy was helpful, but now I was dealing with more than just the loss of my daughter. I was dealing with a wife who was incapacitated, a loss of identity because I'd quit my job, and the loss of our old lifestyle because we'd had to tighten our financial belt. In the midst of all this change, I would have to rediscover who I was.

For the most part, God kept me so busy I didn't have to think much. In addition to the foundation, my primary job was to take care of my family. While people still came to the house to help Tara out, people no longer spent the night and more of the household responsibility fell on my shoulders. I did the best I could, but sometimes things fell through the cracks.

One day Peyton came home from school and said to Tara, "Will you please start packing my lunches?"

Tara was sitting outside wrapped in a blanket as usual, with that vacant stare on her face. She could barely get out of bed to see the kids off to school; the thought of making lunches every day was beyond her. "Sweetie, Daddy is going to pack your lunch. I can't do it right now," she said.

"Please!" said Peyton. "You have to! Daddy packed it today, and all he packed was a pickle!"

A *pickle*? I *know* I packed more than a pickle.

At least I thought I did.

There was a lot going on. It was possible I had started packing her lunch but didn't finish. Tara and I knew how pathetic it must have looked to the teachers at school. They probably just shook their heads and said, "That poor family. Bless their hearts." But it was also a wake-up call for both of us. After that day, I noticed that Tara took some active steps to contain her worst grief to school hours. She also tried to be physically and emotionally present for

Ryan and Peyton when they were home. But for Peyton, the most important change was that Tara started packing lunches again.

Even so, I *know* I packed more than a pickle!

⊶

My inbox was chaos central. I was in the midst of turning over client information to my colleagues, updating past clients before I left, and trying to run the foundation. In addition, probably a hundred people were volunteering either with the foundation or at the house, and they communicated with me by email. Daily, we also received emails from strangers who'd heard our story or wanted to share theirs. We learned a lot of people were connected in ways we couldn't imagine, and it seemed they were all willing to use their connections to help us.

In the midst of all of this chaos, I received an email from a young woman named Brooke. I read her email, and everything around me came to a screeching halt. After reading Brooke's email a second time, I knew I had to share it with Tara immediately.

"Tara, this woman says she got my email from Facebook."

"So? A lot of people do that."

"I know, but listen to this," I said, reading, "'I hope I am not intruding, but I believe my dad has your daughter's kidney and pancreas, and it has saved his life.'"

"Did she say where she's from?" Tara asked, suddenly perking up.

"Colorado."

"Are you kidding? What else did she say?"

"She got our name from an article, and then went onto Facebook and got my email from there. Listen, she writes, 'I totally understand if this crosses some kind of line, or if you don't want to touch base, but we just wanted to reach out and thank you because you've touched our lives, and it's made a huge difference for my dad and for all of us.'" The email was so caring and kind that it was obvious she'd thought about it a long time before hitting send.

By now, Tara was standing behind me, reading over my shoulder. She had been working on writing our letter to Donor Alliance to pass on to the recipients, adding a paragraph here or there as she had the emotional strength and physical energy to do it.

But we'd been told we had to wait six months before we could send a letter to Donor Alliance to forward to the recipients, and it had to be sent by snail mail. So we expected the process to take months—maybe even a year. We never expected that within a few weeks of Taylor's death we'd get an email directly from a recipient, or in this case, his daughter.

Apparently, Donor Alliance didn't expect it either. We called them the next morning and said we'd heard from a Brooke Kartus who claimed her dad, Jeff, had received Taylor's kidney and pancreas. After a flurry of phone calls and some emergency meetings at their offices, Donor Alliance basically confirmed that Brooke was who she said she was. "But can you wait to contact her until we've had a chance to talk to our board? We've never had this happen before."

But there was no waiting. Tara and I had already emailed her. Why wouldn't we? We'd been told there was a chance we'd never connect with an organ recipient and now, just weeks later, we had. We'd immediately looked Brooke up on Facebook and confirmed she lived in Colorado. We couldn't wait to connect, so Tara and I had emailed her. "It was wonderful to get your email. Thank you so much for reaching out. How is your dad doing?"

We were the first donor family with Donor Alliance to connect with a recipient family through social media, and they didn't have a process for handling that yet. A couple of days later, they got back to us and said, "We can't stop you, but would you please sign this legal document releasing us from any liability before you contact her?"

By then, we'd already been chatting with Brooke on Facebook. We learned her dad lived in Colorado and had been unable to work for years because of his diabetes. Over the past few years, the diabetes had taken a toll on his health, his kidneys had failed, and he'd had to go on dialysis. After the transplant, he was able to stop both dialysis and insulin shots. His diabetes was cured! It was amazing to hear how Taylor's kidney and pancreas had made such a remarkable difference in the life of one man and his family.

People asked me how it felt to connect with someone who had received Taylor's organs. It was hard to explain. There was a sense of excitement, but "excited" wasn't really what I felt. For Tara, it was emotional. To her, it felt like a little bit of steam had been released from the pressure of her grief. She had a strong desire to connect with Jeff, to know more about him, and to help him know us and know Taylor. We made plans to visit the Kartus family in June. The kids would be out of school, and we had already planned a family trip to the beach and a weekend in California with Donate Life to present an award. The documentary crew could travel with us, and it just made sense to do it all then.

It felt important to Tara and me that Taylor's gift be acknowledged. It wasn't that we needed to be thanked or appreciated, but we wanted the person who received the gift to appreciate it. Brooke showed us that in her email. She recognized the good gift her father had received.

It was just one more confirmation that our foundation work was important. We could point to something good that had come out of Taylor's death. Jeff was a real person, a cowboy living in Colorado who had a wife, a son, a daughter, and for the first time in a long time, freedom from dialysis and daily insulin injections. Knowing Jeff was out there reminded us of how many more people just like him were out there. He was something tangible for us to cling to as we went forward with the foundation work.

That night in the kitchen, I remember sitting back and thinking, *Of course, we heard from them now. We're supposed to hear from them now.* It just fell in line with everything else God was doing. It was one more sign from God saying we were on the right course and that He would provide for us.

— 22 —

Of Course!

Tara

I watched the celebrities line up in front of the Donate Life signage for photos. Each one arrived with an entourage and paused to smile for the cameras before entering the ballroom. *What am I doing here?* I thought. It was hard to describe how big this moment was for me. After all, it had only been three months since the accident.

Most days I barely got dressed in clean pajamas. The farthest I got from my bedroom was the back porch. Now here I was in a cocktail dress and heels at an invitation-only, opening night, VIP cocktail reception for the Donate Life Film Festival. Looking around, I saw celebrities I recognized. Alex O'Loughlin, currently starring in *Hawaii Five-O*, stood chatting with a group of people across the room from me. Near the bar sat Olympic medalist and pro snowboarder Chris Klug. Producers and directors from shows such as *Extreme Makeover Home Edition* wandered through the crowd with network executives. Most days I could barely talk to my friends and family, and now I was standing in a group of strangers trying to make small talk. What was I doing here? My eyes were preoccupied with the room, but my mind was focused on Taylor. Losing her was the only reason we were here. I'd give anything to have her back.

"What do you do?" a pleasant woman asked. She had shoulder-length dark hair and wore a snakeskin print dress with a matching jacket.

I looked at her smiling face and tried to decide how to answer her question. "We were asked to present an award at tomorrow night's ceremony. We lost our daughter . . ." My voice trailed off, and tears started to flow. By this time, a couple of women had joined us, and someone handed me a Kleenex. I dabbed my eyes. I had on makeup for the first time in months, and I didn't want to ruin it. Through my sniffles, I continued, "Now we have a foundation to increase awareness about organ donation. We named it after our daughter. It's called Taylor's Gift. We've only started, but we believe in what we're doing."

The women in the circle became very compassionate. "Oh," and "I'm so sorry," they said. I appreciated their compassion, but I just wanted to make it through the night without more tears. I knew the best way to do it was to take the focus off me.

"Why are you here?" I asked the dark-haired woman.

"I donated a kidney to my husband."

"Oh, that's great. When?"

"About eight years ago," she said. "It really changed his life."

"That's beautiful," I said, attempting to keep the small talk going.

I introduced myself to the woman, and she said her name was Ann. She asked about my necklace—it was a tiny silver picture frame with a picture of Taylor inside—and we talked about her a little bit. Then Todd walked up with drinks for each of us. The lights dimmed, letting us know it was time for the program to start, and Ann excused herself. Once we were in our seats, someone on stage made a few announcements and then said, "Let me introduce tonight's mistress of ceremonies, Ann Lopez!"

"Todd, that's her! That's the woman I was talking to," I said, watching her walk to the mic.

Ann talked briefly about herself—it turns out she was George Lopez's wife. He was a comedian with a new show on TV that was doing very well, something he never could have done without her kidney. After a brief introduction, she went on to explain the rest of the night's lineup. Suddenly, in the middle of her remarks, she went off-script.

"You know what? Let me stop here. Tara and Todd Storch? Where are you?" Todd and I tentatively looked at each other. He nodded, and I barely raised my hand, but it was enough for her to see me in the crowd.

"They recently lost their daughter, and they donated her organs. Now, they've started a foundation called Taylor's Gift to increase awareness about organ donation." She smiled at us. "I am so impressed with you. Thank you for what you are doing. I just wanted to acknowledge that."

Everyone was looking at me, and all of a sudden the entire room burst into spontaneous applause. It was surreal. Then, as if nothing had happened, Ann gave us a huge smile and went right back to her script.

Todd called moments like these "of course" moments. Of course, God would do something to introduce us and our foundation to everyone in the room. Of course, it would be big, bold, and completely unexpected, so big that, of course, we could only give *Him* the credit. As Todd took a step of faith to quit his job and work for the foundation, this was yet another reminder of how much God cared for us and how He walked alongside us every step of the way.

Before we left that night, Ann Lopez came back over and hugged me. "You have got to keep in touch with me, you've got to!" she said.

Of course, we would.

The next night we presented an award at Donate Life's annual film festival awards ceremony. A number of people we spoke with in the entertainment industry were interested in hearing more about our documentary.

Ana Lucia Cottone was one individual who stood out. At the time, she was an executive at Lifetime Television. She looked like a California girl, young, tan, and blonde, but she was actually from Guatemala and spoke with a beautiful accent. After the presentation, she came up to Todd and me, hugged us, and said she wanted to hear our story. We liked her immediately, but our conversation was interrupted by others who came up to speak with her. She had to leave sooner than expected, but she said, "I really want to connect with you," as she left the room.

"Yeah, right," we joked to each other. "She's a network bigwig; it's not like we'll ever see her again."

She left—but she was back a few minutes later with her card. "Here's my number. I really want to stay in touch with you," she said. Then she was gone again.

The party ended, and Todd and I waited in the lobby for our Donate Life representative. Before we headed back to our hotel, we wanted to thank her again for including us. I'd been trying to hold it together all night, and I knew I wouldn't be able to do it much longer. "I'll go back inside and see if she's there," Todd said. "You can just wait here."

Todd was gone only a few seconds when Ana Lucia came back in the door, looking like she was on a mission. When she saw me she walked over and said, "I'm not done with you."

"What does that mean?" I asked.

"There's just something about you; I don't think I am done with you yet," she said.

My lip trembled, and I bit it to stop the tears that I knew were coming. Seeing my emotions surface, she said, "I know you don't know me, but I'm going to tell you a story."

I was glad; I couldn't do much talking at the time anyway.

"A very long time ago, there lived some Buddhist monks. Their village had been decimated by war and enemies were attacking their culture. To protect themselves, they had to move their village. But part of their religious tradition included this huge Buddha made of mud that they loved and worshiped. They wanted to take it with them to the new village, but they were fearful because they knew if they moved the statue, it could crack and break. Yet they couldn't move on without their Buddha."

I had no idea where the story was going, but Ana Lucia was a good storyteller, and I was hooked.

"So the whole village assembled, and the plan was to carefully work together to move this clay Buddha. But when they started to move it, the Buddha started to crack as they feared. Soon, the cracks got bigger and chunks of Buddha mud fell to the ground." Ana Lucia looked me in the eye. "But underneath the mud was gold."

She placed both her hands on my shoulders and said, "You're going to have to crack before you can find your gold."

I'm sure I said something really smart and impressive back; I think it was, "Oh, wow." But I knew then that Ana Lucia was right. She wasn't done with us yet. She offered to drive us back to our hotel so we could talk more. We've stayed in touch since then. Every time I felt as if I were going to break, or I couldn't hold it together, I'd think of her story, allow it to happen, and look for gold.

❧

My extended family lived in Louisiana, so every year they went to Gulf Shores, Alabama, for a family vacation. We had never been. It was June, only three months since we had lost Taylor, but we thought that it would be good to get away and to have a strong family around us if we needed it. I knew I was a mess, but maybe being around extended family would help distract me. Distractions were good. It would get us out of the house, and we'd get to do something fun with the kids.

199

Once we got to Gulf Shores, we unpacked and went down to the beach. I sat near my cousins, who were there with friends. We were all talking and watching Ryan and Peyton play in the ocean. *This is going to be good*, I thought. *The kids will be distracted, they're happy, and it's all going to be fine.*

"So, you're Ray's cousin?" the guy standing next to me said.

"Yeah."

"You all just got in town?"

"Yeah, we just drove in today from Texas." My eyes were on the kids, and I wanted to make sure they didn't venture out too far. I yelled to Peyton and Ryan, "You guys need to stay close!"

"How many kids do you have?" the guy asked.

Shocked by his question, I burst into tears. I'd not been asked that since Taylor had left. *How do I answer that?*

"I have those two," I said, pointing. That was all I could say.

My cousin saw what was happening and rescued me from the conversation. I walked off down the beach so I could cry without people staring. It was the first time it happened, but it wouldn't be the last. Every time I got my nails done, chatted with a new mom at school, or met a new neighbor, that question eventually would come up. When we went into a restaurant and they said, "How many are in your party?" I'd have to stop before answering the question. Eventually, in counseling Judy helped me learn how to handle it.

"Just say you have three, and change the subject by asking them a question," she taught me.

That usually worked, but it was still a question I would never be comfortable answering again.

⚜

We made it through our first family vacation without Taylor, and we'd held it together. But on the ride home it was just the four of us, and none of us could keep up the brave front much longer. Todd asked me to drive so he could "work" on his laptop. I knew it was just a code word for his wanting to escape, but I was happy to drive. It helped to distract me too. In the back, the kids were each doing their own thing. Ryan was playing video games; Peyton was watching a movie.

About an hour into the drive, without warning, I heard sniffling from Ryan. I dabbed my eyes at the sound. Then Peyton started sniffling. Soon Ryan was bawling, Peyton was crying, and my tears were flowing. Every time Ryan cried, it just set Peyton off, and hearing them cry, well, there was no turning back the flood of grief that was drowning them. I looked over at Todd. He'd closed his laptop and was staring out the window. I knew he was trying not to cry in front of the kids, which only made me cry harder.

Our whole carload was a mess. Then I heard Todd's breathing change. He turned to look at me, and I could see anger boiling beneath the surface. By now, both kids had buried their heads in pillows and were openly sobbing. Ryan was wailing.

Under his breath Todd said, "Are you kidding me?" He raised his fist in the air and shook it at God. "This is what our family is now? This is what You want?" He was as mad as I'd ever heard him. "I can't even console my own children," he said through clenched teeth.

I couldn't look at him because a big eighteen-wheeler semi was passing to my left, and I needed to stay focused on the road. It was a plain white truck, and it pulled right in front of us. I had to hit the brakes hard. As I did, I read the only thing written on the truck—"Taylor."

"Look!" I said.

Todd looked first and then looked at me. "She's here," he said excitedly.

We told the kids to look, and through swollen eyes, they saw it too.

It didn't make our tears go away completely, and it didn't take away all our pain, but it was another "of course" moment. We were on vacation and, of course, Taylor was there too. It was as if she said, "I'm right here. I'm with you," and knowing that helped us to put the brakes on our tears.

Not long afterward, we decided to pull off the road for a stop in Alexandria, Louisiana. We realized it was probably time for a Saturday evening mass, so we looked for a church. With the emotional state we were in, we needed to hear from God.

Looking at the church, I was disappointed. It was a little country parish in a bad part of town. We considered just getting back on the road and saying some prayers out loud in the car. God would surely understand. But instead we parked and went in. When I saw the aging priest, I wondered if we had made the wrong decision. What could he have to say that would encourage us? But boy, was I wrong. During the sermon, he talked about how God had already picked out our cross, and though His path may be hard to follow, He had a divine plan for each of us. The priest said there might be hard days ahead but to keep moving in God's direction because beyond those days would shine days of glory.

To me, his words were another "of course" moment. Of course, God had a plan and, of course, we needed to be reminded that He was in charge. And, of course, He'd get that message to us just when we needed it most. I left that mass feeling that our family had been blessed by God, and we just needed to keep moving forward. To follow Him—no matter how hard it was.

༜

We'd been back from the beach for only a few days when my neighbor Trista, the Grief Fairy, called. "I need to tell you about the email I just got. Can I come over?" she asked.

Ever since that day when I had told her I really wanted to meet the person who had Taylor's heart, she'd been searching the internet to see what she could learn. Weeks earlier, she'd read a post on Transplant Café, an online message board for transplant recipients, where someone had said they thought their sister-in-law had received Taylor's heart. Trista had investigated further, and with my permission she'd reached out to the man who'd posted the message, but it had been weeks and we hadn't heard anything.

"I've got news," Trista said. "I may have found the woman who has Taylor's heart. She's a nurse, a mother of two boys, and I'm waiting to hear if she wants to connect. If she does, is it okay if I give her your email address?"

I couldn't believe it. We'd found the woman who had Taylor's heart, and we might be able to connect! Since the day we made the decision to donate Taylor's organs, it was the one thing I wanted more than anything else. Through tear-filled eyes, I looked at Trista, who was still waiting for an answer, and said, "Of course!"

—23—

The Nurse Responds

PATRICIA WINTERS
TEMPE, ARIZONA

When the third call came, the transplant coordinator said, "We got an awesome heart; this one is really going to happen." And so it did.

As soon as Patricia woke up from the surgery, she said, "Who is she? I want to know who she is!" Somehow she sensed it was from a female donor, but the doctors couldn't tell her more.

While she was in surgery, her husband, Joe, got a call from a friend in Colorado who told him about a local skiing accident and a girl who had died, leaving her heart to a thirty-nine-year-old woman in Arizona. By the time Patricia's heart surgery was done, Joe already knew the donor, so although the doctors couldn't tell Patricia who it was, Joe could. He pulled out his laptop and showed Patricia pictures and videos of the thirteen-year-old donor.

"I can't now," Patricia said. "Please put that away." It was too soon and too much to bear, knowing that the donor was a teenage girl. As the mother of two young boys, she couldn't imagine what those parents must be going through. Though her new heart was beating strongly, it was also broken for the family who had donated their daughter's organs.

She couldn't get them out of her mind.

Over the next few months Patricia felt a pull toward the people who had given her such a precious gift. She wanted to get to know them, so while she was lying in bed with her laptop, she pulled up pictures and videos of the girl. She watched as the family started a foundation, and viewed online clips of news reports in which the mom said she wanted to reconnect with her daughter's heart. Patricia wanted that too. But as a nurse and as a mom, she respected the rules. She wouldn't contact them until the six-month waiting period was up.

But without her knowledge, one of Patricia's relatives had been posting messages on Transplant Café. Under articles about the girl's skiing accident, Patricia's relative posted a comment that said, "I know who got the girl's heart." When the girl's neighbor reached out and offered to connect the commenter to the family, the relative got scared. After a couple of weeks, he finally admitted to Patricia what had been going on and apologized for the mess he'd created.

Patricia was worried that the whole thing could be upsetting to the family. *That poor mother!* Patricia thought. She immediately emailed the neighbor: "I'm so sorry for all of this; I just found out. Of course I'd like to connect with the family."

—24—

First Meetings

Todd

After the plane landed in Denver, I turned on my phone. Tara must have forgotten to turn hers off because I heard hers ping. Then ping, ping. Then ping, ping, ping. I looked at her and said, "Wow, somebody sure wants to talk to you."

She was wrapped in a blanket and leaning against the window. I couldn't tell if she'd been crying or not, but she looked as if she could burst into tears at any moment. As the plane taxied, she reached for her phone. I got busy with mine, catching up on what I'd missed during our flight from Dallas.

Suddenly, Tara got excited. "Todd, Todd," she said, nudging me. "Trista just texted me, and she forwarded an email from Patricia Winters!" Her hand started shaking as she handed me her phone. It was an email from the heart recipient.

"Read it!" she said, obviously too nervous to do it herself.

I opened Trista's email and read the forwarded message. She said her name was Patricia Winters, that she was a nurse and a mom of two boys. She explained how a relative had left the message on Transplant Café and didn't tell her about it until recently. "Please tell the Storches they can contact me any way they want," she'd written to Trista. Then she included her contact information.

We had just arrived in Denver to meet Jeff Kartus, the pancreas/kidney recipient, and his family. Only in God's perfect timing would we also get our first email from the heart recipient. "Well, *of course,* we'd hear from her now," I said.

The email was a big relief to me. I knew how much it meant to Tara to connect with the person who had Taylor's heart. That had been her one desire since we agreed to make the gift. "Do you want to email her back?" I asked.

"I can't. I just can't," Tara said, choking back sobs. "You do it."

I emailed Patricia and told her how happy we were to finally connect with her. "But we're at the airport. We're meeting the kidney/pancreas recipient. You can understand that Tara doesn't want to email right now, but she sends her love."

We were less than twenty-four hours from meeting the first recipient, and now I was a little conflicted. From the moment we made the decision, we both wanted to connect with the people who received Taylor's organs, but I honestly never thought we would. I didn't think we would ever know their names, let alone meet them in person. Personally, I didn't need to meet Jeff to know Taylor's gift made a difference. Nothing in my life was missing that would be made full just because I shook a recipient's hand or looked into his or her eyes.

It was different for Tara. She'd longed for a connection with the recipients since the beginning. She looked forward to meeting them and bonding with them. In some small way, I think she hoped it would connect her with Taylor.

While walking through the airport, my stomach knotted as I thought of all that could go wrong. I worried about Tara. I knew she had high expectations for the meeting. What if it didn't work out? What if the meeting didn't live up to her expectations, and she had some kind of breakdown while we were there? My most important goal for this meeting was to protect her.

But although there was a lot to consider, I still felt an incredible pull to meet them. Our goal was to encourage as many people as we possibly could to register for organ donation. Hearing an organ recipient's side of the story and sharing that in the documentary would be an emotionally powerful addition to our story. It would be hard, but I looked forward to meeting them.

⁂

"I have to get out of here," Tara said. She paced the perimeter of our hotel room. I couldn't remember the last time I'd seen her pace. I had become used to her being inactive, sitting and staring into space for hours.

"Let's take a walk," I said.

We had a couple of hours before we were to meet the documentary crew for dinner, so we decided to walk to the outdoor mall. The 16th Street Mall in Denver is a one-mile pedestrian street lined on both sides with restaurants, retailers, and street performers. As we strolled, Tara stopped occasionally to look in the shop windows.

"I need something to wear to the foundation dinner," she said.

"Maybe you should look while we're here."

We were scheduled to fly back into Dallas late Friday afternoon, and the fund-raising dinner was to be held that night at a friend's house. Though I was surprised she had the desire to shop, we both knew if she wanted to get something before the dinner, this would be her only opportunity.

"I want to find a dress. I want a sundress. And I want it to be Tiffany blue," she said.

"Good luck with that," I said, eyeing the fall collections already in the displays. I knew why she said she wanted that dress in that color. When Taylor was little, her favorite color was purple. As she grew older and became more aware of her own features, her favorite color was Tiffany blue. "Because it matches my eyes," she'd say.

Tara was still discussing the dress she wanted when she spotted one of her favorite stores. "Oh, there's an Ann Taylor; I'm going to see if they have anything."

"See the Starbucks?" I asked, pointing across the street. "I'll wait for you there. When you're finished, come and get me."

I ordered a coffee and found a seat near the window so I could people watch while I waited for my laptop to load. Through the window, I saw Tara leave Ann Taylor empty-handed and walk down the street toward another store. *Good luck finding that dress,* I thought. But I was happy she had the energy to shop. I think being away from Coppell, freed from the fear of running into people who knew her, helped.

⁜

I looked up to see Tara pulling up a chair. I wasn't sure how much time had elapsed; I had become engrossed in my work. A quick glance showed she wasn't carrying any packages. She put her elbows on the table and rested her chin in her hands. She looked bummed.

"No luck?"

She shook her head. "I'm not finding anything. Everything is in fall colors."

"Maybe you're being too picky?" I asked. After all, it was a pretty tall order to find what she was looking for.

"Maybe, but it's what I want."

I looked at my watch. "You've got forty-five minutes left. Do you want to keep looking, or are you giving up?"

"I want to keep looking," she said.

I marveled at her newfound energy. Just a few weeks earlier she wouldn't have had the ability to even dress herself, let alone go shopping for a dress.

Thirty minutes later, Tara was back with a bag in her hand and a wide smile on her face. "You'll never guess what happened!" she said excitedly. "As soon as I left here, I walked outside and said, 'Taylor, you know what I'm looking for.' She's the one who always found the best clothes when we went shopping. Well, the very next store I went into had all of these dark colors, and then I saw this little piece of Tiffany blue fabric peeking from the rack. I went over and pulled out the hanger—and it was a sundress! And guess what? It was my size!"

I couldn't remember seeing Tara so excited. Even I was excited.

"But that's not all," she said, gushing. "While I was walking into the dressing room, I flipped the dress over my arm and the tag fell out. Look at this!" she urged, pulling the dress from the bag and showing me the attached tag.

I expected it to be the dress's price, and from her enthusiasm I expected it to be cheap. But instead of the price tag, she showed me a brownish-gray square tag, and written in yellow cursive at the top was a single word.

Taylor.

"Are you kidding me?" I said, picking up the tag. Finding the dress she wanted, in the way she had, was pretty unbelievable, but that tag made it seem preposterous. "It's the same font we selected for the website!"

"No way!" she said, looking closer. She hadn't noticed that.

I knew the answer to the next question before asking, but I asked it anyway, just so I could see her smile. "Did it fit?"

Like I hoped, she answered with an even bigger grin. "*Of course!* It fit perfectly."

From everything that had happened on this trip—from the timing of Patricia's email to the "Taylor-made" dress Tara found—it was clear God was very much with us. So I'm not sure why we were so nervous on the drive to Jeff Kartus's house the next afternoon, but we were. We were both anxious, maybe even a little scared, wondering if we'd like them and if they'd like us. We had no idea what to expect. We'd never done anything like this before, nor did we know anyone who had.

As I contemplated my feelings, the best I could compare it to would be how I might have felt someday when Taylor started dating. I would want to meet the guy she was with, and I would want to connect with him. Most of all, I would want to know he would take good care of her and keep her safe. That's the same thing I wanted from Jeff.

With only a few more miles to go, we took the exit off the interstate. I silently prayed, asking God to bless our meeting. If things didn't go well, I wasn't sure how Tara or I would react.

ೲ

We pulled up to the Kartuses' house, and the whole family tumbled out before we even put the car in park. It was immediately obvious who Jeff was—the guy in the cowboy hat. Before I could even open my door, Tara was jumping out of the car and running toward him. I wasn't sure whether Jeff and his wife, Vanessa, were huggers or not, but they were now. I watched as Tara hugged Jeff and then said, "Where is she?"

Jeff lifted his shirt and pointed to a scar. "She's right here."

Tara ran her trembling fingers over his scar, and in his slow, methodical way, Jeff said, "I'm taking good care of her."

Thank You, God!

It could have been an awkward moment, meeting a strange woman for the first time and all she wants to do is touch your abdominal scar, but if Jeff or Vanessa were freaked out, they didn't let it show. Tara later told me, "I don't know why I did it, but it's just where my head was. I just wanted to physically touch her again somehow."

"I can't thank you enough," Jeff said, his voice faltering. "Thank you so much. I feel bad for Tara and for you. It's very unfortunate that one had to pass for one to live, but I want you to know how thankful I am that Taylor's life saved mine."

He was so appreciative; it was as if he couldn't thank us enough.

We moved to the backyard and sat on the patio. Jeff was a humble guy and down-to-earth. I watched as Tara engaged him in conversation, asking questions and answering his. Sure, a few tears emerged, but watching her converse felt like I was getting my wife back.

Jeff was open and eager to share his life with us. We learned he had been a diabetic for nearly forty years, but after Taylor's pancreas and kidney saved his life, he was completely cured of the disease.

"My sugars used to be between four and five hundred. My machine doesn't go any higher than five hundred, so who knows how high they were," Jeff said. "But now they're always between 72 and 98." With Taylor's pancreas, he no longer had to test his blood sugar or take insulin. "I gave my insulin away to a family who is struggling financially," Jeff said. "They have a daughter with diabetes and couldn't afford her medication."

Vanessa talked about how much their lives had changed. "Before the transplant, he could barely make it up and down the stairs. He slept a lot. I used to worry about him all the time." She mentioned some of his scarier experiences. "He would get so stubborn, and he refused to eat. But now it doesn't matter; he doesn't have to eat breakfast if he doesn't want to. I can go to work and not worry."

"Now, I have a normal day-to-day routine without having to worry about being tied down by my disease," Jeff said. "And Vanessa can have a normal life because she doesn't have to take care of me all the time."

It was easy to see the strain that Jeff's illness had taken on the whole family, and how different everything was now. It had been a long time since any of them had had a normal life.

Vanessa told us they noticed certain changes in Jeff right away. "He always refused dessert," she said, "but the first time they brought him a meal tray in the hospital, he went straight for the dessert. Skipped the meat and the side dish, didn't touch the fruit—he went straight for the cheesecake. He tore it up in, like, two seconds. He just downed the entire slice. It was amazing since he's never eaten sweets."

Tara burst into tears and started to sob. I tried to wipe my own tears away with the back of my hand.

Vanessa stopped talking, and I could see her looking first at Brooke and then at Jeff. Everyone was silent; she had no idea what just happened. "Are you okay?" she asked Tara tenderly.

Tara got a hold of herself, and through her tears she said, "Cheesecake was one of Taylor's favorite desserts."

Someone handed her a tissue, and I put my arm around her. I wasn't sure what would happen next, but when she looked up at me I could see her eyes glistening. This was the connection she'd been hoping for. The cheesecake made it real for her.

Though he'd had the surgery only three months earlier, and he wouldn't be able to go back to his job, Jeff was already finding volunteer work to keep himself busy and he was driving again. "You've given me a new lease on life, and my wife can now have a life without constant worry," he said.

Jeff was a man of few words, but he made them count. When he talked about the day the medical team came to pick up the dialysis equipment, he simply said, "I was glad to see it go."

It was obvious how thankful he was for the gift he'd been given and how drastically it had changed his life. "I'm not only living for me and my family, I'm living for your daughter," he said.

Tara leaned back in her chair and relaxed a bit. I knew that was exactly what she needed to hear. And I needed it too. Jeff would take care of Taylor's organs, and the gift had transformed his life. But watching Tara as she hung on his every word, I realized it was also transforming her in some way.

Tara told them about the dress she'd found the day before, and we both told stories about Taylor. As we talked, I was reminded of the first time Tara had taken her eyes off Taylor when she was only two or three. They were in a small store, so Tara knew she hadn't gone far, but the fact that Taylor wasn't in sight worried her until she found Taylor one aisle over playing with the toys. When Tara picked Taylor up, it wasn't with excitement or joy but more of a sense of relief, like, *Whew, now I can see she's okay.* That's what I saw in Tara as she spoke with Jeff. I saw a mom who knew her daughter would be okay.

Soon it was time to say goodbye. We were spent, and we knew they had to be too. We hugged and promised to stay in touch. Jeff continued to thank us, but finally I interrupted him and said, "I want to thank *you.* Thank you and your family, especially Brooke, for being willing to reach out and connect with us. You don't know how much this has helped us."

Once back in the car, we didn't even have to say anything. We knew Jeff would take care of Taylor. It was a joyous feeling to know that someone was not only living, but thriving, because of Taylor's gift.

Of course.

Taylor took care of people. That's what she did. She took care of Ryan and Peyton, she took care of her friends, and now she was caring for strangers who—through her gift—were part of our family. In the last few months, I'd heard many stories of Taylor's caretaking that I'd never heard before. Taylor wasn't the kind to come home and tell us the thoughtful things she had done, so each time someone told us a new story of her taking care of someone else—like the girl at the garden dedication whose mom had died—it was a gift to us.

Now we had gotten to hear another story, that of a man and his family, and how Taylor was caring for them from the inside out.

❧

As our plane lifted into the skies above Denver, I noticed that Tara didn't have a blanket wrapped around her this time. Instead she sat erect, calmly reading a magazine. I reached across the armrest and took her hand.

"You know what?" I said. "We were given the *privilege* of organ donation. It wasn't just a decision, *it was a privilege.*"

Her smile was all the confirmation I needed that things were going to be okay.

—25—

One Step Forward

Tara

"Todd, there must be at least a hundred people here!" I said. We had just arrived in our friend's backyard for the first official event of the Taylor's Gift Foundation, and I was awed by the turnout.

"It's happening, isn't it?" Todd asked, as he squeezed my hand.

Only hours before we had met the Kartus family in Denver, and now we were back in Dallas in the backyard of our dear friends Pete and Pauline Stein. The place was filled with friends, family, local business leaders, former co-workers, and community members who just wanted to support and encourage us. I was overwhelmed and nervous. Being around people I knew was much harder than talking to people we'd just met.

"How was the meeting with Taylor's organ recipient?" It was the first question I heard that night, and it was asked over and over again in various forms. "Did it bring you peace?" some asked. I knew what they meant. What they meant was, "Did meeting him fix you? Make you all better? Help you move on?"

The thought of having to carry on small talk, or worse yet talk about losing Taylor, with all these people made me want to ditch my shoes and run home. Instead, I prayed.

I wasn't sure how to answer their questions. It was still so new. We'd just stepped off the plane a couple of hours before, and I hadn't had enough time to process everything. Our experience with the Kartus family felt so intimate that I wasn't sure I wanted to talk about it. Even if I did, how could I explain what I was feeling?

I knew why even the best-intentioned asked me those questions. What else did I have to talk about? For the past four months all I had done was sleep and stare into space. That doesn't make for good party conversation. Fortunately, early in the night I found a topic I was happy to dwell on. Someone complimented my dress. I told them the story and then twisted my arm around to pull the tag out of the back to show them.

"Look at this tag," I'd say.

"Wow! Look at this!" they'd say, pulling another friend over. "You've got to hear the story about her dress! Tara, tell it."

For the rest of the night, I talked about finding the dress. It became my protection and insulation. It gave me something to talk about and another way to marvel at God's goodness without having to mention Taylor or the accident. Finding the dress was a blessing, and being able to talk about it at the party was a double blessing. I was grateful for both. In a way, I felt like Taylor was protecting me.

It was a full evening with dinner, an auction, and a concert. Todd made a short presentation and talked about the foundation's goals. He introduced the advisory board, thanking them for assisting in the launch of the foundation. He told them about Jeff Kartus and his family, and how dramatically different their lives were because of Taylor's gift. "Imagine how many more lives could be saved if we just got more people to register," Todd said.

He concluded by saying, "Meeting the Kartus family brought me a great deal of joy. It was a tangible example of why the work we're doing with Taylor's Gift is important and worth our sacrifices."

As people applauded, I outwardly joined in. But inside, I was thinking how different Todd and I were. While I loved meeting the Kartus family, it didn't bring me *joy*, and it didn't bring me *peace*.

Those things left my life when Taylor died. I suspected they'd never come back to me in the same way.

But meeting the Kartuses did do one thing for me—it gave me strength.

Strength to get up in the morning.

৽

By late June, I found my mornings were getting a little easier. Although I didn't have to be anywhere in particular, I started setting the alarm on my phone and getting up when it went off. "When you get out of bed, make it," my counselor, Judy, said one day. "If you don't, it just calls you to get back in." She was right. So I started to make my bed. During the summer, the kids wanted to sleep in. So on a typical morning, Todd and I would have a couple hours by ourselves before they got up. He'd be out on the porch reading his Bible, and I'd just sit with him. Though we found ways to bond, we were still grieving very differently.

Todd liked to sit in Taylor's room; I didn't even want to see it. It made me anxious to even think about crossing the threshold. But I did like visiting her grave. I would go there almost every day, and sometimes I'd stay for hours. The grave had a temporary marker with only her name on it. I wouldn't even allow them to add the dates. Since the grave itself was so important to me, I wanted to be the one to pick out the headstone. But I couldn't. It wasn't that I was being stubborn; I just couldn't physically make myself describe my child in ten words or less.

It seemed so final.

Taylor's grave, like our home, had become another place for people to drop off signs of their love. People left trinkets—stuffed animals or other knickknacks. Sometimes they would decorate her grave with seasonal signs and streamers. At Easter someone left a flowered cross. My friend Beth Rathe would come out each week and exchange the old flowers for something fresh. I loved seeing flowers in red and black, the East Middle School colors, in Taylor blue and purple, or in red, white, and blue for July. It made me feel good—like people hadn't forgotten Taylor. That was important to me. One of my biggest fears was that people would forget her.

I kept a pillow and a blanket in the car, and on a typical day I would spread the blanket on the shadiest side of her grave, kick off my shoes, and lie down next to her. I'd talk to her, and I would pray.

Sometimes, I'd listen to music on my iPhone, placing one ear bud in my ear and the other on her. I almost always had a hand on her. I liked listening to Steven Curtis Chapman's *Beauty Will Rise* album. It was an album of songs dedicated to and inspired by his daughter Maria, who died in a tragic car accident. The song "SEE" was especially meaningful. It was a description of heaven as if the person were giving a tour to someone who hadn't yet been there. I would play it repeatedly and think of Taylor singing the lyrics. Another song, "Just Have to Wait," was about how I would have to wait to see her again; I cried every time I listened to that one.

One day, while sitting at her grave, I had a major pity party for myself. This wasn't how my life was supposed to turn out. I was mad and frustrated. About that time, I looked up and saw a perfect heart-shaped cloud resting in the clear, blue sky. It felt as if Taylor were reaching out to me—almost like she'd done with the blue dress. I know a lot of people believe that it isn't possible for someone on the other side to reach out, but I saw too many signs of her presence to believe that. Were the signs from her? Were they from God? It didn't really matter. They comforted me and helped me feel connected to both God and Taylor. Moments like that gave me strength to continue moving forward. Sometimes I called these signs "Taylor kisses." I would write about them in my journal, or I'd write letters in my journal to her.

Often I read while I was at her gravesite. My favorite book at that time was *Hearing Jesus Speak into Your Sorrow* by Nancy Guthrie. I would read that book only while I was with Taylor.

I tried to visit Taylor only when Peyton and Ryan weren't home. During the summer, they'd get an invitation to play at a friend's house, and I'd drop them off before heading to the cemetery. Sometimes the time to pick them up came too soon. I'd text various moms and ask if the kids could please stay and play a little longer. "I need some time," I'd text. "I'm falling apart, and I don't want them to see me like this." They always said yes.

When I got home, sometimes Todd would say, "Where have you been?"

"With Taylor," I'd answer. But I knew he already knew. I didn't want to go anywhere else. Even though he didn't feel the same way, Todd didn't tell me *not* to go. He respected my need to be there.

⊶

Todd woke up enthused about going to work. He was creating, leading, and managing a dynamic start-up. A start-up I was a part of but which overwhelmed me each time I tried to participate. In the beginning, I didn't want to hear about it. But lately, as I showed a bit of interest, Todd would see my participation as a good thing and shower me with more details than I could handle. I'd get frustrated because I couldn't take it all in. He'd get frustrated because he had to repeat himself. "We talked about this yesterday!" he said one afternoon. I believed him; I just didn't remember the conversation.

There were other times when I emerged from the fog I'd been in and really wanted to participate and know what was going on with the foundation. In those moments, I'd ask loads of questions. Sometimes, Todd misinterpreted my interest and thought I was questioning him or his abilities.

Todd was so capable and such a can-do guy that often he moved forward quickly, and it was hard for me to catch up. I never wanted him to think I was challenging him or his ideas, but neither did I want to be left out of everything.

It was complicated.

We made mistakes. Lots of them. One of us would blow up, and after we cooled off, we'd come back and say, "I'm so sorry. Let's figure out how to make this work." But it was a struggle. Everything

221

around us had changed—our family, our marriage, and Todd's work were no longer the same. In order to keep it all together, our communication patterns had to change too.

❦

From the moment we made the decision to donate Taylor's organs, I wanted to know the person who had her heart. I wanted to connect with him or her and hug that person. But when Patricia finally reached out to me, I was suddenly hesitant about getting to know her too quickly. For the first few weeks, she emailed or texted Todd. Then as we got to know her better, I felt she needed to connect with me as much as I needed to connect with her. We began emailing and texting directly—usually late at night after our kids had gone to bed.

In the beginning I just shared generic information with her, such as, "I was born in Abilene, and I have three brothers." I learned she had been raised Catholic too. She had been single for a long time and didn't get married until she was in her thirties—at one point, she even thought she was going to be a nun. I found it was easy to connect with her because she was also a mother: she had two boys ages four and six.

One night before I fell asleep, I texted her and said, "Please tell Taylor good night."

"I always do," she texted back.

Soon we friended each other on Facebook. I was dying to see a picture of her but was disappointed when her profile picture was of her kids. Several days later, while in bed, I texted, "Okay, I'm going nuts. I need a picture of you. Can you send me one?"

"No, I'm in my pajamas," she texted back. "I look horrible. My face is swollen from steroids."

After a few more texts, we each agreed to snap a picture and send it—a sort of digital "you show me your bad photo, and I'll show you mine." So I took a picture of my face and sent it to her—no makeup and all.

Immediately she texted back, "You're way too pretty."

After a long pause and some more cajoling, she sent me a text that said, "Okay, this isn't beautiful, but here you go." It was just a quick phone shot, but it was my first glimpse of her. She was sitting on her bed wearing pink pajamas. I could see her stethoscope sitting on the table next to her bed, and my first reaction was, "Ah, there she is."

It was my first chance to see Patricia as her own person, not just an extension of Taylor. Now I had two reasons for wanting to meet Patricia in person.

ஃ

I found comfort at Taylor's grave, but like Taylor's friends, Todd found comfort in her room. I rarely went upstairs, but when I did, and I saw her door open, it bothered me. I started insisting no one go in and that her door stay closed so that I wouldn't have to see inside.

One day, a dear friend confronted me about my insistence that the door stay closed. "Your children won't go in there because you want the door closed. You're making it seem as if her room is off-limits, and you're denying them the privilege of finding comfort there. You find comfort at her grave. They don't have that. Their connection is her room, and you've closed that off from them."

She was right. We opened the door to Taylor's room.

A few days later, I had to go upstairs for something. *You can do this*, I told myself, knowing the door would be wide open. I forced myself up the stairs, slowly exhaling as I took each new step. *It won't be that bad*, I promised myself. But as I reached the top step I had to catch in my breath. I couldn't believe what I saw.

"Todd! Todd! Grab a camera and get up here!" I said, moving closer to get a better view.

Todd came dashing up the stairs, with Peyton right behind him.

"Look!" I said, pointing to the carpet.

Originating from Taylor's room was a giant sunbeam. Though the sun obviously was shining on that side of the house, none of the

223

other rooms on the same side had light spilling out into the hall. The sunbeam radiated from her room and landed on the floor outside of her door, producing a warm sunny spot on the carpet—in the shape of a cross. Todd took a couple of pictures while we marveled at the unlikely occurrence, but Peyton didn't say anything. She just lay down on top of it and pressed her nose into the carpet.

— 26 —

The Stock Market of Grief

Todd

The kids had been sleeping on the air mattress in our room for over three months. Tara wanted our bedroom back. I wanted my wife back. We also wanted to return the mattress so the family who had loaned it to us could use it for an upcoming camping trip. But Ryan and Peyton weren't ready to sleep alone in their rooms. They felt isolated and scared. We compromised by moving them both into the guest room. It was hard to get them to sleep at night at first, but eventually they did it and we were proud of them. We were all taking steps forward, but there were setbacks too.

On the Fourth of July, we went to a concert with Tara's mom and dad. About thirty seconds into the music, Ryan saw the French horns and it reminded him of Taylor. He had to get up and leave. He also didn't like going to St. Ann's. He was trying to avoid things that triggered feelings he didn't know how to deal with. Peyton had her own way of dealing with grief—she clung to Tara. Whenever Tara left, Peyton would want to know where she was going, when she would be back, and how long she would be gone.

Our house seemed like the stock market. While one person's emotional stock was rising, another's would be staying steady, while two more might be dropping. We hoped the general trend was upward, but at this point in the mourning process our emotions weren't stable enough to make any long-term projections.

By default, Tara and I were fix-it kind of people. Our first inclination was to help the kids *get past* their grief. So we went to family therapy. It didn't help. In many cases, it only made things worse for Ryan because it brought up things that were too painful for him to process. Ryan had a lot of feelings mixed up inside of him—he had seen Taylor hit the tree.

"No one knows what I've seen. You're the only one," he'd say to me on his bad days.

He was right. I did know. I had seen Taylor too, but I also knew what it had felt like to look up and see the terrified look on my son's face. More than anything, I had wanted to console him, to turn his eyes away from the scene and tell him it would be okay. But I couldn't. I was deep in the snow, straddling my injured daughter and praying she'd be okay. It had been heart-wrenching to have to choose between consoling my son and helping my daughter. It was even more painful now to look back and know I hadn't helped either one.

Thoughts of being on that mountainside, unable to help Taylor, still ripped me apart inside. After the ski patrol had loaded Taylor on the sled, Ryan and I had to ski down to the lodge.

"Can you do it," I'd asked him, "or do you need to get on my back?"

"I-I can do it," he'd stammered through tears.

"She's going to be okay!" I said, to give him strength and reassure him.

I repeated that phrase, or some version of it, all the way down the mountain. Later, we would find out she wasn't okay, and now I felt as though I had lied to him.

Ryan and I were bonded by sports and music; unfortunately, we also had another bond that no father and son should ever share: we were the ones on the mountain with Taylor. The terrible things we'd seen and the helplessness we'd felt put us in a dark and secretive society of two. We couldn't revoke our membership in this club, we couldn't escape the memories, and we couldn't talk about it.

I would have given anything to take the kids' pain away. Instead, just as Tara and I were learning to deal with each other, we had to learn to give Ryan and Peyton the grace and time to grieve in their own way.

After Ryan had a particularly bad day, I tried to find a metaphor to give him words for what he was feeling and to give him hope for the future. "Your life is like a book," I said. "When you're reading a good book, you just sail through the chapters and enjoy the ride. Then suddenly, something bad happens to the main character. Maybe there is one chapter that is really difficult, and you sort of struggle reading the book because that chapter is hard. You're not sure if you want to keep reading, or if you even want to know what happens next. But when you get to the end of the book, you love how the story turns out, and you recommend it to your friends. That's when you understand why the author put that hard chapter in there. It all makes sense once the story ends." I put my arm around him and said, "Your life is like that book, and God is writing the story. Just know that some day when He is almost finished writing, you'll be able to look back and say, 'I totally get why that chapter was there.'"

That was also my hope.

Someday, I wanted to look back and see the purpose in all of this. For now, each of us just had to keep moving through the difficult parts of the story.

❧

Since I wasn't going into an office every day, I tried to be as disciplined as possible at home. I got up at the same time every morning and went outside to sit on the back porch to read and pray. I had decisions to make for the foundation, and so many things were coming up that I had to seek direction and guidance from Scripture on a daily basis. I liked using the YouVersion app to read the Bible on my phone because I could quickly find related verses or search by topic. One day I started reading James, and for the next several days, I found myself working through his words about suffering, such as, "Consider it pure joy, my brothers, whenever you face trials of many kinds, because you know that the testing of your faith develops perseverance" (James 1:2–3). James also talked a lot about how action should come from our faith—something that resonated with me.

Tara would often join me outside. We just needed to be near each other. Over time, I noticed she was also reading. First, it was books on grief—most written by mothers who'd lost a child. Tara couldn't focus for long periods of time, and stories seemed to hold her attention the best. After a while, I noticed she had started to read devotionals. But lately, I noticed she'd also begun to pick up her Bible and read. I asked her about it one day.

"I think you reconnected with God faster than I did," she said. "You immediately saw a purpose and His divine fingerprints on things. I'm still searching."

At least she was looking in the right places.

Tara

In the hospital in Grand Junction, Todd had promised to be my rock. And he had been. I marveled at his strength. There was only one way to explain it—it was the work of the Holy Spirit.

I often imagined the Holy Spirit swirling around Todd and protecting him. How else did he have the capacity to handle the things he handled? How else could he juggle simple but overwhelming tasks, like answering the hundreds of emails that poured in? Or more complex things, like taking care of a wife who was totally incapacitated and always on the verge of losing it? Without help from God, how else could he deal with setbacks when his own loss was so fresh?

I thought about Pam Cope saying we were handpicked for this. Who were we to be chosen? But aren't we all chosen for something? We had a choice. We could follow God's leading, or we could strike out on our own. We could curl up in grief and shut everyone out, or we could stay the course, even when it got hard—even when there seemed to be no end to the pain.

"Now faith is being sure of what we hope for and certain of what we do not see" (Heb. 11:1). Faith is belief without proof. Though I didn't have evidence, I believed that one day in the future the pain would get easier. I also believed there was a place where Taylor waited for me—and I had faith that in that place all pain would be gone.

⚜

Through July and August, my relationship with Patricia, Taylor's heart recipient, continued to grow through texts and emails. We texted about our kids, our families, and her job as a nurse. Though I still wanted a bit of distance—for example, I wasn't ready to talk to her on the phone—we decided to reserve a date on the calendar for us to visit her in Phoenix. We planned a trip for Labor Day weekend and invited Gary Reaves and his crew from WFAA to come with us to do a story that would inspire organ donations. Patricia agreed, and it was all set. I was scared and excited at the same time.

As a precaution, Todd wanted to verify Patricia was who she said she was. Todd called Donor Alliance to tell them we had been corresponding, and we were planning a trip to see her in a few weeks. Once again, Donor Alliance was caught off guard. I'd only recently sent them a letter for them to send to all of the recipients, and they hadn't sent it out yet, so they hadn't received permission from the recipients to pass on contact information. After a few emergency phone calls and meetings, once again they sent us forms to sign. They also contacted Patricia to see if it was okay for them to release her name to us. Of course she agreed, and we laughed about it in our text messages.

It was real. She was real.

Patricia had Taylor's heart. She also had a stethoscope. In a few weeks, I would put that stethoscope to my ear and hear Taylor's heartbeat again.

I couldn't wait.

❖

Overall, my days were getting better. Though I still had ups and downs—to use Todd's stock market analogy—I was trending upward. Then August hit and school started. On the first day of school, I got Ryan and Peyton off, and then I fell apart. It would have been Taylor's first day of high school.

After dropping them off, I wanted to go to bed, but I also wanted to be as close to Taylor as possible. For the first time since we'd lost her, I crawled into her bed. She was the last one to sleep in it, and the sheets had not been washed. I lay down on her pillow and inhaled the smell of her sheets.

A couple of hours later, Todd came in. "Are you okay?" he asked.

"No," I said, bursting into tears. "She'd be at high school."

"Let's go out and get lunch," he suggested. "We'll go somewhere completely out of Coppell."

And so we did. We went to a quirky little taco place that Todd had found online, and for an hour or two it distracted me. When we got back home, I went back upstairs to her room and lay there. *I have got to get up*, I told myself after I'd been there for a few minutes. *The kids will be home soon. It's their first day of school. You can't do this to them. It's already hard enough on them.* So I did. I got up, made her bed, and went downstairs.

❖

I worried about Ryan. Not only was it his first day of middle school, but it was his first day in his sister's old school—Coppell Middle School East. I couldn't imagine how hard it would be for him. Since our life had become so public, everyone there knew what had happened. In addition, now a huge memorial garden created to honor his sister stood right outside the building. I wasn't able to cope with my old life and Todd wasn't able to go back to his old job, yet we were sending our kids off to school as if nothing had happened in their lives. It was hard to contemplate.

In preparation for Ryan's first day, Laura Springer had hand-selected his classes and teachers. She'd also talked to each of them, saying, "Ryan is not Taylor's little brother. He is Ryan Storch, and he is to be treated as Ryan Storch. He is going to make it on his own. You need to let him be who he is."

Fortunately, Ryan had a great first day of school.

Unfortunately, it was his last good day for a long time.

Starting the next day, and continuing for the next several months, Ryan had one bad day after another. He would call us crying, sobbing so hard into the phone that all we could make out was, "I wanna come home, come home, come home."

Not only was the garden that contained Taylor's memorial pictures constantly in view, but various T-shirts had been made in her honor, and people were wearing them. Blue silicone bracelets bearing her name decorated the arms of both boys and girls.

One day in math class, Ryan's teacher passed out a worksheet of word problems. Problem number five said, "If you were on a mountain, and you skied down at 15 mph . . ." Ryan read the problem, got up from his desk, and left the room in tears.

"Of course you can come home," we said whenever he called. "If you're upset, we want to take care of you and help you through this."

But the truth was we were still trying to figure out our own grief, and we had very few ideas of how to handle his. There aren't 1-800 hotlines for how to handle your preteen son's sorrow. Even when experts were available, they didn't live with us and they didn't know our child like we did.

We did the best we could. But after several weeks of taking him to school only to have him call us to come back home, we had to come up with a new plan. He was missing a lot of classes and it couldn't continue. We even discussed the possibility of homeschooling him. One day, Laura Springer and the school counselors had a frank talk with us.

"He needs to stay at school," she said. "I know you want to, but you can't let him come home every time he asks. I'll be here for him if he needs me, but he has to learn to stay on his own." It was one more hard thing we were being asked to do.

The next day, Principal Springer told Ryan that if he was upset, it was fine for him to go to the counselor's office, but it was no longer fine for him to go home. As soon as the classroom got quiet, or Ryan was asked to focus independently on a task, his mind would begin to race and he couldn't handle it. There were also unforeseen triggers—like the random math question—that would set him off. If it was a little deal, he'd just go stay in the hall until he had control over his emotions. But if it was a big deal, and he was crying, he'd go to the counselor's office, or to Principal Springer's office, and beg to come home. Laura would sit with him and gently say, "I know you think I'm being unfair. But it's all out of love, Ryan. I love you so much that I have to make you do this."

When the school called, I couldn't handle hearing him in pain. I'd hand the phone to Todd because it caused me too much anxiety. Todd ended up being the contact between Laura Springer, the counselors at school, and our family. I didn't have the strength.

But Todd wasn't immune to Ryan's cries either. It got to him too. Some days, he'd hang up the phone and say, "Is it not enough that he lost his sister? Now he's got to figure out how to deal with school?"

Other days, Todd would feel sorry for himself. "We've got to take this on too? I mean, how much can we bear?" Or he'd vent his anger toward God. "My days aren't hard enough? Why does God want us to now parent a child through this?"

Peyton was having her own issues. She was clingy and whiny. It was like she had a leash and I was on the other end. She didn't want me to go anywhere without her. She seemed to regress to an earlier age. Todd knew he shouldn't take it personally. I was just her security blanket, but it was hard on him.

The emotional stocks in our family portfolio were constantly moving up and down. It was like an emotional minefield, with those who felt healthy at the moment trying not to step on those who felt weak. Just like with the real stock market, we couldn't predict what would happen to any individual stock next. We could only hope to manage it so it didn't go off the charts.

— 27 —

Her Heart Is in the Right Place

Todd

When I saw Patricia's name on my phone, I assumed she was providing more details to coordinate travel arrangements for our meeting in a couple of days. She and Tara hadn't yet spoken, so Patricia typically called me.

"I just wanted to let you know," she said, "I am in the hospital with severe abdominal pain." Her voice sounded weak, not at all like the take-charge woman I'd been dealing with.

"It's nothing to do with the heart," she quickly added. "They think it's my gallbladder, and they're going to operate."

"Oh no! Are you okay?"

"Yeah, it's not a problem. Apparently, this happens a lot during the first year following a transplant. But I just wanted you to know I'm doing everything I can to be home by the time you arrive."

"You just need to take care of yourself. We can reschedule and do this in a week, a month, or whenever," I said, as a million thoughts raced through my mind. How would I tell Tara we might have to postpone the meeting? Or worse, that Patricia had to have surgery? It was now September, and Tara had been waiting to meet her since she'd learned of her in June. She'd actually been waiting to meet Taylor's heart recipient since the day we'd left the hospital.

"No, no, I want you to come," Patricia said. "If I'm still in the hospital, you're welcome to come here. I don't care if my hair is a mess or whatever; it's not a big deal to me."

I paused to figure out how I could best respond, then decided to just say it: "Tara won't enter a hospital." I knew the smells and memories of a hospital were more than she could handle.

"Oh, yeah, of course. I'm so sorry. I didn't even think of that."

"Listen, let me figure out some things on this end. Text me your husband's number, and I'll work out the details with him. I don't want you worrying about anything. I just want you to get better."

We hung up, and I sat down. Ever since we'd been in the hospital in Grand Junction and Tara had told me how important it was for her to meet the heart recipient, I'd felt this overwhelming pressure to make it happen. And more importantly, to make it a good experience. Just when it looked like the meeting was finally happening, it appeared it could all fall apart. I started to pray.

God, what's going on here? How do I tell Tara that Patricia is in the hospital and has to have surgery?

My stomach churned. The pressure of making this trip happen weighed me down. I knew how important it was to Tara. But before I made any decisions, I needed to talk to Joe, Patricia's husband, to get more information. I hoped he'd be a less-biased source and tell us honestly whether or not Patricia was up for our visit. Once I got that taken care of, I needed to talk to Tara.

I dreaded telling her.

She had been an emotional wreck all week. I knew it was because she was thinking about the trip. I was afraid she'd be set back by the disappointment of cancelling or postponing. I couldn't fathom how Tara would react if something terrible happened to Patricia. The two women had obviously been growing close, and everything was riding on this meeting.

I got Joe on the phone. "Listen, there's no pressure from us," I said. "This does not have to happen now, but your wife thinks it still can. Can you be upfront with me and let me know if she'll be okay? Or is she just saying she's all right because she wants this meeting to happen so badly?"

Joe was in the same predicament I was. Everyone wanted it to happen, but not at the expense of anyone's health—mental or physical.

"You know, she's going to make the decision. If she feels as if she can do it, she will," he said.

Over the next twenty-four hours, Patricia talked to her doctors and the surgery was scheduled for Thursday. If all went well, she'd be released from the hospital Friday morning. We were due to return to Texas midday Saturday. It was going to be crazy, but, I hoped, worth it. Less than twenty-four hours before we left, and right before Patricia underwent surgery, Tara and Patricia spoke on the phone for the first time. Their conversation was short but cemented the bond between them. It increased their desire for a face-to-face meeting.

Please, God, I begged, *You have to protect Patricia during this surgery, and You have to allow this meeting to happen.*

⁂

Our travel day was tense, until we finally received the text from Joe that Patricia was out of surgery and everything looked good. By the time we landed in Phoenix Thursday night, she was out of the recovery room and eating solid food. I breathed a huge sigh of relief and thanked God for our answered prayer. However, a lot of things still had to happen. We hoped and prayed Patricia would be released the next day and she would feel well enough to meet us. If she did, the meeting would still be on. If she didn't, I knew

Tara wouldn't go to the hospital and all our planning would have been for nothing.

Things continued to look good on Friday morning, but we knew we'd have at least six or seven hours before we would see Patricia. Tara and I hung out in downtown Phoenix, had lunch, and did some shopping. At 2:40, I got a call from one of the WFAA crew members. They had arrived and begun setting up lights, and said we should be there by 4:00. We left in plenty of time, but driving in downtown Phoenix is like driving in a lot of downtowns—not easy to get around. The one-way streets made it difficult for me to find my way back to the highway.

"Do you know where you're going?" Tara asked. She was getting anxious after the GPS seemed to be leading me in circles.

"I'm heading toward the stadium because I know I can get on the interstate near there," I said.

But somehow, I got turned around. At the next stop sign, I pulled up and paused for a second to look around and regain my bearings. "Tara, look!" I said, pointing.

"Oh my!"

Right in front of us was an Arizona State University residential building with architectural grid work on the outside. Hanging on the metal grill was a huge marble sign with white letters that read, "Taylor Place."

Tara and I stared, lost in our own thoughts. I knew we were both thinking the same thing: *Taylor is here with us.* Then a car honked, and we had to move.

"I'm calling Father Alfonse," I said. He answered the phone on the first ring. "We're on our way to meet Patricia, and you're not going to believe what just happened!" I said. "We stopped at a stop sign, and right in front of us was a big building with a sign that said Taylor Place!"

"Well, of course!" he said, laughing. "Don't you think she's there with you? Of course, she is. She's right there with you guys. But please pull over. Don't be driving and talking."

I saw a spot up ahead and eased into it while he continued to talk. As I looked around to gain my bearings, I saw a street sign, nudged Tara, and pointed.

"Father, I hate to interrupt you, but I just want you to know that I pulled over like you asked, and I'm now at the corner of Seventh and *Taylor* Streets."

He laughed again. "Of course, you are!"

Taylor Place. Taylor Street. It really felt like we were getting closer to Taylor's heart.

⚭

I wouldn't consider it hyperbole to say arriving at Patricia's home was one of the most emotional moments of our lives. Walking to the front door, Tara and I held hands. A thousand thoughts swirled through my mind. *What's this going to be like? What kind of person is she? Will I like her?* I remember having to catch my breath as we got to the door. Whatever was about to happen was going to be huge.

Tara wobbled as we made the last few steps up to the door. She had to be nervous; I was. I rang the bell and then stepped back to let Tara enter first. Joe answered the door and welcomed us in. Then Tara saw Patricia. Without saying a word, these two brave women reached out and wrapped their arms around each other. It was more than a hug; it was as if they clung to each other.

My eyes filled with tears. I knew how important this moment was for Tara, and it touched me deeply to see such a positive first impression.

The women continued their embrace—Tara's arms around Patricia's back, and Patricia's arms wrapped around Tara's neck. I tried to blink back tears as I thought about how long Tara had wanted to hug the person who had Taylor's heart. And now she was. Patricia appeared strong, though I knew how fragile she must be, just home from the hospital. I was thankful she had the strength and desire to go through with our meeting.

Almost a minute went by, and I couldn't stand it any longer. I wiped my tears away with my fingertips and joined their embrace in a three-way hug, one arm around my wife and one around the person who had my daughter's heart. The three of us stood there, just thankful to embrace each other.

The best way to explain it was that it felt like falling in love—not the romantic kind, but the kind of love you have when your first child is born. The first time you see them, you instantly love that little person, and know they belong in your family. Until you've had a child, you don't know what it feels like. But once you finally experience that kind of love, it's bigger and broader than you ever imagined. The sensation is hard to describe, but that's how I felt about Patricia. I fell in love with her as if she were the sister I never had.

But my emotions were also complicated. It was bittersweet, knowing that Taylor's heart was here only because she wasn't.

Finally we broke apart. Tara said, "I know we should probably talk or something, but I need to hear her."

Patricia took us into the kitchen and Tara sat down in a chair. Patricia grabbed her stethoscope and helped Tara insert the earpieces. Then Patricia put the head of the instrument high on her chest, just underneath the crucifix she wore around her neck. It seemed as if Patricia wanted to give this gift to Tara as much as Tara wanted to receive it. Tara looked up at me with a mixture of hope and sadness, and I reached out to hold her hand. I had no idea how Tara would react once she heard Taylor's heart, and I wanted to be with her no matter what happened next.

Patricia slowly moved the stethoscope around on her chest. "Tell me if you can hear it," she said.

Tara hesitated for a second, then looked at Patricia and closed her eyes. She nodded softly. Tara was lost in her own world, listening to the rhythmic thumping. She was very composed—peaceful and pained—all at the same time.

I felt such overwhelming relief and gratitude to God for that moment. This is the thing Tara wanted more than any other, and

I'd felt such pressure to get it for her. I'd never thought it would happen. Though I felt like we'd received so many blessings from God since Taylor's death, this was by far the biggest.

After a couple of minutes, Tara opened her eyes and said, "It's so strong."

"Oh yeah," Patricia said. "She is very strong."

Tara took off the stethoscope and handed it to me.

"I want him to hear too," she said.

I took the stethoscope and put it up to my ears.

It's hard to describe what it feels like to know that a heart beating in someone else's chest once belonged to your daughter. It was another bittersweet moment for me. I loved and hated hearing Taylor's heartbeat. I was thankful and angry. I was happy and horribly sad at the same time. There wasn't a single pure emotion; it was an awful, beautiful cocktail of contrasts.

I listened and then handed the stethoscope back to Tara. I wanted her to listen for as long as Patricia would allow.

"I'm so sorry, and I thank you at the same time," Patricia said, bursting into tears. She was a mother, and she knew what this moment meant to us—I could see it on her face. I wrapped my right arm around her, and she hugged me.

"That's all right. I'm so glad you're good," I said.

Tara listened with the stethoscope for a while, then finally took it off and set it on the table. I could see something inside her had settled. That same mixture of relief and strength I had witnessed at Jeff Kartus's house—only a million times more.

We all hugged again and then sat down. Joe had been hanging out in the corner, unsure of what his role was in all of this, but now he joined us at the table.

"How are *you* feeling?" I asked Patricia.

Joe let us know she was okay and though it had been hard, she was doing well. He was protective of her, telling her to sit down while he brought us water. They offered us chocolate Bundt cake, and we talked about our kids. We called Father Alfonse and introduced him to Patricia and Joe. We talked with him for a while, and he prayed for us over the phone. When we hung up, Patricia invited us into the living room where we would be more comfortable. Tara and Patricia sat next to each other on the couch, while Joe and I sat across the room from each other in chairs. As the four of us talked, I could see Patricia watching Tara, to make sure she was okay. And Tara was trying to mother Patricia, making sure she wasn't doing too much.

Patricia understood what it had been like for us to lose Taylor. That understanding probably came from her own near-death experiences. She told us how she had basically been in bed for eighteen hours a day and unable to do much more than lie on the couch for the remaining six. She described how hard it had been to breathe and how she had felt like such a bad mother because she couldn't take the boys to the park or to the zoo.

But Taylor's heart had changed all that.

"Do you want to listen again?" Patricia asked Tara.

"May I?" Tara asked.

"Of course!" Patricia said. "I know I would want to if our situations were reversed."

The two women sat as close as possible to each other. Soon, they were talking privately, lost in their own conversation and oblivious to the fact that Joe and I were still in the room. It was as if they were sisters, with a shared history that neither Joe nor I could relate to.

I was flooded with memories of Taylor. Of seeing Taylor smile. *Can Taylor see this?* I thought about Ryan and Peyton and wished they had come with us. But I also wondered if this was something they should see and do. Would it have been too hard for them? I was glad I didn't have to make that decision right now, and I was unsure if I ever would. What were the chances we would meet again?

Watching the women, I could see they obviously wanted this meeting to last, and Tara and I wouldn't be leaving anytime soon. "Hey, Joe, how about we go out and pick up some dinner and bring it back?" I suggested. "Maybe we can spend some time together and give them a little mom time together."

Joe agreed. As we headed out the door, I turned back to get one last glimpse of Tara. The women were so close and so comfortable with each other. They shared a space, shared their stories, and shared a stethoscope.

It took my breath away to see they also shared Taylor's heart.

—28—

Hearing Taylor's Heart

Tara

When Joe opened the door for us, and I saw Patricia for the first time, my heart began to pound. *There she is, there she is*, I thought. Patricia pulled me toward her, wrapping her arms around me. She held me as tight as she could. I did the same. There was an inexplicable bond between us, and it was created almost instantly. Seeing her, I felt a deep sense of relief. That feeling was intensified a thousand times when, a few moments later, I sat in her kitchen and heard my daughter's heart beating.

At first, all I heard was a diluted whooshing sound as Patricia searched with her stethoscope for the perfect spot on her chest. When she found it, the sounds became crystal clear.

Bump-*bump*. Bump-*bump*. Bump-*bump*. The rhythm was instantly familiar, and I recognized her heart calling out to me. It was the same distinctive sound I'd heard so many times before—lying beside her, with my head on her chest in the hospital, lying with her in her bed at home, even the very first ultrasound when she was still in my womb. A gush of warm emotion rushed over me, and I melted from the inside out. Taylor seemed to speak to me, saying

"I'm here. I'm right here." It was hard to comprehend that despite all we'd been through in the past few months, Taylor's heart had *never* stopped beating.

An overwhelming sensation of love filled me. I felt a connection with Taylor and with Patricia. I knew it wasn't physical; there was no reason for us to bond so quickly or for me to connect with Taylor's heart in the way I had. The connection was a spiritual one. The Holy Spirit is the great Comforter, and I felt as if He had embraced me and wrapped me in the comfort of knowing my daughter was safe. I finally felt the connection that I had so longed for. It was overwhelming, in such a beautiful way.

⚬

After the guys left to get food, Patricia and I sat alone in her living room, and I felt safe asking her a very intimate question.

"I'd like to hear her heartbeat like I used to—without a stethoscope. Can I put my head on your chest?"

"Of course," Patricia said, wrapping her arm around me and pulling me closer. With my eyes closed, I pressed my ear against her warm skin, marveling at the sound of my daughter's heart pumping in Patricia's chest.

Bump-*bump*. Bump-*bump*. Bump-*bump*. BOOM.

Suddenly there had been a loud kick. I waited a second, then sat up and looked at Patricia.

"Did you feel that?" she asked.

"Yes. I did."

I put my ear back to her chest—and BOOM! It happened again, like a huge kick. "What was that?" I asked.

"That was Taylor," Patricia said with a smile on her face.

"Does she do that often?"

"It's never happened before," she said. "But while you were listening, I was praying to God and asking Him to give you a sign from Taylor."

I was speechless.

"Just as soon as I finished praying, I felt it," Patricia said. "I've never felt anything like that before. But until you said something, I didn't know if you could feel it too."

By now, we were both tearing up again. The same warm feeling that washed over me in the kitchen flooded through me again. It was a precious gift from God, from Taylor, and from Patricia. I would never forget it.

∞

The guys were gone a while, and as Patricia and I continued to talk, she asked me to tell her more about Taylor. I talked about how fun she was, the silly things she did with her friends, and how she always took care of the outsiders. I told her about how I would lie next to Taylor at night and we'd talk about her day. And boys.

"Right before she fell asleep, she always did the same thing," I said. "She'd tuck her Pooh bear *behind* her." I had thought that was so odd. I told Patricia how one night I asked her about it. "Why don't you snuggle with him?"

Taylor had said, "Because when I'm really tired, and I turn over, he's just there. I don't have to find him."

"I thought it was kind of silly," I told Patricia, "but once she said it, I totally understood. He was just there for her when she needed him."

"She liked Pooh?" Patricia asked, a smile forming at the corners of her mouth.

"She loved Pooh!"

"Did I tell you I have a Pooh tattoo on my right hip?"

"No way!" I said, laughing.

She showed me her Pooh tattoo and told me all about her Winnie the Pooh collection, which was now in her boys' rooms. It felt like the invisible bond we had the moment I walked in the door had only grown tighter.

When the guys returned, I told Todd about Patricia's love of all things Pooh and then about the kick in her heart after she prayed to God for a sign of Taylor. As he listened, his eyes grew wide and a smile spread across his face.

"Of course!" he said when I finished.

I witnessed a deep sense of peace settle over him.

I recognized it, because I felt it too.

Finally, at midnight, we tore ourselves away. Patricia had just gotten out of the hospital, and she needed to rest and recover.

None of us wanted our visit to end, so we decided to meet for breakfast in the morning before Todd and I headed to the airport to catch our flight. The next morning, the good feelings continued. Patricia brought her stethoscope so I could listen one more time. It was so hard to say goodbye to her. We both wanted to connect again, but we were unsure of how or when it would happen.

But we each had faith it would.

ↂ

On the flight home, I turned to Todd and said, "This was a gift from God."

He smiled at me.

It was similar to what he'd said to me on the plane home from Denver, but now I understood it at a deeper, more profound level than I had before. Knowing that Taylor's heart had *never* stopped beating was a powerful and overwhelming thought; I was in awe. From the beginning of time, God knew that Taylor's heart needed to be with someone who wanted to connect as much as we did. And now He had made that happen. So many donor families want to meet their loved one's organ recipients but never have the opportunity. I knew God's hands were all over this—I could see His fingerprints in everything that had happened. It was only because of His grace that we had the privilege of experiencing this.

Though I didn't like it when Pam Cope first said it, by now I had come to believe we had, indeed, been handpicked for this. After meeting Patricia, I believed she had also been handpicked by God to give Taylor's heart a new home.

❖

Though the story began as a local piece about hearing Taylor's heart, our story and the foundation ended up receiving national attention when *Good Morning America* showed the piece to their audience and the hosts were clearly moved by our story. A week later, both Patricia and Joe and our family were invited to go to New York to tell our story in person on *The Today Show*.

Those who are grieving like to be distracted. Sometimes they choose inappropriate ways like alcohol or drugs, but for Todd and me, it seemed God had blessed us with some healthy distractions.

Like Ryan and Peyton.

Blue sundresses with a Taylor label.

Or friends who made me earn points by planting tomatoes.

And now this trip.

It was such a blessing to have something to look forward to. And I couldn't wait to see Patricia again.

—29—

Trust While Doing

Todd

I felt as if I had learned to trust God in new ways when I quit my job and we started Taylor's Gift. But I still struggled knowing what my roles and responsibilities were in this new partnership. I knew I was supposed to trust God to make things happen, but did that mean I should sit back and not do anything? Just wait for Him to do it all? Or was I supposed to do something—use the gifts and talents He'd blessed me with to further the mission of Taylor's Gift Foundation? And if so, how much of me and how much of Him?

Until this point, there had been very little of the old Todd *doing*. I had spent most of the previous months responding to the things God brought our way, and I had no doubt He had blessed us abundantly. However, as we prepared for the New York trip and for the *Today Show*, I wrestled with whether or not I should call some of my media connections to see if we could do more interviews while we were in NYC. Didn't it make sense to maximize our time and the foundation's exposure? On the other hand, so far I hadn't made any calls to media—they called us—so maybe I should sit back and see what else God would do.

It was a dilemma that got at the heart of who I am.

Am I a doer or a truster?

Around that time, I came across Psalm 131 in the Message version of the Bible: "God, I'm not trying to rule the roost, I don't want to be king of the mountain. I haven't meddled where I have no business or fantasized grandiose plans. I've kept my feet on the ground, I've cultivated a quiet heart" (vv. 1–2). That passage spoke to me. I hadn't fantasized grandiose plans. I had kept my feet solidly on the ground, and I didn't want to rule the roost. I just wanted to help sick people get healthy through organ donation.

I decided God would want me to use the talents and connections He'd blessed me with to further what He was already doing. I was also pretty sure those on the list waiting for organs would want the same. I was doing what I was doing not for any glory for me—I wasn't trying to be king of the mountain—I just wanted Taylor's life and death to have a purpose and meaning. So I picked up the phone and called a friend of mine in New York with lots of media connections. I told him about Taylor's Gift and how we were trying to get the message about organ donation out to as many people as possible. "We're going to be in New York in a couple of weeks to do *The Today Show*. Is there anyone else we should connect with while we're there?"

"I know a lot of people who would be interested," my friend said. "Let me make a few phone calls and get back to you."

I'd done what I could do. The rest was up to God—that's where the trust came in.

That's also where God worked.

◦⊰◦

I finally felt as if I'd found the balance between trusting and doing. As we prepared for the New York trip, I captured a couple of thoughts on my blog:

252

I am constantly drawn to two things. The first is what my grandfather instilled in me: It's not what happens to you that matters, but how you react to it that does.

The second is Taylor's favorite verse, from Luke 18:27 (NIV): What is impossible with men is possible with God.

More than anything else, these two thoughts were my vision for Taylor's Gift. Yes, we'd lost our daughter and that wasn't fair. We didn't have a choice about whether she lived or died. But faced with her loss, the question remained: How would we react to it?

The foundation was our answer.

We also knew that moving the needle on the number of organ donors wouldn't be easy. And, frankly, the kind of media attention we were getting was in the realm of the impossible. What nonprofit less than a year old could land segments on the two most-viewed morning shows? But what was impossible with men was possible with God. We were proof of that.

Whenever I dropped Taylor off at school, I would say, "Make someone's day better." I liked to think that's what we were doing with Taylor's Gift. We were working to make someone's day better through the gift of organ donation. While reflecting on the things that had happened over the past few weeks and the things scheduled for the next few days, I wrote:

> None of this would be possible without God choosing us for this journey. We are blessed. This is just a small step in the life-changing work that Taylor's Gift Foundation will make in this world. Taylor is proud of all our work, but there is so much more ahead of us.

c⅜o

The last time I had been in New York City with my family was at the beginning of November 2006, when I'd run the New York Marathon. Tara, Taylor, and Ryan had come to cheer me on; Peyton was too young, so she had stayed at home with grandparents.

I had planned my work schedule around the event so I could be in the city with my family for a few days. I would work during the day, and when I finished I'd join Tara and the kids in exploring Manhattan. The city was special to Tara and me. It was where our relationship had moved from friendship to something more. We had taken the kids to the top of the Empire State Building and to Little Italy, where we had pointed out the restaurant Tara and I ate in when we were dating. It had been one of the best trips we'd ever been on. We had been thrilled when the kids loved it as much as we did.

As the plane descended into New York, I pointed out buildings in the skyline to Ryan and Peyton. I had an immediate sense of déjà vu. I remembered pointing out the same buildings on our last trip. It was the same son, but this time, a different daughter.

Patricia, Joe, and their boys were staying in the same hotel as we were, and they were waiting for us in the lobby. We had introductions all around, lots of hugs, and a few tears. It felt like a reunion.

After checking in, the whole crowd went out for dinner. We had a great time talking, laughing, and getting to know one another better. When we returned to the hotel room, Tara and Patricia were still texting back and forth when suddenly Tara said, "Ryan and Peyton, Mrs. Winters has her stethoscope. Would you like to hear Taylor's heart?"

Patricia was thoughtful enough to have brought her stethoscope, and she thought the kids might want to hear their sister's heartbeat again.

"I would!" Peyton said eagerly.

"I don't want to," Ryan said.

There wasn't a right or wrong answer. So Ryan and I stayed in our room while Tara and Peyton went up to Patricia's, where Peyton heard her sister's heart beating for the first time since her death.

Tara told me later that as soon as Peyton heard it, she looked up and locked eyes with Patricia, and they both smiled. Tara snapped a picture at that exact moment and showed it to me. It was incredible to see.

The next morning, I woke to the sound of rain and got up to read my Bible. In my journal I wrote:

Sitting in the Essex House Hotel in New York City. Began the morning with the Bible. I love reading the YouVersion on the iPad. Today starts with Psalm 126, "And now, God, do it again. Bring rains to our drought-stricken lives."

God is raining His blessings and glory and love on us. Yes, it is raining outside, and the rain pounds the window over our hotel room. I know You are here. I know You are with me.

Before we left the hotel, I prayed God would bless our story by using it to inspire and motivate viewers to become registered organ donors.

⁂

Being behind the scenes of *The Today Show* was an amazing experience, not only for the kids but for the adults too. Tara and I sat on the couch with Patricia between us. The three of us held hands. There was an energy among us, but no one was nervous because we had each other. Though the footage they showed made us tear up, we all stayed strong. Throughout the interview, I felt like I was at the center of God's will. I knew that sharing Taylor's story was helping to save lives—like Patricia's.

Later in the day the kids wanted to see the Empire State Building. On the way, I thought about Ryan and wondered if he remembered the last time we had visited. A feeling of nostalgia washed over me—we were doing the same things we'd done on the last family trip, only this time with Peyton. Back then, Ryan had been the younger brother—the middle child. Now he was the older brother and the oldest. Things had changed for all of us.

Being at the top of the Empire State Building is really cool. But until I'm up there, I forget that it can also be a little scary. That high up, the wind is stronger than you expect, and for some reason, looking down makes the distance to the ground seem a lot greater than when you're on the sidewalk looking up.

That night, like always, I had my camera with me. I lined up the kids and Tara so I could take their picture. Looking through the camera lens, I realized it was the same spot I'd taken a picture of Tara, Taylor, and Ryan years earlier. I was flooded with memories of Taylor and our last trip to New York, but I tried not to let my emotions show. I didn't want to ruin the experience for anyone else.

But it didn't get any easier. Ryan and Peyton chose the very same coin-activated binocular viewer that he and Taylor had argued over last time we were there. At the time, I had only one quarter, and they had to take turns. Watching Ryan go through the same motions, this time with Peyton, I thought about how much things had changed. Who was I back then? That dad would never have suspected how limited his time with his kids really was. Just like the quarter would buy only so many minutes with the binoculars, time would run out and the view would never be the same.

I was still in a nostalgic mood as we made our way back to the hotel. We passed street vendors selling jewelry, handbags, and sunglasses. A dark-haired woman had children's artwork for sale. The colors caught my eye, and I saw that they were a combination of painting and calligraphy, and each picture spelled out a child's name. When I looked up from the table, the picture on display made me stop and look again. In flowing letters and vibrant colors, it spelled: TAYLOR.

Once again, I felt as if she were with us.

I stopped to take her picture.

⚬⟡⚬

Over the next few weeks, as the stats came in, we began to see the number of registered donors increasing nationwide. To me, it was a confirmation that we were doing exactly what we should be doing. The numbers were proof. It was very satisfying to know that our story and Taylor's Gift had played at least a small part in getting that needle to move up.

I thought back to the conversation I'd had with Tara about how one day I wanted to see Taylor and hear her say, "Good job, Daddy! You did it!"

What would she think about all of this? I closed my eyes and thought about all the people we'd met and how our world had grown. *What do you think, baby? We're not there yet, but I am giving it everything I've got.*

A vision came to mind of Taylor laughing and saying, "Let's do this, Dad. Let's get this stuff done. This is how we can save the world!"

And for a moment, all felt right.

—30—

The Bike Rider
Leaves a Message

JONATHAN FINGER
COLORADO

For the first time since his teens, Jonathan was once again riding his mountain bike. It was an exhilarating sensation. After spending so many years on the couch, tethered to a machine, the open air felt like freedom. Though it had taken eight years, Jonathan finally had a new kidney. After his mother's donated kidney had failed, he had vowed to do everything he could to make sure the next one—if there was a next one—lasted as long as it possibly could. Now that he finally had it, he was eating right, exercising, and making sure he kept his scheduled doctor's appointments.

It was at one of those appointments that the social worker came in with a large manila envelope and said, "This is from the donor's family. Do you want to see it?"

Jonathan had wanted to connect with them from the beginning. In fact, he'd started a letter to them several times but had

259

never quite found the right words to finish it. He eagerly took the envelope, and when she left the room, he opened it.

Jonathan already knew what to expect—he'd been told the donor was a young female. Since he assumed most organ donors were much older, he thought that meant she was in her fifties or sixties. He liked to think she'd been sick for a long time and that her family was ready for her to go. But when he opened the envelope, a picture of a young girl slid out onto the floor. Jonathan was stunned. He picked up the photo and studied it, then emptied out the contents of the envelope. There were multiple pictures of the young girl and her family, accompanied by a four-page letter written by her mom.

Jonathan was immediately engrossed. The letter described who the young girl was, what she believed, and all the things she had done in her short life. It made him feel incredibly emotional. In an instant, he felt a connection to her and her family. Even without knowing them, he already thought of them as family. He remembered the letter he'd begun to write months earlier when he didn't know anything about her. Now that letter wouldn't suffice. He'd have to rewrite it before he sent it off.

But before he could, a virus set him back. Though it didn't put the kidney at risk, he was hospitalized for a while. He postponed writing the letter until he was better.

Too soon, November arrived, and the holidays were sneaking up on Jonathan. He worried that sending the letter through Donor Alliance would take too long. He wanted the family to know how thankful he was *before* Christmas. He debated about what he should do.

On November 16, while watching the local news, he saw a story about the Avalanche—the local NHL hockey team, who was playing the Dallas Stars that night. Both teams were honoring a girl who'd lived in one team's state and had died in the other's. He immediately recognized the picture of the girl they showed on the news. This was his donor!

As the story continued, Jonathan knew he couldn't wait any longer. Instead of mailing his letter, he picked up the phone and dialed the 1-800 number listed on the foundation website, and left the most awkward message of his life.

—31—

First Holidays

Tara

After returning from New York, Todd and I had to stop by Austin Elementary, where Taylor and Ryan had gone and where Peyton now attended. While we were there, a custodian stopped me and said, "Can I talk to you a minute?" She went on to tell me how her fifteen-year-old son was facing a medical issue with his heart, and it was affecting his behavior and attitude. He was leaving home and not coming back, not taking his medicine, and exhibiting other self-destructive behaviors.

"How do you cope with this?" the woman asked.

Our situations weren't the same—Taylor had died in an accident; her son was facing a long-term illness and possibly death if he didn't make some adjustments in his lifestyle. However, I understood her fear and the feeling that things were spiraling out of control. I knew how helpless she must have felt, so I said, "When I feel like you do, I pray." I then asked if I could pray for her and her son.

She nodded, trying to hold back the tears.

I knew I didn't have any concrete answers for her. Tragedy strikes different people in different ways, and the only sure thing is that

God understands our pain and will help us get through it. That was the best I could offer—a way to connect with Him. Todd was with me and joined me in praying for her. On the way home Todd said, "It really touched me when you ministered to her. Knowing how much pain you are still carrying, it was just so beautiful to see you reach out to her even in the midst of your own grief."

His words meant a lot. He was right; I dealt with a lot of pain, and I wasn't sure I could say it had lessened much. But I had come a long way from those initial days. Some days I still felt like I had a long way to go.

A few days later, I was reading Scripture when I came across 1 Peter 5:10. "The suffering won't last forever. It won't be long before this generous God who has great plans for us in Christ—eternal and glorious plans they are!—will have you put together and on your feet for good" (Message).

I already knew the good days on earth were temporary; my faith told me the bad days would soon end too. My hope was in God, not in my own ability to fix things.

∾

Among the amazing people we'd met was Ralph Strangis, the play-by-play announcer for the Dallas Stars. Ralph wanted to use his NHL connections to support Taylor's Gift, and he had worked tirelessly with the Dallas Stars to put together a fund-raiser.

The plan was to present Taylor's Gift Night at American Airlines Center, the home stadium of the Dallas Stars, on November 16, when the Stars played the Avalanche, the Colorado team. One team was from the state where Taylor had lived, and the other team was from the state where she'd died; both teams joined to support one cause.

Coaches, broadcasters, and staff from both the Stars and the Avalanche planned to wear blue Taylor's Gift ties. During warmups, players from each team would wrap their sticks in blue tape, and during the game, tables would be set up in the arena to give fans an opportunity to register as organ donors. They could also support the foundation through donations in the merchandise stores. In exchange, they would receive Taylor's Gift wristbands. Ralph would interview us during the first intermission, and the Stars would donate proceeds from ticket sales to the foundation.

It was an unbelievable opportunity and our whole family planned to go.

❖

On November 16, my parents and Todd's parents met us at the house, where we hung out until it was time to leave for the hockey game. I was always nervous before foundation events. They often required me to speak publicly, and I hated that. Even private conversations could be awkward. People wanted to hear our story, and I didn't want to tell it for fear of breaking down in public. But despite my anxieties, the awkward moments were worth it if they resulted in more people signing up to become donors.

I invited our parents into our bedroom to show them some things on the computer. "Here's what the new website looks like," I said, pulling up the latest version. I talked about how much work it took to create it and all of the volunteers and companies that were involved. "And we just got a 1-800 number," I said. "It's so cool because people can leave messages on it. When they leave a message, it transcribes it and emails it to us."

While I was showing them, an email came through with the subject "Google Voice."

"Oh, look! We just got one," I said. "Let's see what it says." I clicked it open and began to read the transcript of the call out loud.

"Hi, my name is Jonathan Finger, and I received one of your daughter's kidneys. You sent me a letter. It was blue—" I stopped reading and looked up to see four sets of wide eyes staring back at me. "Todd! Where's Todd?"

"I think he's upstairs working on the foosball table," his mother said.

I ran to the living room and yelled, "Todd! You've got to come here right now!"

Todd came right down. This time, instead of reading the transcript, I turned up the speaker and played the voice message so we could hear what he sounded like. When it finished, I played it again. And again.

We marveled at the incredible timing and the fact we all got to hear the call together.

It was such a blessing to have received Jonathan's call. It had been more than six months since I'd sent the letter to Donor Alliance, and we hadn't heard from any of the other donors. I was afraid no one else wanted to make contact. But with Jonathan's call, we had now connected with three out of the five. And in time, I believed that we would eventually connect with them all.

That night, I didn't have to be anxious at all. Just as God had given me the blue dress to talk about at that first fund-raising dinner, He gave me Jonathan to talk about at the hockey game.

"You'll never believe what happened today," I said when people wanted to chat, and then told them about the phone call.

It took us a couple of weeks to respond to Jonathan, but we finally did. Like Patricia, our early communication with Jonathan was through texts and emails. We learned that this was his second kidney transplant and he'd been on dialysis for eight years! He talked about the freedom he had now. I couldn't imagine a bigger life change.

Because of Jonathan's tech background, he and Todd also started to communicate via online chats. Soon Jonathan volunteered his talents for the new website. He became an active volunteer for the foundation.

As Todd and Jonathan worked together, they found out they shared a lot in common. Like Todd, Jonathan played several instruments, and they had a shared love of rock music. One day, while they were chatting online, they discovered they even shared the same birthday, though Jonathan was a few years younger. Just as

Patricia and I had connected so deeply, now Jonathan and Todd were doing the same thing. Once again, it was as if God had orchestrated the whole thing.

oŝo

We knew our first holidays without Taylor would be hard, and we made intentional choices to minimize our pain. At Thanksgiving, for example, we didn't want to do anything we'd ever done before. We thought that meant we didn't want to be around our families and all the painful reminders of Thanksgivings past. So we rented a little cabin in Broken Bow, Oklahoma. It was far enough away from our memories and within our little budget.

We packed a ton of food and lots of games for the kids and looked forward to some great family time. Todd wanted to grill out, and I wanted to chill out. He looked forward to chopping wood, teaching the kids how to whittle, and making a fire in the fireplace. At night, he planned to take the kids outside to look up at the stars. We all wanted to make new family traditions so reminders of our old ones weren't ever-present.

Unfortunately, what we got was a lot of time alone with our thoughts. The first morning, Todd woke up and couldn't walk. He'd dislocated his back while moving the foosball table, and apparently his back had locked up on the drive to the cabin. He spent the entire trip sitting in a recliner because he was in so much pain. No fires, no grilling, no staring at the stars, no chopping wood, and no whittling. The only time he got up was to hobble to the table for meals.

I cooked every single breakfast, lunch, and dinner, and made all the snacks. I played games with the kids, drove to the local pharmacy for Todd's prescriptions, and when it wasn't raining (which was rare), took walks in the woods with the kids. There was very little chilling for me and a whole lot of doing. A few days into the trip, I began to resent Todd. I wanted him to be there for me emotionally and physically; instead, I was taking care of him.

It wasn't until later that I realized he'd probably felt the same way about me for months. How selfish of me to feel that way.

⋄

Thanksgiving Day wasn't easy. I knew it wouldn't be. I woke up missing Taylor. All day long, past Thanksgiving Day memories flashed through my mind. I would briefly indulge them—Taylor's first Thanksgiving, later years of her eating her favorite casseroles, or watching the parades on TV. When the memories got too painful, I'd shove them away.

Around 11:00, I put the food in the oven and sat down with Todd while I waited for it to finish cooking. He was watching a pregame show in anticipation of an afternoon of football. Without warning, James Brown, one of the hosts of *The NFL Today* on CBS, introduced a Thanksgiving story about blessings and inspiration. I had been lost in my own thoughts, but those words caught my attention.

A video began to play, and I watched the mother of former Cincinnati Bengals receiver Chris Henry tell her story. Chris had died eleven months earlier in a tragic accident. At the time, his mother had made the difficult decision to donate his organs. As the eight-minute story unfolded, I watched as she met the four recipients—four lives that his organs had saved, four families that had been forever changed because of his gift.

I couldn't help it; I started to cry.

Each of the recipients talked about how much they wanted to thank her for their life-changing gift. One recipient's husband said, "Life isn't about the number of breaths you take; it's about the moments that take your breath away." Meeting the mother of his wife's donor was one of those moments.

I knew exactly how each of them felt.

Chris's mother explained how the recipients had become like family to her. At the end of the piece, she said, "People of faith believe that people journey into one's life for a reason. Of course

268

my family will never be the same, but it will also never be bigger. For that, on this and every other day, I will truly, truly be forever thankful."

By this point, I was bawling. The kids, sensing the change in my mood, had wandered in to see what was going on. I tried to pull myself together and use it as a teaching moment. "Look how many people are talking about organ donation now. Did you ever think you'd see that on an NFL pregame show?"

If a national conversation about organ donation was starting, that was something to be truly thankful for. It felt great to see the exposure the issue was getting. But at the same time, I knew the only reason we even paid attention to the issue was because Taylor was gone. It was impossible not to feel sadness along with our gratefulness.

That Thanksgiving taught us a lot of lessons. We'd thought that being away from family would ease our pain, but being left to our own thoughts, without the added chaos of our family to distract us, just left us with a different kind of pain.

Most of all we learned we couldn't run from our pain—it only followed us.

❧

We made it through Thanksgiving, and our friends asked what we were doing for Christmas. My standard response was, "I just want to go to bed and wake up on the second of January." We both knew we needed to celebrate and put up decorations for the sake of Ryan and Peyton, but it was beyond our ability. Finally, friends suggested that if we got out the tree and a few boxes of decorations, they would put them up for us. So that's what we did. We left the house, and they came over and decorated the house beautifully. Nothing was in its usual place, so it was at once familiar and completely different at the same time.

It was perfect and it was a huge gift to me.

Todd

Grief was an ocean with waves continually crashing along the shoreline. Sometimes the waves were small—powerless to do much. Other days their power was enough to rock me in their wake, but if I was strong enough I'd meld and move with them so they couldn't harm me. The worst were those that pounded against me all day, threatening, like a riptide, to pull me under. Just as I'd catch my breath, an eight-footer would rise up and crash over my head, leaving me gasping for air.

Right after Taylor died, people would ask, "How are you?" As the months passed, that slowed down a bit. However, with the holidays so close, I found myself answering that question more frequently. The answer was never simple. It truly depended on the moment. For example, the fifteenth day of each month was hard because it reminded us of March 15, the day Taylor died. On those days, I often found myself supporting Tara in some way. But as Tara and the kids developed better coping skills, it was as if I could take a break from being their protector. It was then I found myself starting to slip into the abyss of grief.

That's what happened on December 15, the worst of the nine "fifteens" I'd experienced since Taylor's death.

That morning, I found myself listening to, and involved in, conversations with people planning their upcoming ski trips. Each one reminded me of my beautiful daughter. I remembered how excited she had been just nine months earlier as she got ready for our ski trip. She had been so excited to get out on the slopes and experience it all.

I'd learned enough in therapy to know that trying to run or hide from the waves of grief wouldn't help. I had learned to embrace the water. Tread. Stand. Paddle. Just let the waves rock me. It's when you fight against the waves that you lose your footing and go under. Riding them will take you back to shore. So after those morning reminders of what I'd lost, I tried to get busy. I spent most of the day in my office working on operations and accounting issues for Taylor's Gift. And the seas calmed for a bit.

But late in the afternoon the waves were back, slamming against my mind. I had gone to finish some Christmas shopping, and while I was running some errands those persistent waves seemed to find their way into my car, making it hard to think. I pulled into a parking space as my brain sloshed. It felt like seaweed: tumbling in the waves but never going anywhere.

During those moments, I tend to get very reflective and often I try to write, jotting down notes so I can think things through more thoroughly. It was my way of riding the waves until the swells stopped. But the memories kept coming—wave after wave of them. It felt like a high tide of grief, and my arms were tired; I couldn't swim anymore. I put down my pen. Nothing seemed to calm the raging waters of my grief.

By the time I got home, I was tired and sluggish. The back pain that had plagued me since Thanksgiving ached down to my toes. Maybe the grief exaggerated it that day; it was hard to tell. All I wanted was sleep. It was the only thing that would stop the emotional tides and the physical pain.

Around 8:10 p.m. we heard a knock at the door. I opened it to find the entire Coppell High School choir; they were Christmas caroling. Tara and the kids joined me at the door, and as they sang I felt the waves calm and roll back out to sea. *Thank you, God! This is exactly what I needed.*

After a couple of traditional carols, they finished with "Man in the Mirror," a song about looking at yourself and making a change. Tara and I immediately got the message, and as we did, we both teared up. Somehow, in the beauty of that moment, my pain dulled.

Before they left, the group presented us with a check for fifteen hundred dollars—money they'd raised from programs the choir had put on to support Taylor's Gift. Tara and I were touched by their selfless generosity.

As we said good night and closed the door, I knew we were blessed—genuinely blessed to be part of such a wonderful community.

That night I went to bed early. I hugged and kissed Tara and the kids, including a hug and kiss to Taylor in heaven. I said my prayers, and before I fell asleep I got out my notebook and wrote. The next day I would post it on my blog:

> I miss her so much, but know she is with me all the time. Thanks for being there with me, Christ. Thank you for allowing me to process this grief and put it to good use each and every day . . . and when I don't feel I can, continue to show me the path.
>
> Another day. Another 15th.
> Good night.

—32—

Change of Hearts

Tara

Christmas was miserable.

We spent it with my family in Louisiana. Like we had done with Thanksgiving, we chose to spend the day away from home so we wouldn't have to relive all the memories of Christmases past. My extended family went the extra mile to make Christmas a merry time for Ryan and Peyton. They surrounded all of us with love, laughter, and tons of Cajun food.

We were in survival mode. There's not much else to say about Thanksgiving, Christmas, and New Year's, except to thank God we made it through them. At least, I figured, the New Year meant we'd made it through our first year of holidays.

A few days later I headed to Walmart to pick up a few supplies. At the entrance, I suddenly stopped. Though it was only the first week of January, I was visually assaulted with an overwhelming abundance of pink and red. I'd been so worried about Thanksgiving and Christmas that I hadn't even considered Valentine's Day. It was one of my favorite holidays to celebrate with the kids. Every year I decorated the house and had presents for everyone at the table. I always made a pink-and-red dinner with ham, strawberries, pink mashed potatoes, and cherry 7-Up. It was my day to say, "I love you so much I'm about to burst!"

I felt as though my heart had already burst while standing in Walmart. And it only got worse as February 14 got closer. A few weeks later, when I went to buy candy for my kids, I found that the things they loved best were all packaged in threes. Three Hershey's kisses. Three SpongeBob candies. Three chocolate-covered marshmallow hearts. *I don't have three anymore.*

Valentine's Day not only snuck up on me, it sucker punched me when I wasn't watching.

One more holiday to dread.

⚘

A few days before Valentine's Day, I heard the front door open and in walked Ana Lucia Cottone, the network executive we'd met at the Donate Life Film Festival. She was the one who'd told me the story about the clay Buddha that cracked, exposing gold underneath. We'd kept in touch and become good friends. I loved her no-nonsense style. She would say whatever was on her mind.

We'd often talked about getting together again, and knowing that pink and red were out for this Valentine's Day and "blue" was in, Todd wanted to surprise me by flying her in.

"I'm here for a week!" she announced.

I took one look at my messy house, hugged her, and burst into tears.

Ana Lucia was, in fact, the exact Valentine my heart needed. She wasn't the kind of person who let you lie around and mope. While she was extremely sympathetic, gentle, and kind, she was also willing to do whatever she could to help us get on with life. I must have looked like I really *needed* that help. By the evening of her first day, she said, "Do you ever look at yourself in the mirror and just talk to yourself?"

"No."

"You need to see yourself go through this," she said, standing me in front of a mirror. "You need to take a good look at yourself."

I looked at the face in the mirror, and it was a shock. I'd lost a lot of weight, my cheeks were gaunt, and my eyes were sunken. I looked five years older. Up to that point, I had no idea how bad I looked.

"Look at yourself and say, 'I'm going to be okay,'" she said.

Studying myself in the mirror, I resolved to do better. I had concentrated all of my available energy on taking care of Ryan and Peyton. I wasn't doing anything for myself.

But Ana Lucia wasn't just about making me better. She wanted the whole family better. When she found out we hadn't sat at the kitchen table and eaten dinner as a family since Taylor had died, she made us do it. It was hard at first, because no one knew where to sit. Were we supposed to leave Taylor's chair empty? Ana Lucia didn't care. She sat in a different chair every time, disrupting our old family traditions and helping us create new ones.

Though I was proud of the progress Ryan had made—he was adjusting well to school and had started staying through the whole mass at St. Ann's instead of leaving—it wasn't enough for Ana Lucia. She noticed that Ryan and Peyton were still sleeping in the guest room, one in the bed and the other on the floor.

"All right, this is what we're going to do," Ana Lucia said. "Ryan's room is going to be his hangout. Peyton's room will be her playroom. And we're moving both of their beds into the game room. That way, they can each sleep in their own bed but still be in the same room together."

"No, I don't really like that idea because they need to be in their own bedrooms," I said.

"But they're not in their bedrooms now, right?"

"You're right," I admitted.

So I discussed it with the kids, and we all agreed. We invited friends over to help us move the furniture. When we finished, Ryan and Peyton each slept in his or her own bed in the same room.

Ana Lucia's presence was like a fresh breeze in a stale house. She shook up our entrenched grief patterns and showed us new ways of seeing ourselves. She reminded me that it wasn't enough to just get through; I needed to learn to take care of myself again. I knew she was right. If I took care of myself, I'd also be better at taking care of my husband and kids. It was the best Valentine's Day gift I could have asked for.

Todd

March loomed large.

As January became February, March cast its shadow backward onto my heart. Not only did the upcoming March present the one-year anniversary of the skiing accident and Taylor's death, but it would also be our first spring break without Taylor. As the one-year anniversary drew closer, I couldn't stop thinking about it. Just as Tara and the kids' emotional stock seemed to be rising, mine seemed to be tanking.

In addition, I was filled with self-doubt. I was worried about how we were going to hold everything together financially. Not only did we have a lot of start-up and ongoing costs for the foundation, but the donations weren't coming in like I'd hoped. This put our foundation work and our family's financial position in jeopardy. If money didn't come into the foundation, I didn't get a salary.

After several days of being in a horrible mood and doubting everything in my life, I started asking myself some angry questions. *What the heck am I doing here? Why am I doing this? Where is God?* I didn't see God working, and I began to wonder if He'd left and I hadn't followed—or worse, that maybe He'd never been in this in the first place. I felt alone and I wanted out. I was in a bad place, a place no words could describe. I called Judy, our counselor, and asked if I could come in for an emergency appointment. She agreed.

The appointment was set for the afternoon, but before I left I had a talk with Tara. "I'm beginning to think that it's just me who wanted to do this, that it's not God's plan for us," I said, referring to my foundation work.

"What makes you say that?"

"I feel as if I am trying to control it, and I don't want to. Where is God in all of this? I need a sign from Him that this is what He wants and that He's still in charge. I'm just not seeing it."

Tara tried to comfort me, but she didn't have any answers either.

On my drive to Judy's office, Pauline Stein called. She was the friend who'd held the first Taylor's Gift fund-raiser in her backyard. She was a close adviser to the foundation and an even closer friend. As we talked, I could feel my anxiety and tension building. I was short with her, and I knew she heard it.

"You sound stressed. Are you?" she asked.

"On a scale of one to ten, I'm about an eleven hundred," I said.

"Tell me what you're stressed about."

So, I unloaded on her. I told her I had a lot of self-doubt. I was worried about the finances. Donations hadn't been coming in to the foundation like we'd hoped, and there were a lot of expenses. "I'm not even sure I'm doing what God wants anymore."

Pauline comforted me with words of affirmation and then prayed for me. Our conversation helped me be in a better place. Her call meant a lot. She reminded me I wasn't alone in this.

I arrived on time for my appointment with Judy and filled her in on my day. "But I felt a little better after talking to Pauline," I said.

"Why is that?"

"She reminded me of why I started this in the first place and that this was God's work, not mine, which He's proven so many times." Even as Pauline had said it, I knew God could prove it again.

Judy gave me some great advice about taking care of myself and being patient when I didn't see results right away. I knew she was right. I hadn't been eating or sleeping well, and I rarely exercised anymore. By the time I left her office, I felt as if there were some things I could do to help improve my mood. But I wasn't sure there was anything I could do to improve my situation. Only God could do that.

At the end of the day, I thought about stopping by a local restaurant and bar owned by friends who had done a lot to support the foundation. It was the Coppell watering hole and the center for local politics and conversation. But as I got in the car, I felt a strong compulsion to go straight home, so I did. When I arrived, Tara met me at the door with a smile on her face. "You're never going to believe what just happened."

She told me that while I was out, a boy Taylor's age had come to the door and asked for me. When she told him I wasn't home, he handed her an envelope and asked her to give it to me.

"He said it was an anonymous donation and his mom wanted him to give it to you," Tara said.

She looked for a car and didn't see one, so she asked him to write his mom's name and phone number on the envelope so we could call and thank her. And then he left.

Tara handed me the note from the envelope. It was short and basically said, "We see all the sacrifices you're making, and we appreciate all that you're doing. Keep going."

"That was nice," I said to Tara. It was so encouraging and just what I needed after the day I'd had.

With an even broader smile on her face, Tara handed me the check that accompanied the note. The first thing I noticed was that it was not a donation for the foundation; it was for us personally. I burst into tears when I read the amount.

The check was for *nine thousand dollars.*

I was stunned at the generosity and timing of the gift. It was as if God Himself had written the cashier's check and handed it to me personally. I looked at the check for more clues as to the donor and noticed it was dated *two days* earlier.

The whole time I had doubted, God already had a check prepared. Of course. *Who was I to ask God for a sign?*

How great He was to give me one anyway.

Tara

With only a few days left in February, I was dreading the month of March, but something happened to change all that. I was in the living room when I got a phone call from Eleanor, my sorority sister from college. She now lived in Pacific Palisades, and we hadn't talked in a while, so I picked up the phone eager to see how she was doing.

"I know this is a long shot," she said, "but I have tickets for *The Ellen DeGeneres Show* coming up, and I was wondering if you could come out and go with me?"

"Are you kidding?" I asked.

"No, I bid on these VIP tickets at my kid's school auction last year, and I just never had the chance to use them. I called today, and they said the only day they have VIP seating available is on March 8."

"That's, like, ten days from now . . ."

"I know it's crazy, but I'd love for you to come with me if you can."

"I would love to! Let me talk to Todd and get back to you."

I was a little concerned about whether or not I should take off and go. March 8 was exactly one week before the anniversary of Taylor's death—a day neither Todd nor I were looking forward to. In addition, we had a lot going on with the foundation and I had started to play a bigger role in things. Did it make sense for me to be gone with all of this going on?

But when I spoke to Todd, he didn't have any reservations. "You should go have a girls' trip with Eleanor. You deserve to have fun," he said.

"Are you sure?"

"Why not? You get to have a great time with your friend, and as a bonus you get to see the show too. I'll take care of the kids," he added. "Let's just figure out how to get you out there. Hopefully, we can get a cheap ticket."

I called Eleanor back and said, "It's a go! I'm just not sure how I will get there, yet. Todd is looking for a cheap ticket."

"I've already taken care of it," Eleanor said.

I was surprised, but I shouldn't have been. That was just like Eleanor.

"Wow! Thank you!" I managed to say, grateful and relieved. "I can't wait to see you again."

A couple of days later, I debated whether or not to call Ellen DeGeneres's producer; I still had her number because we'd talked to her several times in the fall. They were interested in our story but couldn't make the timing work. So if I told her I'd be in the audience, I just hoped she'd be able to give Ellen a copy of Taylor's poem. I decided to give it a try and picked up the phone.

When the producer answered, I said, "I'm not sure you'll remember me. But my name is Tara Storch, and we discussed my daughter and Taylor's Gift, the foundation we started in her honor—"

"Oh, my gosh. Yes, I remember you," she said. "How are you?"

We chatted briefly, and then I said, "I'm going to be in your audience on March 8, and I would love to meet you in person while I'm there."

"Of course! Let me give you my cell phone number. When you get here, you'll be standing in a long line. Just text me, and I'll come down and say hi to you while you're in line."

I thanked her, and we hung up. I thought about Taylor and her poem. I wished she could be there with me. *Taylor, honey, I haven't forgotten. I may not get you on the show, baby, but I'll be in the audience, and I'll do what I can to share your story.*

Later that night I texted Dina, the friend and volunteer who handled all of the media for Taylor's Gift. I told her I was going to be in the audience of Ellen's show on March 8.

Dina texted me back a single question: "When did Taylor turn in her 'I Am' poem?"

I thought about it a moment and remembered it was the Monday before we'd left on spring break. I wanted to be sure, so I checked a calendar before I texted her back.

"March 8. Of course!"

—33—

The Teenager's Mother Wants to Reach Out— but Can't

ASHLEY ZOLLER
SOUTH DAKOTA

Dueene was terrified while Ashley was in surgery. With doctors cutting her daughter's eye she feared something would go wrong. If anything happened to Ashley, she didn't know what she would do.

When Ashley woke up from surgery, Dueene was by her side. She watched Ashley look around the room, and waited to see if she noticed a difference in her vision. When Ashley finally looked at Dueene, she simply said, "I need to go to Texas."

Dueene smiled. Obviously, the anesthesia was still affecting her. Dueene brushed the hair out of her daughter's face.

"You have beautiful eyes, Mom," Ashley said.

"Thanks. Can you see them better now?"

"Yeah, you used to look like a ghost. Your face was white, and you had dark circles where your eyes should be."

Dueene smiled. She could tell the surgery had been a success.

The next morning, the doctor handed Ashley a card with varying type sizes.

"What do you see?" he asked.

"I can see the really small letters now. I couldn't see them before."

It was another indication the transplant had been a success.

Dueene knew things had really changed when, a few days later, they were both back at JD's Pizza, their family-owned restaurant. A customer asked Ashley, "What was the first thing you saw when you woke up from surgery?"

Ashley thought for a moment and said, "When I looked at my mom I thought, 'Wow, she's a cool mom.'" That was a special moment. Ashley had never said anything like that before. It was such a difference from her angry outbursts in the restaurant before her surgery. The words meant a lot to Dueene, and she treasured them.

Though the surgery was successful, the recovery was rugged. It would take eighteen months for Ashley to fully regain her stamina, and she endured a lot of pain during that time. But as the pain gradually lessened, Dueene noticed that Ashley's personality softened. She was more likely to ask for a hug than to start a fight.

Dueene noticed other differences in Ashley too. Though she was still obsessed with monster trucks, and cake, she was now also obsessed with Texas.

"When can I go to Texas?" she'd ask several times a day. "I want to go to Texas."

"You don't know anybody in Texas, I don't know anybody there, so why do you want to go to Texas?" Dueene asked her repeatedly.

But there wasn't an answer. Ashley just kept saying, "I just want to go."

Dueene found Ashley's constant talk about it amusing; it was just one more personality quirk that made her daughter unique.

⁂

One day, Dueene got an envelope from Ashley's doctor. Inside was information on her daughter's cornea donor—a teenage girl named Taylor. In the letter, Taylor's mother described how her beautiful daughter had died in a tragic skiing accident. She said Taylor was a caretaker who always looked out for the special needs students at her school.

Students like Ashley, Dueene thought. Then she read that the family lived in a suburb of Dallas. *Was this why Ashley wanted to go to Texas so badly?*

It was too much to absorb. Dueene couldn't imagine life without Ashley. Now another mom was living without her daughter, and that daughter had donated her cornea so Ashley could see. It was heart-wrenching to think about what the donor family had been through.

Dueene wanted to reach out, but what would she say and how would she say it? She tried to explain it to Ashley, but Ashley couldn't grasp the concept that a girl had died, and that because of her death Ashley now had her cornea.

Dueene knew it was far too confusing for Ashley to make sense of it. It was too overwhelming for Dueene. She cried on and off for a week and then tried not to think about it.

— 34 —

I Am Outgoing and Friendly

Tara

When we got to the studio, I texted Kara, the producer, and told her I was outside. I held two Taylor's Gift T-shirts. I'd rolled and tied each one with a blue ribbon and attached a silicone foundation bracelet to each bundle. I'd also enclosed an envelope that contained a handwritten card, pictures of our family, and Taylor's "I Am" poem. I hoped to give them to her and Ellen.

I quickly got a reply: "I'll come find you in line."

The outside of the studio was exactly as Kara had described—a massive line with hundreds of people in it.

"Tara?"

I looked up. It was Kara. She introduced herself and gave me a quick hug. I introduced her to Eleanor, and we chatted for a few minutes. Then I said to Kara, "It's not a coincidence that I'm in the audience today. Exactly one year ago today, Taylor turned in that poem saying she wanted to be on the show."

"A year ago *today?*" Kara asked in disbelief. "Wow. That's not random."

We chatted a few more minutes before she thanked me for coming and said she had to get back to work.

"Here's a shirt for you and one for Ellen. If you have a chance, please give it to her," I said as I handed her the gifts.

"I'll give it to her after the show," Kara promised. "The show will start around four. Hopefully, I'll see you before, but if not, I'll come say hi afterward."

⚬⟡⚬

We checked in, and a woman guided us to our seats.

"That's such a pretty turquoise sweater you're wearing, we're going to sit you right here," she said, pointing to the aisle seat in the front row. I knew the look of the audience was important for a show, but I doubted it was my sweater that nabbed us the front row. "I'll bet Kara got us these great seats," I whispered to Eleanor as she sat down beside me.

It felt surreal to be inside the studio. All I could think was how much Taylor would have loved being there with me, and I started to tear up.

Then music started playing and the lights began flashing. The energy in the room picked up as the show began taping. "I've got to stop crying," I told Eleanor. "I want Todd and the kids to see me in the audience, but they'll never show me on TV like this. There's no crying at *The Ellen DeGeneres Show*, for goodness' sake," I joked.

I knew I was at this once-in-a-lifetime event because of my daughter. I also knew Taylor would want me to enjoy the moment, so I resolved to relish the experience to its fullest. But it would be a struggle. Happiness, for me, was ever elusive.

The music swelled, and then Ellen appeared. Unbelievably, she looked directly at me, gave me a sweet smile, and pointed to her right wrist.

She's wearing the Taylor's Gift bracelet!

My hands flew to my face to cover my tears. I couldn't believe it. Kara had said she would give it to her after the show, but she was already wearing the bracelet! The music increased in volume, and Ellen started dancing in the aisles.

"Here she comes," I told Eleanor.

She danced into the audience and stopped in front of me, grabbed my shoulders, and said, "I got your note. I want to talk to you later. I read the poem and Taylor sounds like an amazing girl."

"Thank you," I said, hugging her. "Thank you for the laughter you've brought into our house."

Still dancing, she smiled at me and said, "You're doing good."

Then she danced away and continued to move through the audience.

It's hard to explain what I felt in that moment. Relief, certainly. So many things we'd done had been for the foundation, to increase organ donation registration across the United States, but this was something I'd done for *my daughter*. It had always been a dream of Taylor's to be on Ellen's show, and now she had done it. It was a personal celebration for Taylor.

We did it, baby! We did it! You're finally here!

The energy in the room was high, and with the music pumping and the lights flashing, it took me a few minutes to figure out exactly what I was feeling. But as I relaxed in my seat to enjoy the show, I recognized an old, familiar feeling I hadn't felt in a long time.

Joy.

⊶

As the show entered its final segment, Ellen sat alone on the set. After the last commercial break, she said, "I recently found out we have someone special in our audience today. Tara Storch, will you join me on stage?"

Did she just say my name? I was stunned.

I stood up and started to tremble. *This is it. This is the moment*, I thought as I steadied myself. The day had now gone from being

287

about Taylor to being an incredible opportunity to tell people about our foundation and educate them about organ donation—and I was petrified. I hated talking to large groups, and now I would be talking to millions of viewers. I knew I'd done it on *The Today Show*, but Todd had been with me then. This time I would be all alone. One slipup and the opportunity would be gone.

Please, God, don't let me stumble as I speak.

I made it onto the stage and sat down in the chair, and Ellen clipped a microphone on me and gave me a sweet pat on my arm. I said another quick prayer and took a deep breath. When I took that breath, a sense of calm washed over me. *You can do this*, I heard inside my head. Somehow, I knew I could. I felt warm and loved, as if the Holy Spirit had enveloped me in His peace. I sat back in the chair and readied myself for whatever came next.

Ellen briefly introduced our story and talked about Taylor's poem and how much it had touched her. She then asked me about Taylor's Gift.

When I told her that Taylor had turned in the poem this very day, a year ago, Ellen got choked up. Miraculously, I held it together long enough to read the poem, and even smile at the line where Taylor said she wanted to be on *The Ellen DeGeneres Show*. As I read, I saw photos of Taylor on the monitors in front of me. When I finished, Ellen said, "What an amazing, amazing girl." Then she told the national audience she was putting the poem and the link to the foundation on her website.

In the final seconds, I had the presence of mind to say that just because someone agreed to be an organ donor on their driver's license didn't mean they were on their state's list. I reminded Ellen and the audience how important it was to double-check and that they could do it through our website.

When the show ended, Eleanor and I were able to visit with Ellen backstage. She was friendly and warm, and we didn't feel rushed. She talked with us and said she felt a special connection with Taylor's story and wanted to stay in touch. It was an unbelievable day. I'd helped make one of my daughter's dreams come true.

God had orchestrated this day in His own time. It was both a personal acknowledgment of Taylor and a public acknowledgment of our work at the foundation. But more than anything, it was a public example of Romans 8:28 and how everything works for good for those who love the Lord.

One of the lines in Taylor's poem was, "I say with pride that I'm a Christian," and now she had said it to a national audience from the set of her favorite talk show. The things she stood for, and the things she put in writing, were now made public in her death in a way they never could have been in her life.

Only God could have done it that way.

Of course.

Todd

We knew that spring break would be hard. Weeks before it happened, everyone around us was already talking about their plans and asking about ours. We couldn't afford a big trip, but we wanted to do something. We had been tiptoeing around the upcoming anniversary and trying not to talk about it, but finally Tara and I decided we needed to get it out in the open. A couple of weeks out, we took the kids for ice cream and asked them to make a list of ten places they wanted to go during their week off.

Tara and Peyton planned a couple of girls' days, while Ryan and I would do guy stuff. We all wanted to go to the zoo as a family, and we talked about going ziplining.

Though we had a plan, we weren't excited about it. Tara and I would have preferred to ignore the whole thing, but we did our best to be enthusiastic and fully present for the kids' sakes. They deserved that much and more.

On March 14, Tara and I were home alone. Both kids were at friends' houses. About 3:30, I stopped what I was doing and got up from my office to find Tara. She was already on her way down the hall to meet me.

"You know, this is about the time it happened," I said.

"I know," she said, and we hugged and cried.

But the moment didn't take us out. Taylor's life had ended, but Ryan's and Peyton's hadn't. Neither had ours—whether we liked it or not. After we cried, we pulled ourselves together, packed a few things, and when the kids got home we left for Wimberley, Texas, to go ziplining. And it was good. We had time in the car together as a family, time away from home, and the opportunity to make new memories doing something we'd never done before.

While we were in the hotel, I had a conference call with our creative agency. They wanted to unveil the new public service announcements they had just finished.

While the commercials were downloading, I asked Tara and the kids if they would rather leave or if they wanted to be a part of it. They all wanted to stay.

As the call started and the commercials played, I watched how my family engaged with the creative team. Everyone loved the work that had been done so far, and the kids were really into it. Ryan offered a couple of suggestions.

"I think you should change that," he said, pointing out one creative element he didn't like and including what he thought it should be.

The team responded enthusiastically, "That's a fantastic idea."

"I think the color isn't quite right," Peyton said.

"No, you're right, and we'll fix that," they agreed.

I marveled at how involved the kids were and how they also had something to contribute. Early on, they weren't always so supportive—it was too painful for them, while they were dealing with their own pain. Now, months later, as I watched the kids interacting with the creative team over the computer, it was especially sweet to see Peyton noticing little details and wanting to have input. The foundation had truly become a part of the family.

❖

The pain was still there. The loss still hurt. But we were all steadier now. We could talk about Taylor, or the foundation, without it sweeping us out to sea emotionally. In those times when our emotions did sweep us away, we recovered and found our footing much more quickly than we had in the past. As a family, we stood together in the ocean of grief, holding on through the swells and doing our best to keep each other afloat. It wasn't always easy, but it was a beautiful thing to see.

And I thanked God for it.

Over the past year we'd suffered great loss, but we'd also gained some things. Our marriage was now stronger than it had ever been, and so was our faith. We had a deeper connection with each other and with God. While the three recipients we'd connected with certainly didn't replace Taylor, the hope for their futures replaced the despair we had in Taylor's death. Being an organ donor was Taylor's gift to them, but it was also her gift to us.

❖

On the fifteenth, I wrote a note to Taylor in my notebook:

I'm not falling apart like I thought I would. A gift from you and God. One year without you. How did I ever make it?

That night as Tara and I sat together in the kitchen, I said, "If we can make it through this, we can make it through anything." But the truth was that we had done more than make it. Though it had been the hardest year of our married life, I loved Tara even more now than I did a year ago.

Tara

By June 2011, we had mostly resumed our usual activities. I know some people would call it returning to normal, or a new normal, but I didn't like those terms. In my mind, we'd never be normal again. But we were surviving. While there were still fluctuations in the stock market of our emotions, to use Todd's analogy, if we weren't trending upward, we were at least holding steady.

One day we were getting ready to leave the house as a family to head to Fossil Rim, a wildlife park. Before we left, the phone rang, and I answered it.

"My name is Dueene Zoller, and my daughter, Ashley, has Taylor's cornea," the caller said.

I took a deep breath and exhaled slowly while she continued.

"I got your letter, and I am so sorry I never wrote back," she said. "I can't imagine what you're going through."

It had been more than a year since I'd sent out the first letter, and we hadn't heard anything—I didn't think we ever would.

I went out onto the back porch so we could talk. Dueene told me she was sitting in her truck in the parking lot of JD's Pizza in Rapid City, South Dakota, where they lived. She said Ashley was a twenty-year-old special needs child.

"How's she doing?" I asked.

"Really good," Dueene said. She explained how Ashley's eye had been coning and how that had caused severe headaches. "The new cornea made the headaches go away." She told me how Ashley had woken up from her surgery and said, "I need to go to Texas!" and how odd Dueene thought that was until she received our letter. "Maybe there's a connection there?" she asked. She also told me that when she looked into Ashley's eyes, she saw Taylor.

"Thank you for calling!" I said. I could tell it was hard for Dueene to reach out. Ashley was obviously her whole world, and the thought of losing her daughter had to be hard for her to conceive. But I was thrilled to have connected with her and to hear how well Ashley was doing. I told Dueene how we'd met some of the other recipients and how we hoped one day to meet Ashley too.

The conversation was short and sweet. Now we had connected with four out of the five recipients. Wow!

After we hung up, I went into the house and told Todd and the kids about the phone call. It excited the kids, but after they heard the news, they were ready to go to Fossil Rim. In a funny kind of way, it was almost normal for them to hear about these kinds of unexpected calls, and I was pleased that they no longer triggered prolonged episodes of grief.

When we finally headed out to Fossil Rim, I stared out the car window and prayed. I thanked God for Ashley and Dueene and that they had reached out. In the hospital, we'd been told we might never connect with even one recipient, and now we'd connected with four amazing people. I couldn't wait to one day get to heaven and introduce them to Taylor.

But somehow, I felt that Taylor already knew them.

I still hadn't found the peace I'd been looking for, but I resolved that I probably never would. This wasn't the way our story was supposed to be written. The natural order of things is that children are supposed to outlive their parents, grow up, get married, and have their own children. However, though we were having to rewrite our story, this wasn't the end of Taylor. Through organ donation, Taylor had already outlived herself and continued to do so each day through Jeff, Patricia, Jonathan, and now Ashley.

And with God's help, now we were learning how to live on without her.

Part 3

New Beginnings

— 35 —

The Cowboy

The Gift of Giving Back

Jeff Kartus
Colorado

The cowboy was no longer confined to the house, and because he didn't have to worry about low blood sugar, he was free to do as much physical labor as he liked. So every morning Jeff volunteered at a local stable, feeding and watering the horses and cleaning stalls. Jeff adored horses, and he didn't mind getting dirty taking care of them. But even more than caring for the horses, he enjoyed helping the people who boarded their horses there.

One of the regulars at the stable was a woman named Kim. She suffered from a chronic pain condition that affects the nervous system and can be debilitating. Kim could no longer walk and had to employ a Hoveround power wheelchair to get from her truck to the barn. But she was determined to ride her horse, Copper, no matter what. Kim had figured out a way to mount Copper by standing on the Hoveround. She'd get off by doing the same thing in reverse.

Jeff kept an eye on her during her mounts and dismounts and while she was riding. He videotaped her lessons so she could watch them later at home. And he always cleaned up after Copper. There was no way Kim could handle a shovel to clean up after him herself.

Kim told Jeff that riding Copper made her feel whole. But it was also an important part of her therapy—since a horse's gait most closely mimics a human's gait. Through riding, Kim's body built up the stamina she needed to walk short distances, which made all the difference in her quality of life.

Jeff understood. Before the transplant surgery, he'd also been confined to a wheelchair. He knew how important it was to be independent. Jeff was happy to do what he could to help Kim retain her independence.

⋄

One day, Jeff was cleaning stalls while Kim was out riding in the pasture. He heard a horse running, and looked up to see Copper running past him, his saddle askew, headed toward the stable. Jeff was confused. Did he really see what he thought he saw? Or was he losing his mind? As a result of his accidents, he'd had a lot of head trauma, and he couldn't always tell if what he saw was real or something in his head. As he tried to figure it out, he heard Kim's guide dog, Alexei.

Jeff looked out toward the fields and saw Alexei barking. Kim was lying next to her on the ground. Something had gone terribly wrong. Kim couldn't dismount without using her Hoveround to get off. Jeff knew she'd either had a seizure and fallen off or she'd been thrown. Either way, he knew she must be injured and was possibly in a lot of pain. All those car accidents flashed through his mind. His body tensed, remembering the injuries—the broken ribs, neck, and back.

Jeff knew he should call an ambulance, but when Kim had had her last seizure she'd begged him not to. He understood. He'd had enough seizures due to low blood sugar and knew what that felt like. Each time an ambulance came, they just wanted to take him to the hospital. After so many trips, he started refusing to go and begged Vanessa to take care of him at home.

But this was different; Kim had been thrown from a horse. What if she was really hurt?

Before he could make a decision, Copper circled past him again. Jeff knew he had to do something about the horse. Kim loved her horse almost as much as she loved her husband. If anything happened to Copper, it would devastate her. He took another quick look at Kim and saw she was now sitting up. That was a good sign.

He went after the horse.

Fortunately, after racing toward the stables, Copper just trotted back to his familiar pen, and Jeff was able to open the gate and let him in, securing it behind him. Kim's saddle was still askew on Copper's back, but Jeff would have to leave that for later. At least the horse was safe. He had to get to Kim.

He looked out toward the field and saw she was still sitting up. He could run out there, or he could even take a horse, but he couldn't bring her back that way. He would have to get her Hoveround and drive it out to her. He ran to where she'd parked it, but he was unfamiliar with how to operate it and couldn't get it started.

He could think of only one other option. Jeff would have to drive his truck out to the pasture. He knew this was against the rules, but he felt he didn't have any other choice. He jumped in his truck, put it in gear, and tore through the fields.

As he drove across the pasture, with his heart pounding and his mind racing, Jeff wondered if this was what Vanessa felt like every time she raced to one of his accident scenes. It was a scary feeling to know someone you cared about was injured and not know what you'd find when you arrived. As the truck bumped and bounced through the fields, tossing dirt clods into the air, he thought about Vanessa having done this very same thing so many times for him. Now he was able to do it for someone else.

Pulling up next to Kim, Jeff could see she was alert and talking.

"I'm not sure what happened," Kim said when he reached her.

Jeff checked to make sure she wasn't injured before gently lifting her into the truck.

"Is Copper okay?" she asked.

Jeff assured her that Copper was fine. He closed the door, loaded Alexei into the bed of the truck, and drove as gently as he could back to the stables. Other than a few bruises, including a bruised ego, Kim seemed fine.

"Thank you so much!" she said. "I don't know what I would have done if you hadn't been here!"

Jeff was thankful. Kim was fine, but it could have been worse. Jeff thought about all the accidents he never walked away from—the times he was put in the hospital to fight for his life.

Kim's husband later thanked Jeff for rescuing his wife. "Though riding is so good for her, it can also be dangerous. I wouldn't let her keep doing this if it weren't for you," he said.

"I'm just glad I can help," Jeff said.

❧

Eighteen months after meeting Todd and Tara, and twenty-one months after his kidney/pancreas transplant, Jeff still thought of Taylor every day. It was hard not to. His life was completely different from the one he'd lived before the transplant. Because of her gift, he was able to do what he'd always wanted to do—help others.

—36—

The Nurse

The Gift of Time

PATRICIA WINTERS
ARIZONA

Patricia beamed as she and her family walked through the gates of the Magic Kingdom and entered the happiest place on earth. After months of lying on the couch, barely having enough energy to watch her boys play by themselves on the floor, she couldn't believe she was finally here with them. Seeing the joy in her boys' eyes when they looked up and down Main Street was all the proof she needed that the park really lived up to its claims.

"Where do you want to go first?" she asked.

The boys were too overwhelmed to answer.

"Let's head over this way," she said, spotting a sign that pointed to "The Many Adventures of Winnie the Pooh."

For years, Patricia had just wished for enough energy to take the boys to the playground minutes from their house. Now, less than a year after her transplant, they were spending three days together as a family, walking, talking, riding rides, and making memories. It truly was a dream come true.

As the kids chatted about all the things they wanted to do at the park, Patricia thought of all the things she could now do that she couldn't before. The biggest one was that she could now *breathe*.

With her ever-present illness, the past few years had been especially hard. Medical bills had mounted, then Joe had lost his job, and then they'd lost their dream house. But she didn't care about that anymore. Though the house was beautiful when they moved in, she'd been sick most of the time they'd lived there and couldn't really appreciate it. Now it held only negative memories. The new house felt like a fresh start. Though their home was smaller, their fun had increased.

That wasn't the only thing that had increased. Patricia felt as if her heart was bigger. She couldn't really explain why. Could it have been all the lessons—like patience and compassion—she'd learned from being ill? It was hard for her type A personality to slow down, but she'd had to because of her illness. Now she had a greater understanding of those who moved a little slower than she did—such as the elderly and disabled. Or was it because she didn't take anything for granted anymore? Ordinary events took on greater meaning. "Each birthday and holiday is so special," she said. She believed that having a long-term illness made her a better parent because she started looking at things through the eyes of her children.

But her perspective changed in other ways too.

The illness and financial problems had been hard on her marriage and other close relationships. Patricia found herself having to forgive those closest to her for things they'd done that hurt her. In the past, Patricia would have just walked away, but now she had a new perspective about what was really important. "Knowing you were almost snuffed out can be a gift because it clarifies things for you," Patricia told her friends. "You learn that houses and things don't matter. People do."

Patricia felt as though her old heart was limited in how much it could love, but with Taylor's heart her capacity had grown. One of the easiest ways for her to see it was when she was with Tara. Patricia would say that she wasn't a huggy-touchy-feely kind of person and that she didn't express her love that way. But when she was with Tara, she did. "Every time I leave her, my heart aches," said Patricia. "I just have this sense of loss when we say goodbye. It's a new feeling for me."

Patricia has a greater sense of purpose too. She knows that life is a gift, and she doesn't want anger, lack of forgiveness, or other relationship problems to get in the way of whatever time she has left. Instead she resolves issues quickly so she can get on to what she needs to do—such as being a mother. Though being a mother to Jack and Sam is her most important job, Patricia still works as a nurse, teaching prenatal classes. In addition, she helps out with Taylor's Gift, supporting the Storches in their foundation's mission.

If her boys ever look back on those dark days, Patricia hopes they will see her determination and perseverance. It would have been so much easier to give up, but she didn't. She fought hard because she loved them so much. She also knew it wasn't her fight that won the battle. There were so many times during her illness that she shouldn't have made it, and yet she did. The only explanation that made sense to her was that God had divinely intervened in her life to keep her alive until she got the perfect heart.

So through the Storches' decision, Taylor's gift, and God's grace, Patricia was able to give her boys the gift her own dad wasn't able to give her—more time.

And for that, she is eternally grateful.

—37—

The Bike Rider

The Gift of Freedom

JONATHAN FINGER
COLORADO

The Register's Annual Great Bicycle Ride Across Iowa, better known as RAGBRAI, is the oldest and largest bicycle touring event in the world, with more than twenty thousand riders. It's like the Tour de France in Iowa, only instead of French countryside there's corn, lots of corn. But Jonathan didn't even know that much about the seven-day tour when he agreed to form a team with some of his online piano forum friends. He just thought it sounded like fun.

After researching the ride, Jonathan knew it would be a demanding physical challenge. The ride was nearly five hundred miles long, from the Missouri River to the Mississippi River, and the route wasn't flat—the first two days alone would have climbs of about four thousand feet each—and Jonathan would have to ride sixty to eighty miles a day up and down rolling hills. The ride would take place the last week of July 2011. He agreed to do it just a few months after his transplant in the fall of 2010, which didn't leave him a lot of time to recover and train.

In addition to having a new kidney to take care of, Jonathan had a history of heart problems that would complicate his ability to physically push himself. To participate in RAGBRAI, Jonathan would have to train hard for months, and some of that time included the Colorado winter months when he wouldn't be able to bike outdoors. Even under perfect training conditions, Jonathan knew he would be physically pushing his body further than it had ever been pushed. Even training as hard as he possibly could wouldn't guarantee that he'd have the strength and stamina required to make it to the end of the seven-day tour.

But Jonathan was determined to do it. The team would be riding for his favorite charity—Taylor's Gift Foundation.

As Jonathan trained for RAGBRAI, and began to take longer rides on his bike, he found riding gave him more opportunities to think. There was a cadence to pedaling. The sound of the sprocket teeth making their way through the bike chain had its own rhythm—calming and invigorating, peaceful and energizing, all at the same time. When he shifted gears, there was a clicking sound as the derailleur and chain shifted from one sprocket to the next. Relearning how to gear a bike and how to pedal were key parts of his training. It became the music that underscored his thoughts.

Day after day, as the wind hit his face and the sun warmed his back, he rode and he thought. He noticed how his thinking had changed. For years, he had been so busy thinking only of himself—his health, his dialysis, and his physical needs—that he hadn't been able to spend much time thinking about others. As he rode, he began to reminisce about his relationships with friends and family. It was as if he had a new freedom to think about others rather than just himself. Having that emotional freedom, alongside his new physical freedom, would take some getting used to as he began seeing and feeling the world differently.

❖

After training for months, Jonathan headed to Iowa to meet up with his online friends. The first few days of RAGBRAI went pretty much as expected. The ride was tough but manageable. Most teams rode together, one rider in front to reduce the drag for those behind, switching to a new front rider with fresh legs when the leader tired. But Team Taylor's Gift was small, and it soon became apparent that there were big differences in skill and endurance levels. Jonathan had been riding seriously for less than a year, and he hadn't been able to build up all the stamina he needed. He couldn't keep pace with the others, and they would often have to slow down to keep pace with him. Jonathan eventually told the other riders it was okay for them to go on without him. He'd just catch up to them at the final stop at the end of each day.

Alone with the cadence of his pedaling, Jonathan's thoughts turned inward. He knew he was stronger than he'd been since his teens, when the kidney disease had taken over. But how strong was he? Who was he?

For years, he'd seen himself as a vulnerable patient—someone who needed to be taken care of. When he was sick, he'd often feel weak and fearful. It was hard when he felt that way, and he knew it affected all of his relationships. But riding through Iowa on his bike, surrounded by hundreds of people yet all alone, Jonathan started to change the way he felt about himself. Each day's ride gave him new confidence and helped him know he wasn't the weak link in the chain anymore; he was the strong one, the overcomer who had survived against all odds. He began to think about what this meant for his relationships. He knew now he wouldn't have to be the focus of a relationship; for the first time, he could give and receive love equally. That one thought was exciting and freeing. From now on, his relationships wouldn't have to be defined by who could take care of him.

❖

A few days into RAGBRAI, Jonathan stared at the approaching hill—Twister Hill—and wondered if he had enough left in him to make it to the top. The hill was already taking out more experienced riders who had dismounted to push their bikes to the top. Jonathan had already come so far physically, mentally, and emotionally that he didn't want to give up. But he was afraid he might have to. His legs were spent, and his hands and arms were numb from gripping the bike handles. He knew he could walk his bike up the hill and still be proud of the job he'd done. There would be no shame in pushing his bike to the top. It wasn't the destination, it wasn't the prize, and it wasn't even the end of the ride. This was just another obstacle in a much longer tour.

But as he approached the hill, he thought back to that dark day in the hospital when he'd wanted to die. Father Seraphim had stopped by, and Jonathan had asked him if it was okay to give up. Father Seraphim had assured him that it was his choice but reminded him of how valiantly he'd fought to make it that far. Jonathan remembered that exhaustion and how much he'd wanted to give up. Yet somehow he'd found the strength to push through, and years later he could see how that decision had paid off with a new kidney and the promise of a new life.

At the base of the hill, Jonathan's legs were screaming in pain. The sweat had soaked through the jersey on his back and mixed with the sunscreen on his face. As it dripped off his forehead, his eyes stung. But once again, Jonathan made the decision to fight. He shifted gears on his bike and pressed hard on the pedals, trying to maintain his speed as he ascended the hill. He knew that the victory was virtually meaningless. Even if he made it to the top, the ride and the mental fight continued for another twenty-five miles that day alone—and there were two more days ahead of him. But Jonathan chose to fight his way up the hill, even knowing the fight wouldn't be easy.

"We always think we're at the end of our rope, but we're not," Jonathan said. "It's such an important exercise to realize we can do much more than we think we can."

Wearing his Taylor's Gift "Be a Hero" jersey, Jonathan triumphantly made it to the top of the hill that day and rode to the finish line. It was a physical accomplishment, but it was also a mental journey—much like his life.

"I feel like I have more capacity to love now than I did. I haven't always had the energy, or the desire, or the resources to make decisions and be a proactive part of anything, and now I can," he said.

Taylor's gift has given Jonathan freedom. He has more time, greater health, the ability to play music, and the ability to push himself physically. But perhaps his greatest freedom isn't a physical one—it's an emotional one. Jonathan now has the freedom to love others fully.

—38—

The Teenager
The Gift of a Future

ASHLEY ZOLLER
SOUTH DAKOTA

"Ashley, time to get up!" Dueene said.

Ashley opened the door to her room. "Good morning, Mom."

Ashley was already dressed and ready to go; Dueene smiled at her daughter. For years, Ashley had woken up every morning ready for a fight. If it wasn't about her clothes, it was about her breakfast—usually she argued with Dueene about both. Some mornings they would fight over Ashley taking her medicine, and other days Dueene would have to force it down her. But ever since her corneal transplant eighteen months earlier, Ashley had changed. In fact, she'd become a different person.

Dueene poured herself another cup of coffee and watched Ashley hungrily wolf down her breakfast. Most mothers of twenty-year-old daughters didn't marvel at their daughters' eating habits, but Dueene did. After nearly two decades of trying to get Ashley to eat, she was finally doing it. Ashley seemed to have more of an

311

appetite following the corneal transplant. In fact, over the past year she'd put on ten pounds and was continuing to gain weight. This was a huge accomplishment. Dueene remembered bringing her three-pound baby home from the hospital and doing everything she could to coax her to eat. Years later, she still weighed only twenty-five pounds. By the time Ashley was in high school, she seemed to have stagnated at eighty-four pounds.

But since the surgery, Ashley had blossomed to more than ninety pounds—a huge milestone. She was healthier than she'd ever been.

ം

Dueene worked seventy-five to eighty hours a week in the restaurant. When it was slow, she had time to think. In December 2011, she spent a lot of that time thinking about Ashley's future. In a few days, Ashley would turn twenty-one. That milestone birthday also meant that, as a special needs student, this would be Ashley's last year in public school. *What will she do next year?*

As Dueene stacked cups and folded pizza boxes, she knew they needed a plan for Ashley, but she wasn't sure what. On one hand, Dueene welcomed a break from parenting. Ashley had required her full-time attention, twenty-four hours a day, seven days a week, for more than twenty years. Dueene had given up a lot of her own hopes and dreams to be available for Ashley's special needs. If Ashley were able to live in some kind of group home, Dueene would experience freedom she hadn't had since Ashley was born. But Dueene also knew if Ashley were living anywhere else, she would miss her terribly.

One day, Dueene was preoccupied with thoughts of Ashley's future. "What's going on?" one of her longtime employees asked. As Dueene wiped down counters, she expressed her concerns. "I want Ashley to be independent and to have her own life. Everyone deserves to have their own life. But I'm not sure how that's going to happen yet."

"But you're doing everything you can," the employee said.

She was right. Dueene was doing whatever she could to help Ashley learn to live independently. In addition, several times a week a companion came in to teach Ashley specific skills. Together, they would go to the mall, the grocery store, or volunteer in the community. At home, the companion helped Ashley do her own laundry and learn basic household skills—such as how to clean the toilet.

"I've seen a lot of progress in her skills," the employee was quick to add.

Dueene knew she was right. "Things are getting better. I feel as if I haven't taken a deep breath in twenty years, but I'm going to start taking a lot of deep breaths soon."

⚮

Ashley entered the restaurant immediately after school and plopped down on a bench in one of the Aztec-themed booths.

"Do you want something to drink?" Dueene asked.

"Sure."

As Dueene disappeared behind the counter and grabbed a glass, she asked Ashley about her day.

"At school, I had to wipe off all the tables. I had to work with a bully. His name is Justin. He pushes me."

"Did you push him back?"

"No."

"Good for you, Ashley." Dueene wanted to reinforce her daughter's good behavior.

In the past, when Ashley was in one of those kinds of moods, she would have decked him. One of the characteristics of Williams syndrome children is that they're fearless in the face of danger. Although Ashley was smaller, she'd take on anyone, no matter what size they were. At that time, Dueene would have been scared for the bully—Ashley's anger was that explosive. But since the transplant, her outbursts had disappeared.

"What did the teacher do?" Dueene asked, setting a drink in front of her daughter.

"He's not allowed to come near me anymore."

Dueene ran her fingers through her daughter's straight hair. Ashley had begun straightening it because she thought boys liked it that way. Dueene smiled. She knew Ashley had recently started showing more grown-up preferences. For her upcoming birthday, she wanted clothes, but not the pink and purple girly kind she had in her childhood. Instead, she wanted rocker clothes from the Hard Rock Café. Ashley also had a boyfriend—a young man with special needs whom she'd met at Walmart. The two friends socialized occasionally with a group, or they talked and texted when Dueene allowed. It was obvious that Ashley had begun to pay attention to boys—and they were paying more attention to her.

Dueene's twenty-year-old daughter was beginning to act like a teenager.

❖

While Ashley was doing her homework, Dueene got busy in the kitchen, prepping for the busy night ahead. When the dinner rush started to build, Dueene moved to the counter to take orders and did her best to keep customers moving through the counter line. She also tried to keep her eye on Ashley in the dining room. It was an old habit.

In the past, it seemed Ashley was always agitated and angry. If the restaurant was crowded and people got in her space, it would set her off and an outburst would follow. Dueene had trained herself to look for the initial signs of Ashley's outbursts, so she could intercede and prevent a full-blown scene from taking place in front of customers.

But with a steady stream of customers and an employee out sick, Dueene was so busy she didn't have time to keep a watchful eye on Ashley. It wasn't until the end of the night, after everyone had left, that Dueene realized the place had been full all night and Ashley had not only kept out of trouble but she'd helped out too.

"How did it go?" Dueene asked as Ashley carried dirty dishes to the kitchen.

"Good. I like meeting new people here," Ashley said.

Dueene had to pause a second. *Who was this kid?* Ever since the transplant, Ashley seemed calmer. More at peace with herself. And though Dueene was always on the lookout, there hadn't been any outbursts. In fact, it had been quite the opposite—Ashley had actually been helping out at the restaurant.

Dueene's mind flipped through a few recent scenes. In June, when the Sturgis Motorcycle Rally was in town and the place was packed, Ashley had waited on several tables of bikers. And they'd left her tips. "They were cool," Ashley had said.

More recently, a sweet older couple from Alaska had come in, and Ashley had become friendly with them. She had a knack for remembering names and faces, and Dueene knew that if the couple ever came back, Ashley would remember them. As she counted the receipts, Dueene realized her daughter was growing up. She was treating people more kindly, she'd stopped having outbursts, and she'd started helping around the restaurant. Ashley seemed more capable of taking care of herself than ever before.

Until the surgery, Dueene hadn't understood how painful Ashley's headaches were or how much they had impacted her behavior. Now that they were gone, Ashley was a different person. And Dueene was just beginning to see how much she had changed.

Right after Ashley's transplant, Dueene noticed physical changes in her daughter. Though she'd had trouble sleeping since she was a baby, following the surgery she began to sleep more. Her depth perception was also better. Before the surgery, Ashley had trouble staying on the sidewalk while walking; she rarely had that problem anymore. And going up and down stairs had also gotten easier.

Ashley reported other changes to Dueene. She could see faces better, and people no longer looked like ghosts. Her grades improved, and she began doing better in school because her reading had improved—she could finally see the text.

"And I can type faster," Ashley told Dueene one day after school. "I can see the letters better on the computer."

In the future, Ashley would still be in therapy for her other Williams syndrome–related issues, but now she had the vision and clear mind to be able to work hard on those things without eye pain and headaches distracting her. For a girl whose life had always been hard, the transplant helped make it a lot easier.

⋯

Dueene wanted to thank the Storches, but it took her nearly a year to finally contact them because she wasn't sure what to say. She knew her life had been tough raising Ashley, but Dueene had always adjusted. She couldn't imagine how Tara would ever adjust to losing Taylor.

The phone call was brief and not nearly as difficult as Dueene had expected. The connection between the families was made. For a few weeks after Dueene called, Ashley texted Tara occasionally, and Tara texted back. The Storches told Ashley they hoped to see her one day in Texas. Ashley wanted that too. She still couldn't understand how Taylor had died and donated her cornea so she could see again. But she could understand the pain of a mother losing her daughter.

⋯

As Ashley's twenty-first birthday drew closer, Dueene knew there would be difficult decisions for her daughter in the year ahead. But now that her headaches were gone and her attitude had improved, Ashley was able to make great progress with her therapists and the other professionals who were teaching her how to live independently. In the months since the transplant, Dueene had grown more confident that one day soon Ashley would be able to lead an independent life.

Taylor's gift had given them both a future.

And that was a gift they could enjoy together.

−39−

Outlive Yourself

Todd

Currently, only four in ten adults in the United States are registered to be organ donors, yet there are more than one hundred thousand people awaiting an organ transplant. How long they will wait depends on a number of factors, including how sick they are, their blood and tissue types (rare types generally have to wait longer for matching organs to become available), and how long they've been on the list. Whether the wait is a few weeks, or as in Jonathan's case, eight years, the wait is too long. In the best-case scenarios, these patients are in medical limbo waiting for an organ so they can resume a full life. In the worst cases, they pray just to survive.

While awaiting a transplant, patients can have mounting medical bills that put pressure on their personal finances. Many have to divert their resources from other necessities such as housing, or even medications, to pay the bills they've incurred. Even with medical insurance, the lifetime maximum for many policies is a million dollars. For patients who require ongoing tests and treatments, that figure is too low. Patients can easily exceed the lifetime maximum coverage cap, and then they have to begin paying out of pocket for additional treatment. The longer a patient must wait for an organ, the greater the potential financial crisis is for them and their family.

During the wait, a patient's health only worsens. It's one thing to receive a new heart as soon as doctors recognize the need. It's another to physically waste away, hoping you will still be a viable candidate for surgery when the organ finally becomes available. Many people on the list die while waiting. Even those who live long enough to receive a needed organ often suffer additional medical complications due to the long waiting period, which makes their recovery that much more difficult.

Deteriorating health and financial situations can also lead to relationship issues. Marriages become strained as the couple deals with the emotional, financial, and physical consequences of a long-term illness. Relationships with friends and family members change as the patient requires more care. Patients move from being an equal in their relationships to being the needy one. Lives are placed on hold as patients quit jobs or school, find new childcare because they can no longer care for their children, and withdraw from public spaces and social situations where they risk contracting a virus. The longer someone waits for a transplant, the more likely the emotional and relational strain will lead to depression or a desire to just give up.

At the same time, those who have donated a loved one's organs face their own anguish, just as Tara and I did, as they try to deal with their loss. We were blessed to have a strong marriage and a community that surrounded us and loved us—even when we were hard to love. We know not everyone has this kind of support. Whom do patients turn to when they need assistance? Who lets them know it's okay for a husband and wife to grieve differently? Who reminds them there is purpose in the pain?

Whether it is a patient awaiting an organ or a grieving family who donated organs, their faith is often shaken by their circumstances. At Taylor's Gift Foundation, we want to wrap our arms around these individuals and help them through these bleak days, pointing them toward a brighter future. Though the foundation initially set out to educate youth about organ donation, we realized there were other needs—education and awareness, as well as financial and emotional support. Very quickly, we further clarified the purpose of Taylor's Gift Foundation to encompass all that we're doing.

Our mission is increasing organ donation to Regift Life, Renew Health, and Restore Families.

We've spoken to thousands of people in numerous states and helped organize grassroots events across the country. Working with our creative partner, Firehouse Agency (http://www.firehouse agency.com), we've created award-winning television commercials and billboards that have been seen by millions. We've provided scholarships to high school students and sponsored organ donor recipients to give them the opportunity to ride on the Donate Life Rose Bowl Parade float to help raise awareness about organ donation. We've comforted grieving parents and helped draw attention to individuals who needed lifesaving transplants.

As I write this, we've been doing this for only about two years, yet we've already seen the needle move. In that time, more than two million new organ donors have registered in Texas, and more than thirteen million have registered across the United States. We know the work we've done has played a part in that increase.

But perhaps our biggest accomplishment is that we're starting to change the conversation about organ donation. It's not about death; it's about life.

Most Americans have a life insurance policy that, upon their death, leaves financial means to help their family continue *their lifestyle*. Organ donation is the only gift we can leave that helps people continue *their lives*.

You may not need a transplant today, and I hope you never will, but the chances are good you know someone who already has, or who one day will. The waitlist can be greatly reduced (if not eradicated) if enough people register. But as a small family foundation, we can't do it on our own. We need you to register—and then talk about this issue with your friends and family. Sometimes it's as simple as saying, "Do you have life insurance?" and after they respond, telling them there is another gift they can leave that may be more important. Organ donation doesn't cost anything; you can't take your organs with you, and it saves lives when you leave them here.

More importantly, a conversation about what you plan to do when you die forces you to examine how you're living. Taylor wasn't an organ donor advocate. We didn't sit around our dinner table at night and discuss this issue as a family. Since we didn't know Taylor's explicit wishes, we decided to donate because of who she was and how she lived her life. She had a kind and generous heart and always took care of outsiders. We knew without a doubt this was what she would want.

It was her life, not her death, that led us down this path.

Just like a Boy Scout who goes to a campground and leaves it in better shape than when he arrived, Taylor left the world a better place, not only for her organ recipients, but also for their friends and families.

I've had a lot of time for self-reflection over the last few years, and I've come to the conclusion that I am at my best when I am helping and serving others. My grandfather's words were true: it's not what happens to you that matters, but how you react to it that does. Life is better when we're focused on others. I am thankful that God gave me that insight very early. As a result, I have been able to fuel my grief toward something good—something that serves others.

Taylor already knew that. She lived it, and I want to be like her in that way.

I look forward to seeing her again and hearing her say, "Good job, Daddy! You did it."

—40—

The Gift of Hope

Tara

My friends Beth Rathe and Kathy Quirk were the ones who put fresh flowers on Taylor's grave weekly. They also picked up the trinkets that people left and put out seasonal displays for the holidays. One hot summer day, more than a year after Taylor's death, the three of us were talking at Taylor's gravesite when Beth said, "It's time to get it done."

"You really need to do this," Kathy added.

I knew what they were talking about. I'd made a great deal of progress during the fifteen months since Taylor had died, but there was one thing I still hadn't done—chosen a permanent headstone for Taylor's grave.

"I just can't do it," I said.

"You can, and we'll help," Beth said.

Like so many pivotal moments during my journey, I needed my friends to help me make it happen. They asked me what I wanted, and I gave them permission to work with the people who would create the designs to be etched on her headstone.

A few weeks later, we all sat down in Kathy's kitchen to review their work. As soon as Beth opened the manila folder, I burst into tears. She quickly shut it.

"No," I said, grabbing a Kleenex and wiping my nose, "we have to do this. Let's just get it done."

We were all crying as we looked through the drawings for a permanent memorial for Taylor. Yet, with the Holy Spirit's comforting help, we made some decisions and sent our notes back to the designers for revisions. A few days later, they emailed me a revised drawing. I didn't like it, so I emailed them back with more detailed notes, and we repeated this process for weeks.

I wanted it to be perfect.

And I didn't want it to be final.

But by July 2011, I knew I had to force myself to make it happen. I drove to Fort Worth and sat down with the lady who was designing the layout of the stone on her computer screen. I gave her the photo of Taylor I wanted to be etched into the stone. Underneath the photo, I chose a volleyball and a heart to represent her life. On the other side, we put a cross.

I wanted her headstone to reflect her interests, her love, and her faith. Those three symbols, the volleyball, the heart, and the cross, accomplished that.

In the upper righthand corner, I had Luke 18:27 inscribed: "What is impossible with men is possible with God." Since Taylor's death, that verse had been proven true in our lives, both personally and with the foundation.

In the upper lefthand corner, I had Romans 8:28 inscribed. It was the same Scripture that Father Alfonse had come across on the night of Taylor's funeral. He had been saying that God had a purpose in all of this, and randomly opened Peyton's new journal and read: "And we know that in all things God works for the good of those who love him, who have been called according to his purpose."

◦⊰⊱◦

A few weeks later, I stood next to Taylor's grave in the sweltering August heat and watched the crew install her marker. Using a tape measure, they marked a space on the grass slightly larger than the headstone and then placed their shovels upright and stood on them to break through the initial layer of sod and hard earth. After the first cut, they turned over shovelfuls of brown dirt and placed them in a pile.

Watching them, I was reminded of Ana Lucia's story of the clay Buddha cracking only to reveal the gold inside. I had definitely cracked, but I had also found gold. Our marriage was stronger, we had a clear purpose in life, and though it had been shaken, my faith was now more precious to me than ever before. I had been comforted by the Holy Spirit and drawn into a more intimate relationship with God, and though I would never be thankful for Taylor's death, I was thankful for God's comfort and the spiritual growth I'd experienced.

I had feared this moment because I was afraid the tombstone was the "final nail in the coffin," and it would be an ending. But as I looked out over the emerald green cemetery grass and blue sky and saw the white clouds in the distance, I knew Taylor's death wasn't the end. Taylor also lived on in the lives and hearts of people she'd touched at school, at volleyball, and at church. Her gift became a new beginning for Jeff, Patricia, Jonathan, and Ashley. Her story inspired countless people to donate their organs, which meant that in some small way, she would live on through more recipients whom we would never meet. And she also gave us signs that she was still a part of our lives just when we needed reminders the most.

In the early days of grief, I wondered if I would ever have two good days in a row. As time passed, there were three days, then five, then there were good weeks. Back then, I was desperate to know if I would ever be happy again—it didn't feel possible. But now I know that though the pain will always be with me, it will change form and lessen over time. I'm happy again. I've found happiness in the ordinary things—watching Peyton swim, listening to Ryan chatter at the dinner table, or feeling their arms around my neck. Their humor cracks me up and I have gigantic belly laughs at their antics, something I once thought I would never have again. This new joy is more pure and precious to me than ever before.

As the workers picked up the heavy granite stone and carefully laid it on the surface they'd prepared, I saw Taylor's image, and next to it the cross. I thought about Jesus dying on the cross. The Son of God had a purpose in death. Though many thought His death was an end, on the third day they discovered that Jesus's purpose was part of something much bigger. Something eternal.

God created each of us for a purpose.

I'd always known my purpose—it was to be a mother to my three kids and a wife to Todd. But when one of those kids was taken from me, I felt like my purpose had been taken too. Some people talk about empty-nest syndrome when their kids go off to college. For a long time I felt as if my nest had been kicked and the pieces had gone flying everywhere. But once I got over the initial shock of losing one of my babies, I saw there were two more who needed me more than ever. What I came to realize over my months of searching was that my purpose hadn't changed—I was still a mom of three. But Ryan and Peyton need me in different ways now than Taylor needs me. We were a five-piece puzzle that had to be put back together with only four pieces, and we were all working hard to create a new picture of what our family would look like going forward.

Todd quickly knew his purpose was in the foundation. I rediscovered during those months of grieving that part of my purpose as his wife was to help him fulfill his God-given purpose. Now that he is working out of our home and we have the foundation, it is easier than ever for me to be a part of what he's doing.

Our purpose comes from God, who is the Author of our stories, our lives, whether we like the plot or not. He was the author while

Taylor was alive, and He was the Author of her story even in her death. But her death is not the end of her story. God is still sovereign and He is still writing. Taylor's next chapter continues—it just continues in a new setting. And mine continues as a mother of three, though I don't see one the way I used to.

I thought about Taylor, wrapped in Jesus's arms, her head on His shoulder and her ponytail tickling His neck, smiling down on us as we've muddled our way through a few dark chapters. She got to the happy part of her life's story faster than most people.

Todd and I know that each day only brings us closer to the day our stories will once again merge with hers—we have the same Author of Life.

When we die as believers, life doesn't end. It's just a new beginning of life with God.

Eternal life.

And that is the story we all look forward to living.

Todd and Tara

The title of this book is *Taylor's Gift*, but this isn't just Taylor's story, or even just our story. It's the story of a cowboy who now has the strength and ability to give back to the community, a nurse who can be an active mom and fully present for her kids, a biker who can give of himself completely, and a teenager who for the first time can see her future. It's the story of countless recipients who received organs because someone heard Taylor's story and registered to be an organ donor. It's also the story of the infinite number of gifts they will give to *their* friends and family.

Taylor's gift is a gift that keeps on giving.

To others.

To us.

But the greatest gift we've received through this journey didn't come from Taylor. It came from God.

The gift of hope.

No matter how tragic our circumstances, God was always there for us.

Whether we acknowledged Him or not, He was always there.

And whether we heard Him or not, He was always present.

He will be there for you too.

Of course He will.

You are His gift. You are His child.

Acknowledgments

After people hear our family's story, they often mention that it has inspired them. But through the good days and the bad, what has inspired us is the love and encouragement of our friends and family. We could fill another book with all of the names of those who stood by us, but we hope that in reading this book they will recognize their part in our story and our appreciation for their role in our lives.

A very special thank-you goes out to:

Bill Taylor, who was the first by our side when we needed him most. We can't fully imagine or understand how you handled everything that was thrown at you. You have been there for us in so many ways: emotionally, spiritually, silently, and physically. You have handled the roles of brother, uncle, and doctor with such grace that it amazes us. Thank you for loving us deeply and always being there.

Kary, Juli, Chris, Bernie, Kristin, and Curt, who were able to be by our side at the hospital during such a difficult time. Your presence, love, and hugs helped carry us through.

All of the friends and family who took care of us when we came home and for months afterward, especially Daniela Centeno, Pam and Randy Cope, Ana Lucia Cottone, Chris and Kim Dicken, Susie

Evans, Tresha Glowacki, Mandy Goddard, Greg Goyne, Kathy
Gutierrez, Paul Haggan, Jeff Hook, Jeremy Lipsey, Lisa Marshall,
Mary Marshall, Linda Medina, Jeff and Kathy Quirk, Beth Rathe,
Dina Conte Schulz, Candy Sheehan, Pauline and Pete Stein, Terry
Storch, Jason and Dana Thompson, Angie Thurman, Trista Wojick,
Judy Ordemann, and Nancy Yingling. Your conversations, clean
laundry, foundation advice, baskets of food, care of Taylor's grave,
laundry soap, tomato plants, meals, cards, letters, and so much
more were physical tokens of your care and concern for us. And
thank you to the many more who have loved and supported our
family during this time, both for things we know about and the
many unseen acts you've done.

Matt, Beth, Allie, and Emily Sunshine—our Suntorch family!
We have described our friendship to many as "family without the
blood," and we love you deeply. So many of our special memories
include you. You are forever family to us.

Laura Springer, who in our opinion is the best school principal
in America and also a true friend. Your laughter, hugs, and smiles
always seem available at the perfect time.

Taylor's dear friends Courtney Quirk and Kate Dicken. You
opened your hearts to try to be "big sisters," and for that we will
be forever grateful.

To Steve "Hutch" Hutcheson: you will always hold a special
place in our family. You gave Taylor the nickname "T" and surrounded her with your beautiful faith. Thank you for your prayers
and strength.

Everyone at the Center for Sales Strategy, especially John Henley, Jim Hopes, and Steve Marx. If more companies were run
with the same integrity and compassion, the world would be a
better place.

Father Alfonse, who helped us understand purpose in pain and
showed unconditional love in the worst of times. Thank you for
your advice and care. We'll never forget the day you emphatically
encouraged us to write a book.

Andrea Doering at Baker Publishing, who was brave enough to reach out to grieving parents and ask if we had ever considered writing a book. Your act was a (divine?) confirmation of Father Alfonse's suggestion, and we are so thankful for you.

Jennifer Schuchmann: from the moment we talked with you, we knew you were the one to help us write this book. We know that if we had met earlier in life, we would have been the best of friends. You have a special place in our family now; you know inside jokes, what makes us tick, and how to pull us out when we turn inward. Your gift of writing is truly from God. You have handled our story with such grace and respect, and for that we are forever grateful.

Kathy Helmers at Creative Trust and the entire Baker Publishing team. Thank you for helping us through this journey. We have felt loved and protected by your experience and guidance.

Taylor's Keepers—Jeff Kartus, Patricia Winters, Jonathan Finger, Amanda Zoller, and an unnamed liver recipient—for being open to connecting with us and loving us like family. We feel a special connection to you like none other. You each have helped us have hope and strength in ways we can't truly explain.

Our extended family: thank you for all of the thoughts, prayers, laughter, notes, hugs, and encouragement. We know this has been a hard journey, and we thank you for never giving up on us.

Our parents: we know this has been tremendously difficult for you. We don't know the perspective of a grandparent, but we do know the meaning of your love for us. You have constantly surrounded us with support and prayer. Thank you for your unconditional love.

All of you have been Christ's hands and feet and have loved us when we were the hardest to love. May this book be a testimony of your love and friendship, and may it inspire others to go and do likewise.

Ryan and Peyton, who are our daily reminders that God is good. Thank you for loving us unconditionally during the worst of our grief—you've inspired us with the courage you've shown in the face of yours. Though there is a piece missing from our five-piece puzzle, the remaining pieces are tightly locked together into a new picture. Thank you for walking so bravely and faithfully through a tragedy you didn't ask for. You are our biggest blessings and our deepest love.

Finally, to God, His Son, and the Holy Spirit: thank You for Your comfort and protection during the hardest times. We marvel at how You have brought all of this together for Your good, and we hope our words honor You and give You all the glory.

Todd and Tara Storch

About the Authors

Tara Storch is wife to Todd and mom to Taylor, Ryan, and Peyton. Along with her husband she cofounded Taylor's Gift Foundation to "increase organ donation to Regift Life, Renew Health, and Restore Families." She has more than twenty years of sales and marketing experience, is an active volunteer, and is a community leader. She is a passionate speaker for their mission and helps with many aspects of the foundation including marketing, merchandise and events. She has told their story on *Good Morning America*, *The Today Show*, *The Ellen DeGeneres Show*, and other national media.

After the death of his daughter Taylor, **Todd Storch** pursued his God-given passion to promote organ donation and help others. As cofounder and president of Taylor's Gift Foundation, Todd leads an amazing core team and volunteer network. In less than two years, Todd has spoken to thousands of people across the country and, through the foundation's efforts, has helped contribute to the certification of nearly two million organ donors in Texas and over twelve million nationally. Todd has more than twenty years of experience as a senior executive in radio and digital media sales, and extensive experience helping companies build their digital and interactive divisions. Most importantly, Todd is husband to Tara and father to Taylor, Ryan, and Peyton.

Jennifer Schuchmann specializes in collaborations with celebrities and newsmakers. Among her many books, she is the coauthor with Kurt and Brenda Warner of the *New York Times* bestselling *First Things First*, with Dan Woolley of *Unshaken*, the only book written by a survivor of the Haiti earthquake, and with Jim Cymbala of *Spirit Rising*. She is also the host of "Right Now," a panel-driven television talk show that airs nationally on the NRB Network. Learn more about Jennifer at WordsToThinkAbout.com, or follow her on Twitter @Schuchmann.

gⁱve LiFE

Help us help others by donating to the Taylor's Gift Foundation at TaylorsGift.org/give. Your contribution will go toward aiding families touched by organ donation.

outlive yourself

By registering to be an organ donor you have the privilege of one day saving someone's life. It's the greatest gift you could ever give. Register today at TaylorsGift.org.

♡ Taylor's Gift™